Beans, Greens, and Sweet Georgia Peaches

Beans, Greens, and Sweet Georgia Peaches

The Southern Way of Cooking Fruits and Vegetables

Damon Lee Fowler

BROADWAY BOOKS

New York

BROADWAY

BEANS, GREENS, AND SWEET GEORGIA PEACHES. Copyright © 1998 by Damon Lee Fowler.
All rights reserved. Printed in the United States of America. No part of this book may be
reproduced or transmitted in any form or by any means, electronic or mechanical,
including photocopying, recording, or by any information storage and retrieval system,
without written permission from the publisher. For information, address Broadway Books,
a division of Bantam Doubleday Dell Publishing Group, Inc.,
1540 Broadway, New York, NY 10036.

Broadway Books titles may be purchased for business or promotional use or for special
sales. For information, please write to: Special Markets Department, Bantam Doubleday
Dell Publishing Group, Inc., 1540 Broadway, New York, NY 10036.

BROADWAY BOOKS and its logo, a letter B bisected on the diagonal, are trademarks of
Broadway Books, a division of Bantam Doubleday Dell Publishing Group, Inc.

Library of Congress Cataloging-in-Publication Data
Fowler, Damon Lee.
Beans, greens, and sweet Georgia peaches : the Southern way of cooking fruits and
vegetables / Damon Lee Fowler. — 1st ed.
p.   cm.
Includes bibliographical references (p. 294) and index.
ISBN 0-7679-0128-2
1. Cookery (Vegetables)   2. Cookery, American—Southern style.   I. Title.
TX801.F65   1998
641.6′5′0975—dc21   97-22153
                                                                        CIP

FIRST EDITION

Book Design by Deborah Kerner

98   99   00   01   02   10   9   8   7   6   5   4   3   2   1

In loving memory of my aunt,
Alice Holmes Vermillion,
the best vegetable cook
I've ever known

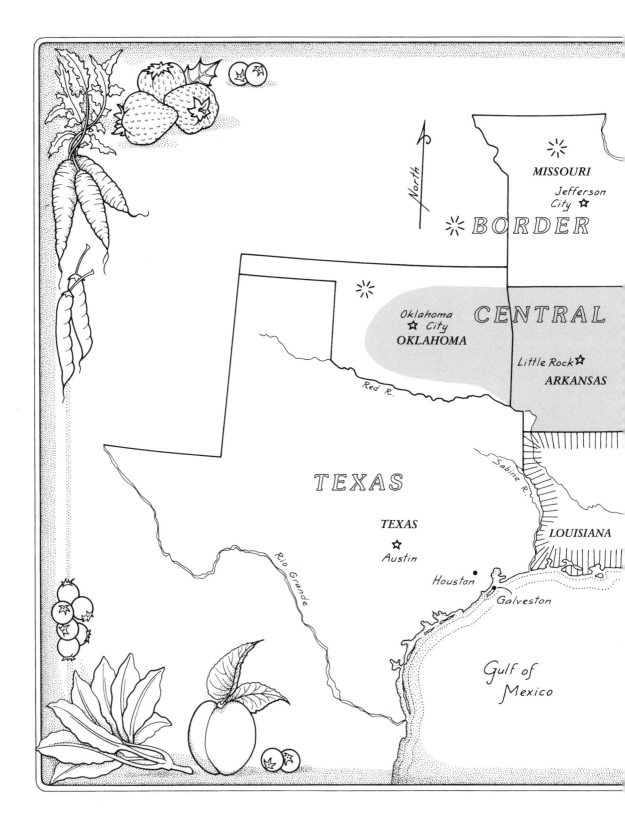

North

MISSOURI

Jefferson City ☆

BORDER

Oklahoma City ☆

OKLAHOMA

CENTRAL

Little Rock ☆

ARKANSAS

Red R.

TEXAS

Sabine R.

TEXAS ☆ Austin

LOUISIANA

Rio Grande

Houston

Galveston

Gulf of Mexico

MARYLAND

Washington, D.C.

Annapolis

Charleston

WEST VIRGINIA

Williamsburg

Richmond

VIRGINIA

Jamestown

Ohio R.

Frankfort

STATES

KENTUCKY

MOUNTAINOUS SOUTH

Raleigh

NORTH CAROLINA

Nashville

Tennessee R.

SOUTH

TENNESSEE

OLD SOUTH

Columbia

SOUTH CAROLINA

Atlanta

ALABAMA

MISSISSIPPI

GEORGIA

Charleston

Savannah

Atlantic Ocean

Montgomery

DEEP SOUTH *

Mississippi R.

Jackson

Mobile

Chattahoochee R.

Baton Rouge

New Orleans

Tallahassee

FLORIDA

Miami

* Deep South is sometimes called "Gulf South" and includes Texas.

Florida Keys

© 1997 Jackie Aher

CONTENTS

➤

Acknowledgments

Southerners only sound as if their mouths are full of grits all the time; usually, they aren't. But our mouths really are open most of the time where food is concerned. We're either eating or, the next best thing to it, talking about eating. This is a lucky break for any writer interested in Southern food.

In order to get the essential character of the Southern way with produce, I talked to as many good Southern cooks as I could find. Getting them to talk wasn't difficult; getting them to hush was. Fortunately, they tend to be generous souls; I often got recipes without asking for them. Many recipes came from friends and relatives, and even from people who were complete strangers to me when I asked for their help. I have a file of twice as many recipes as follow on these pages, a testament to their generous spirit. Those who gave me recipes are credited in the text. Space prevents my listing you all here, but I thank y'all with all my heart.

The first people I must thank are the ones who will protest that they were only doing their jobs—my agents, Elise and Arnold Goodman. Without their believing in me, the idea for this book would never have blossomed, much less sold. My editor, Harriet Bell, with her keen eye, keener taste buds, and enthusiasm for good food and writing—not to mention her friendship—made this book great fun to put together.

As always, Marcella and Victor Hazan continue to be my inspiration and the rule by which I measure my own work. They have touched every aspect of my life and career with a generosity that still fills me with awe. Without them, I would never have had the courage to make the fateful leap into a new career.

Karen Hess is my friend, teacher, counselor, and moral guide in one. She is never too busy to help me with a problem in research or cooking technique, or to just lend her ear when my spirits are lagging. Such merit as my work has owes her a large debt.

John Martin Taylor has been constant with his friendship and professional support. His friendship and, through him, that of his sister Sue Highfield and partner, Mikel Herrington, have been a continuous joy and inspiration.

Jackie Mills, Andria Hurst, and Judy Bess Feagin at *Southern Living* magazine have provided great technical and moral support. Jackie gave me recipes, and Judy talked me through recipe-testing problems.

Just when I think she's forgotten me, I get a call out of the blue from my drill sergeant, Nathalie Dupree, to catch up on gossip, see what I'm up to, and to make sure that I'm staying as busy as she thinks I ought to be.

As only Southerners can, Ruth Adams Bronz and I became very close friends in a short period of time. When we were barely acquainted, she carted me all over New England with no more recommendation than that we were both Southern and loved food. She's my one-woman therapy group. And speaking of therapy, one phone call from Marie Rudisill has been known to get me through six months without going off the deep end. Her wit and wisdom have been both my life preserver and my compass.

Fellow writer Martha Giddens Nesbit has been an ever-present and reliable friend and technical support. When I think I can't go on, I watch Martha juggle a successful marriage, two growing boys, and two careers, and think I've got it easy after all. Martha also introduced me to our mentor and Macon Mama, Clara Eschmann, who shares my creed: Thank God for Bourbon. Clara let me run off with some of her books without scolding me—much.

"Jane's Canners," the brigade of women who make pickles, relishes, and chutneys for St. John's annual bazaar, were game to be invaded by a man and help me test the canning recipes in this book. Headed up by the parish's capable (and first female) senior warden, Jane Pressly, and co-chair Betty Shepherd, they were Evelyn Birchall, Nancy Cope, Mary Ellen Greenwood, Cathy Jarman, Louise Mauer, Laurie Osteen, and Millie Summerell.

My neighbor Tom Edenfield had nothing whatsoever to do with this book, but he badgered me about not being mentioned in my first one until I promised to put his name in here. There you go, Tom. Yet another neighbor, Richard Galloway, gave me free access to modern office equipment and let me regularly raid his herb garden. Still another, Renee Zito, loaned me antique books. Virginia Scott lent me several cookbooks from her collection and let me keep them for a lot longer than most would. My friends and former architectural clients Susan and Rick Sontag have been a tremendous support—in both professions.

As always, my parents have been generous in their support. They spent years and untold amounts of money helping me become an architect, but they also have thrown their unqualified support behind me as I drift into another career—and have been amazingly silent about the tremendous debt that I owe them. This time, they also actively helped with recipe research.

My best friend, Jim King, allowed me to subject him to test runs of every single recipe in this book and has been generous and unflinchingly honest with his opinion, whether I wanted to hear it or not.

Finally, my gratitude and love to all traditional Southern cooks everywhere, from Shreveport to Sri Lanka, who have never stopped believing that the Southern way with flavor is good and worth preserving, who have kept the faith in the face of culinary fads and packaged food—who remain steadfast in a world that is changing faster than a Southern belle's mind.

Thank God for every one of you.

THE SOUL OF SOUTHERN COOKING

VEGETABLES AND FRUIT

The words "Southern cooking" inevitably have great conjuring power, though what they conjure may not always be very close to reality. The first thing that the words usually evoke, at least for most people, seems to be fried chicken; and, you might well wonder, why not? Celebrated the world over, there are surely few things to eat that can equal its perfection. I've heard fried chicken called the "soul" of Southern cooking, a point that surely few would argue.

And yet, if I were to choose one thing that characterizes the many diverse cuisines that make up what we call Southern cooking, what I would call its "soul," it would not be fried chicken. What I would choose is produce. For the real heart and soul of a Southern table, whether that table is in Tidewater Virginia, the Carolina Lowcountry, or the depths of a Louisiana bayou, is not the meat in the middle of it but the vegetables and fruit that surround it.

Yet Southern vegetables have not—at least in our century—enjoyed much of a reputation. In fact, for years they've been the subject of much malignment and derision. One might almost say that Southern vegetables have made our foodways not famous but infamous. If you are persistent and finally pry people away from notions of fried chicken, the best they will probably do in recalling Southern vegetables is "slimy" okra, or boiled collards, or overcooked green beans—a sad, and grossly mistaken, impression.

In direct contradiction of that impression, the South has often been called "America's garden," and not without justification. From the very beginning—even before heavy-duty European colonization—ours has been a mostly agrarian society; our economy depended almost completely on growing things. Though every farm and plantation had the usual barnyard animals, animal husbandry was not a highly developed art until recent years. It's important to remember that whenever people live close to the land in this way, regardless of where they are, produce inevitably has a high profile in their diet. This is especially true of the South, even of today's urbanized, industrialized, and internationalized South.

Few modern Southerners would raise their own frying chickens, even if their local zoning laws would permit it, yet it isn't unusual to find a vegetable patch in the midst of urban Atlanta. In less urban settings, the most elegant of gardens in the most fashionable of suburbs will, at the very least, sport a few tomato plants. Southerners will put up with a lot, but don't mess with their fresh tomatoes and okra.

Now, there's no one vegetable or fruit that can be singled out as the most representative of a Southern garden. I would even hesitate over tomatoes and okra. For, while a single vegetable may figure prominently in the diet of a particular region or community of the South, as rice did for centuries in the Carolina Lowcountry, or as collard greens do even now among African American families, what really characterizes the Southern table is not any single fruit or vegetable but the fact that there are so many. From early spring, when much of the rest of the country is still frozen, until the late frosts of our relatively mild winters, literally hundreds of varieties of fruits and vegetables are to be found growing in Southern gardens and enjoyed on Southern tables. It's on the strength of this diversity that the once legendary reputation of Southern cooking was built.

The greatest obstacle to understanding Southern cooking is that which makes the region itself so difficult to grasp: the sheer size of it. Stretching from the Mason–Dixon line to Key West, from North Carolina's Outer Banks to the plains of western Texas, the South (including Arkansas, Oklahoma, and West Virginia) incorporates nearly a million square miles of land.

In short, the South is many places and has many faces—a land of felicitous harmonies and jarring contradictions. It is, at once, the earthiness of the rolling upcountry farmland, my home by birth, and the urbane elegance of my adopted home on the Colonial coast. It's the rugged wilderness of the Ozark Mountains and the electric wilderness of South Beach, Miami; the lush bottomland of South Georgia and the arid plains of West Texas. It's the forthright, earthy subsistence of mountaineers and genteel civility of coastal planter aristocrats. It's Mr. Jefferson's Monticello and Dori Sanders's produce stand in Filbert, S.C. It's string quartets in Charleston and jazz in New Orleans, Jessye Norman and Patsy Cline, tent revivals and Elvis.

Obviously, Southern cooking can be—and is—as complex and varied as all that. From hoppin' John to fried rice, the variations are endless, for all these different elements have made their contributions to the Southern pot. But even with all these differences, one can distinguish a common thread—and that is the union of the English cooking practices, which came to dominate all other cuisines both native and immigrant, with the sensibility of the African cooks, which transformed it.

The most useful thing to know about all the different cuisines of the South is that their foundation is basically European. Legends of Native American cookery notwithstanding, the European settlers swept aside the indigenous cultures and brought their own culture—and cooking practices—with them. While the settlers did learn from the Native Americans, most particularly about the many plants that have become so intrinsically a part of our diet today, their fundamental cooking practices did not change; they simply adapted new ingredients to their old foodways. So, the basic structure of Southern cooking remained European—and, since it was the English colonists who eventually dominated, mostly English.

Now, in other parts of the Anglo colonies, that's just about as far as it went. The basic structure survived little altered from what it had been in England. But the cooking of the South very quickly went in its own direction. The difference, of course, lay in who was doing most of the cooking—the African slaves. For the better part of three centuries, African cooks dominated Southern kitchens, particularly those of the wealthy and influential upper classes. As those cooks established themselves in those kitchens, and gradually began to change the food that went on their white masters' tables, their cooking practices eventually changed those of the white mistress and even trickled down the social ladder to poor white families. Gradually, as generation upon generation adapted, the cooking of the entire region was transformed.

There are many clues that give away the African influence on Southern foodways. Most obvious are the many African ingredients that are so common in Southern food: rice, peanuts, okra, legumes such as black-eyed and cow peas, and sesame seeds. (Ironically, peanuts are not native to Africa, and ultimately, nor is okra, but both were already an established part of the African diet when slaves began to be imported into America.) It also seems pretty certain that we owe the popularity of such diverse vegetables as Asian eggplant, Central American tomatoes, American sweet potatoes, and European collard greens to the influence of those African cooks as well. While none of those vegetables are

African in origin, they were either already known to African cooks before they were brought into America, or they resembled vegetables with which they were already familiar.

Aside from ingredients, there are a number of Southern specialties that are distinctly African—if not in origin, at least in sensibility. There are bean and rice dishes, including (and especially) the bean pilau we call "hoppin' John," those many pots of greens and gumbo, and fritters of all kinds. Another telling clue is that in the midst of all the radical changes that were happening in other areas, baking, which remained mostly the province of the white mistress, changed only nominally. And baking was something over which the African cook had little control.

Now, the intention here is not to throw credit too far in one direction or the other. I have mentioned it because, historically, while African cooks have been given full credit for skill, they get very little credit for innovation. But even as we celebrate that innovation, we must keep in mind that it occurred within the framework of European cooking practices, in what were basically European kitchens, sometimes (though admittedly probably less often than not) hand-in-hand with the white mistress. The real magic of Southern cooking is not solely its European foundations or African innovations but the masterful union of the two traditions.

Nowhere is that union better displayed than in the way Southern cooks have with the produce of the garden. Whether it is a savory gumbo, or a sumptuous peach cobbler, or a fried apple or a green tomato pie, the Southern touch is subtle, carefully balanced, full of flavor, and yet never overblown. So perfect is the balance that one is sometimes hard-pressed to tell what is European, what is African, and what is Native.

The strength of the Southern way with produce has always lain in the freshness of its ingredients. Even with our modern air freight, real just-picked freshness is only possible when the fruit or vegetable has been locally grown in its natural season.

In *Mrs. Hill's New Cook Book* (1867), Annabella Hill asserted that vegetables intended for dinner (which was at two o'clock in the afternoon) "should be gathered early in the morning. A few only can be kept twelve hours without detriment." I wouldn't want to hear that lady pronounce on the average supermarket produce section. Such sensibility has unfortunately been lost to most of us, but some of it can be recovered, even if you live in the middle of the city. With a little care, you can still find reasonably fresh produce for these recipes. All it requires is that you redevelop a seasonal mentality and take a little more time and care to seek out locally grown fruits and vegetables. A seasonal mentality simply means becoming more conscious of the rhythms of planting and harvest in the area where you live, learning to appreciate the fuller flavors of in-season produce.

To that end, the recipes in this book are divided into seasons in accord with the time of year that they ripen *where I live*. Therefore, these divisions aren't meant to be taken as gospel. Even in the South, the exact season for a fruit or vegetable can vary. But by organizing them in accordance with their distinctive seasons—at least in Southeast Georgia— a rhythm begins to develop. Once this rhythm is established in your kitchen, then you start to appreciate the fuller flavor of seasonal cooking. You'll prefer spring asparagus and find yourself passing by the bland, out-of-season variety in the fall, because then fragrant new turnips are available, which you know are going to taste so much better.

About the Recipes

In sifting through the hundreds of recipes that came my way for this book, whether they arrived in written form or actually steaming on my plate, I had one primary aim—to paint as diverse a picture of the Southern kitchen as possible. To do so, I've painted with a very broad brush. Historian that I am, I have included a number of lovely historical dishes that had all but disappeared from our tables along with others that have only come to it in recent times. There are recipes from traditional African American cooks who have hardly been out of their hometowns and from expatriate Southerners living as far away as Berkshire County, Massachusetts, and Rome, Italy. There are things that I learned from the most elemental country cooks to the most accomplished professional chefs.

What you will not find, however, is complicated restaurant cooking or a lot of what is nowadays fashionably referred to as "fusion" cooking. Though I've included recipes from professional chefs, they don't necessarily represent the cooking that those chefs do for their patrons but, rather, the kind of cooking that they do for themselves—at home. And as for so-called fusion cooking, in which concepts and ingredients are borrowed willy-nilly and dumped together in an abstract composition—well, you can probably guess what I think of that. I don't consider black-eyed pea–stuffed ravioli with a *coulis* of collard greens and a hot-sour mango sauce to be Southern; I consider it to be something Italian that got out of hand. It can be argued that traditional Southern food is "fusion" cooking, since it is to a large extent borrowed from Europe, Africa, the Caribbean, and Native America. Well, in that sense, any of the world's great cuisines can be considered "fusion" cooking. But what is missing from the whole fusion concept is the two elements that are essential to the lasting success of a cuisine—foundation and balance.

So, what I looked for when I began to search out recipes, whether from old cookbooks or my neighbors down the street, was the traditional taste and aroma that sparked a keen sense of recognition on my palate. I did not want flavors that startled but, rather, those that enveloped and reassured me with their familiarity. In short, I looked for flavors that were distinctly Southern, that brought to my tongue and imagination the memory of the tables of my childhood—even if it was something I'd never had on that table.

Those flavors and aromas of the Southern table are difficult to pin down and describe. As our region is many different things, so is our cooking: the flavors are in part African, yes, but they are also in part English and French and Native American and Caribbean; they are full of high-flown elegance and down-home familiarity; they taste of crisp mountain air and of salty coastal breezes. But one thing is sure, whether served to you from a pine table in a rough mountain cabin or from a mahogany sideboard in the polished elegance of a Lowcountry townhouse, they are flavors and aromas that all of us recognize and share, flavors that define us to ourselves and identify us to the outside world.

Flavors and aromas that say—taste this—that's what it means to be Southern.

THE SOUTHERN KITCHEN

EQUIPMENT, INGREDIENTS, AND METHODS

Equipment

The most reassuring thing about Southern cooking is that for centuries it has been done by simple people using the simplest of tools. There are very few special pieces of equipment that you are likely to need to successfully turn out the recipes of this book. If I have a sharp knife and a cast-iron skillet, I can do just about anything. Nonetheless, there are a few items that you will find useful to have on hand. This is by no means a complete kitchen list; I'm taking for granted that you know you need things like pot holders, spoons, and dishrags.

CAST-IRON PANS: Despite the new superengineered cookware that is available, Southern cooks continue to prefer these durable pans for a number of reasons. Their low conductivity makes them retain heat well and provide that heat more evenly than other cookware. A well-seasoned cast-iron pan is indispensable for frying chicken (or anything else) or for baking cornbread, and a cast-iron Dutch oven makes the best gumbo imaginable. Most Southerners believe that a well-seasoned cast-iron pan adds to the flavor of the food that cooks in it. This may be imaginary, but I do think that cast iron makes a discernible difference. It's a good idea to have several sizes of cast-iron pans on hand: a large (12-inch), deep pan for frying and braising, a medium (8- to 10-inch) pan for smaller batches of food and cornbread, and a small (6-inch) pan for half-batches of cornbread. A 4-quart Dutch oven with a lid should answer for the stews, gumbos, and wilted greens.

To season a new iron pan, preheat the oven to 250 degrees F. Wash the pan in soapy water, then rinse and dry it thoroughly. Rub the inside of the pan well with lard or olive oil and place it in the oven. Let it bake for an hour, turn off the oven, and let the pan sit in it overnight. The next day wipe the pan out, rub it with more lard or oil, and repeat the baking. The pan is now ready for use.

To maintain cast-iron pans, never, ever put them in a dishwasher or wash them with soap. If anything sticks to the pan, scrub it loose with coarse salt, a plastic scrubber, or a natural bristle brush, thoroughly rinse and dry the pan, then rub the inside well with a cloth that has been dipped in fresh lard or olive oil.

It's also good to have several sizes of heavy-bottomed stainless or porcelain-lined pots (enameled cast iron is okay) and kettles, at least one heavy-bottomed sauté pan with sloping sides, and an unglazed earthenware baking dish. If you enjoy putting up your own conserves and pickles, a large, enameled canning pot with a jar rack is useful not only for that process, but for cooking big batches of corn on the cob, artichokes, Lowcountry boil, or gumbo.

SCALE: Wherever possible, I give weight measures for vegetables so that it is simpler to shop for key ingredients in the market. It's still sensible to weigh ingredients for many recipes—especially when you are baking. For example, it's easier to know how many sweet potatoes you are going to need if the recipe says 3 pounds instead of "3 cups cooked, mashed." But be warned about scales; not all of them are created equal. Test the accuracy of your scale with 2 level cups (dry measure) of sugar; it should weigh exactly a pound. If the measurement is off, take it into account when weighing ingredients for a recipe.

KNIVES: This is no place to be cheap; buy the best knives you can afford and keep them razor sharp. A heavy 8-, 10-, or 12-inch chef's knife, a 2$^{1}/_{2}$-inch paring knife, and a serrated knife (for slicing tomatoes and citrus fruit) will take care of just about any job in the kitchen. In general, the heavier the knife is, the easier it will be to use, because the weight of the knife does most of the work. Other indispensable cutting tools are a good sharp vegetable peeler and a pair of heavy-duty kitchen scissors.

MISCELLANEOUS TOOLS: A large, fine-mesh wire strainer is useful for draining small vegetables, rinsing rice, or can be put to work pureeing vegetables when you are caught without a machine. A food mill is also especially useful for pureeing and often does a better job than the food processor or blender. If you plan to can any of the preserves, pickles, or condiments in this book, you'll also need a wide-mouthed funnel for filling jars and a large pair of canning tongs for handling the jars after they come out of the hot-water bath.

The Home Canning Process

Most of the recipes in this book for pickles, relishes, and other conserves can be processed, or "canned" for prolonged storage. Canning is a sealing process by which heat builds steam in the top (or headroom) of a jar of conserve. As the steam escapes, it creates a vacuum, pulling the lid of the jar into a tight seal. Once properly sealed, the jar can be stored at room temperature.

Canning is not a difficult operation, but if you have never done it, there are a few key fundamentals that you should be familiar with before trying it.

NECESSARY EQUIPMENT

For all preserves, it is important to use the right jars and lids. Old commercial jelly and pickle jars are not designed for home use. Put them in the recycling bin and buy jars specifically made for home canning. For sealing the jars, use only new metal lids and rings that are free of rust. Never reuse old lids, as the sealing compound may be damaged. New jars are usually packed with lids, and replacements are available wherever the jars are sold. Do not use the old-fashioned glass-lidded jars with clamps and rubber rings. No matter how clean the jars and lids appear to be, they must be sterilized before using them.

There are two types of home canning processes: steam-pressure canning and water-bath canning. I prefer the water-bath canners, because the pot is more versatile and can be used for things other than canning. It is a deep enameled kettle fitted with a rack that keeps the jars from bouncing on the bottom of the kettle or bumping into each other during the processing. The rack also makes it easier to put the jars into the boiling bath.

Aside from the proper jars, lids, and processor, it is helpful to have a large pair of canning tongs for handling the jars, a stainless wide-mouthed canning funnel for filling them, and plenty of clean cotton or linen kitchen towels.

PROCESSING CONSERVES

Before canning, everything that touches the pickle or preserve must be sterile. Sterilize jars covered in boiling water for at least 10 minutes; boil the lids for 1 minute in a stainless pan, then turn off the fire and let them remain in the water until you are ready to use them. Don't touch the insides of the jars or the lids with your hands after the jars and lids are sterilized.

Use a wide-mouthed funnel to fill the jars, and don't touch pickles, fruit, or other conserves with your bare hands. Transfer the food to the jar with stainless tongs, spoons, or forks. For whole pickles and fruit preserves, leave no less than 1/2 inch of headroom at the top of the jar and cover them with the pickling or preserving syrup by at least 1/4 inch, leaving an overall headroom of 1/4 inch in the top of the jar (pack them tightly so they won't float). For jams, marmalades, relishes, and chutneys, leave 1/4 inch of headroom. Once the jars are filled, place the canning lids on them with the tongs. (Avoid touching the inside of the lid with your bare hands.) Screw on the rings until they are just lightly tightened. Don't tighten the rings too much, or the air will not be able to escape, preventing a proper seal.

To process the conserve in the water bath, the jars are submerged in boiling water. The water must cover the jars by at least 1 inch. Don't worry that it will leak into the jar; steam builds up in the "headroom" and prevents this from happening. As this steam is forced out, it creates the vacuum that seals the jar. Different preserves require varying lengths of processing time in the bath, so refer to the individual recipes for times.

When the jars first come out of the bath, they are very hot and fragile and must not touch each other or any cool surface. As you take them from the bath (using the canning tongs), place them on clean, double-folded cotton or linen towels. Never allow them to touch one another or the bare counter, or they could crack. As the jars cool, the vacuum formed in the top will pull the dome of the lid inward, making a "popping" sound. Let the jars sit for at least 24 hours before storing them. Any that do not seal can be reprocessed, but jars that don't seal after the second try should be stored in the refrigerator and used as soon as possible.

A FEW PRECAUTIONS ON STORAGE

All unprocessed conserves must be refrigerated. They should keep for up to 2 months *if packed in a sterile jar.* Processed conserves should be stored in a cool, dark cupboard or pantry. *Do not* eat any conserve with a bulging lid. I try to use canned goods within a year, though most will last a lot longer.

In any case, if you are ever in doubt about any conserve, *don't eat it;* throw it out. It's better to lose a little bit of work and material than to end up being poisoned.

Ingredients

You will be relieved to know that a well-stocked Southern pantry is in many ways a well-stocked American one. Even if you're not from the South, if you are at all enthusiastic about cooking, many of the ingredients that are called for in this book will already be on your pantry shelves. Nonetheless, there are some that are specifically regional, which you may not already have on hand.

If you have any trouble finding these ingredients, listen around you at work, among your neighbors, or among the patrons of your local market for the soft drawl of a Southern accent. It is axiomatic that you can take a Southerner anywhere in the world and they do not change; they just keep right on being Southern. Chances are, they can tip you off about where to find good collards and okra, or where you can find grits, white cornmeal, and soft wheat flour. Failing that, I have provided addresses and phone numbers of select mail-order sources for some of the essentials at the end of the chapter.

DRY GOODS

F L O U R :   Southern cooks prefer flour milled from soft wheat. This type of wheat has a lower protein and gluten content than the hard red-wheat flours that dominate markets outside the South. The lower gluten content is critical for producing tender pastry, fluffy biscuits, and light cakes with a delicate crumb. Widely marketed brands of soft-wheat flours include White Lily, Dixie Lily, and Martha White. If you live where the King Arthur Flour brand is sold, look for their unbleached soft-wheat pastry flour. If none of these are available where you live, some mail-order sources are listed in the Sources section at the end of this chapter.

All-purpose flour is the most commonplace and universally available type. It's a blend of both soft- and hard-wheat flours, often mixed with a little barley flour to enhance its workability. For most of the recipes in this book, all-purpose flour is fine unless the recipe says otherwise. I used to hear it said that the blends of these flours marketed in the South tended to be weighted on the soft-wheat side, but I've used flours from all over the country and frankly can't see any real difference. For baking, I've even made biscuits, pastry, and cakes with all-purpose flour and gotten good results. While soft-wheat flour is preferable and will make it easier for you to achieve success, every recipe in this book was tested using all-purpose flour.

Bread flour is blended to have an extremely high gluten content, which makes yeast doughs stretch and allows for more air to be trapped so that the bread rises higher. Unfortunately, what makes this blend desirable for yeast dough makes it undesirable for baking-powder breads and pastries. High-gluten flour makes biscuits and pastries tough and heavy. Therefore, bread flour cannot be substituted in any of the recipes, unless the flour is used only as a thickener or a breading for coating vegetables that are to be fried.

CORNMEAL: In the South, you can take for granted that "meal" means cornmeal. What you can't take for granted is that it means white cornmeal. Though white meal is the preference in most places, there are pockets of the South where yellow meal takes precedence. Yellow meal has a more robust, slightly sweet flavor, but white meal is more delicate and, to some people, richer-tasting. I prefer white meal, but use whichever you prefer.

The important thing about cornmeal is how it is made. Stone-ground meal has by far the best texture. Stone-ground means that the corn was milled on an old-fashioned millstone. The package may read "water stone-ground," which means that the mill was powered by running water. It doesn't really matter; the corn can't tell if it's a motor or a waterwheel that is making the stone turn. It gets crushed all the same. Unbolted meal has none of the bran removed, so it is more flavorful and interesting, but it is also more per-ishable, so if the meal is unbolted, make sure that it is fresh and not stale-smelling. Unbolted meal is almost always labeled as such. If the package doesn't say so, it is proba-bly bolted meal.

Stone-ground meal is available in natural and health-food stores, specialty groceries, and some supermarkets. For mail-order retailers of stone-ground meal, see the end of the chapter.

GRITS: There are two basic types of grits: hominy grits and whole-corn grits.

Hominy grits is the most universally available; it's made from dried corn from which the husk is removed. There are three types of hominy grits. Avoid instant grits like the plague, and pass over the "quick" grits if you can. Stick to regular hominy grits: the package cooking directions will say that it takes at least 20 to 30 minutes to cook. To be really good, the grits should be cooked even longer.

Whole-corn grits is ground from the whole grain; none of the outer husk is removed. It has the most flavor and is the best and most satisfying grits to use. Mail-order sources for grits are listed in the Sources section at the end of the chapter.

Before you write to me about my grammar, please read the discussion of the singularity of grits on page 44.

SALT: Most markets offer three types of salt: sea, kosher, and regular table salt. For all my cooking, I use only sea salt. For flavor and subtlety, it has no equal. It is more expensive than table salt, but if you can buy it in bulk from a natural or health-food store, the difference in cost isn't enough to worry about. A close second to it is kosher salt. Many cooks prefer kosher salt in part because the flakes make it easier to pinch when measuring the salt. Both kosher and sea salt are pure and have a clean salt flavor, so you'll find that you actually use less of them than you are accustomed to with table salt.

Table salt, the most common variety, has a harsh, chemical taste. If you've always used it, chances are you don't notice the taste. If you don't believe it, buy a little sea or kosher salt. First taste it directly on your tongue, then clean your palate and taste the table salt. You'll be surprised how awful table salt tastes by comparison.

SUGAR: Our consumption of this innocent product has gotten way out of hand, in part due to all the soft drinks that the average American puts away every day. But I'll spare you the health lecture. My only problem with sugar is the way it has come to be overused in cooking, especially with vegetables. For most of the savory recipes in this book, sugar has no place.

However, when a recipe calls for sugar, the type to use for the most authentic Southern flavor is pure cane sugar. In some of the recipes, I specify turbinado or demerara sugar, a partially refined cane-sugar product whose granules are larger than regular white sugar. Its color is a lovely light brown, and the flavor is mellower than that of fully refined sugar. It isn't the same as modern brown sugar, which is merely refined sugar with some of the molasses added back. Whenever possible, I use turbinado or demerara sugar instead of regular brown sugar, and the recipe will specifically call for them. If you can't find either of these sugars, regular brown sugar can be substituted. The reverse, however, is not always true. In the event that a recipe does call for brown sugar, it means commercial brown sugar; don't substitute turbinado or demerara unless the recipe states that it's safe to do so, because they react differently in cooking.

MISCELLANEOUS INGREDIENTS

ANCHOVIES: Salt-packed whole anchovies are the finest quality. In larger cities, they are readily available in Italian and specialty markets. Elsewhere, they are not as easy to find. Next in quality are anchovy fillets packed in olive oil in glass jars. A distant third are oil-packed canned fillets. As convenient as it is, I don't care for anchovy paste that comes in a tube and don't recommend it.

BREAD CRUMBS: Don't throw out those old, dried-out loaves of French bread and yeast rolls; make your own bread crumbs (in the food processor or with a box grater) with them. Once you start making your own, you'll really appreciate how much better they taste than the commercially produced variety.

CAPERS: The pickled flower buds of the trailing plant Capparis spinosa, which is native to the Mediterranean, capers have long been imported and used in Southern cooking. The finest are packed in salt; these are available at Italian groceries and specialty markets in larger cities but are difficult to come by in most places. Capers packed in brine, which are almost universally available, work just fine in these recipes.

Salt-packed capers must be well rinsed before they are used.

OLIVES: Use only imported Greek or Italian brine-cured black or green olives. Yes, they are traditional, especially in port cities like Charleston, Savannah, and New Orleans. The most economical way to buy them is at Italian, Greek, or other specialty groceries where they are sold in bulk.

TOMATO PASTE: The imported variety that comes in a squeeze tube like toothpaste seems to have the best flavor and is the most convenient to use. There's never a half-used can of the stuff moldering in the back of your refrigerator. However, any all-natural tomato paste is suitable.

COOKING FATS

BUTTER: There is no substitute for good butter. Use unsalted butter, the best you can find.

DRIPPINGS: Drippings are the rendered fat from bacon or salt-cured pork. Whenever you make bacon, save the drippings. After they cool, pour them into a glass jar, seal it well, and store it in the refrigerator. You can also make the drippings as you need them. Fat levels differ, but an average slice of bacon should give you about 1 tablespoon of drippings.

LARD: Lard is discussed in the section on pork products (page 21). Look for lard without preservatives (some butchers carry it), or render your own. If you buy lard, check the package. It should be dry, and the lard should be creamy white and have a clean, pleasant, faintly oily smell. If it is yellow and has a strong odor, the lard is rancid.

OILS

VEGETABLE OILS: Much touted these days as being a healthy alternative to animal fats, these oils do not have a long tradition in Southern kitchens. The oldest and most famous, olive oil, has always been known and used by upper-class Southern families, both for limited cooking (generally reserved for salads) and for medicinal uses. Most of the other oils, including the now popular peanut oil, have come into common use only in the last century.

For most deep-fat frying, I still prefer lard, in spite of all the negative things that the naysayers have laid at its door. However, if you are avoiding animal fats, you can use filtered, refined vegetable oils for all your deep-fat frying. The best of them is peanut oil.

For sautéing, where only a small amount of fat is required, the most traditional Southern flavor is to be had from animal fats—rendered bacon drippings, lard, and butter. Their distinct advantage is flavor: a little of them goes a long way. The less flavor the fat has, the more of it we tend to use. With that in mind when searching for animal-fat substitutes to use in these recipes, what I looked for first was flavor. The best flavor to be had is from cold-pressed, unfiltered oils, such as an extra virgin olive oil, unfiltered corn oil, or peanut oil. These oils are loaded with flavor, so a little of them adds big things to the pot. You generally won't find them in your supermarket; with the exception of olive oil, cold-pressed oils are usually available only at natural-food and specialty groceries. They cost more, but they are worth it.

If you are accustomed to working only with refined oils, there are a few things you should know about the cold-pressed, unfiltered variety. Because these oils are not filtered or refined, they still contain some of the flavorful solids of the vegetable or seed from which they are pressed. These solids spoil more easily; therefore, unfiltered oils are a lot more perishable than commercially produced oils. Buy them from a vendor that has high turnover and store them in a cool, dark place, well away from light and heat. If you don't use the oil very often and your house is warm all the time, the refrigerator is the better place to keep it.

Corn Oil: Corn oil is not especially traditional in Southern cooking, but if you are avoiding animal fats, it makes a good substitute for those fats in certain types of cooking. For deep frying, regular commercially produced, refined corn oil does an acceptable job, though it is not as good as peanut oil. It has very little flavor on its own, and it stands up fairly well to high heat. For sautéing, cold-pressed, unfiltered corn oil has a rich, almost buttery flavor that makes it a good substitute for butter or bacon fat, especially in dishes that contain corn. Look for it at natural-food or specialty groceries.

Olive Oil: As Southern cooks have begun to use more and more olive oil in their cooking, reasonably good extra virgin olive oil has become more widely available in the South; even supermarkets are beginning to carry more than one brand at a time. If, however, your supermarket stocks the oil on a top shelf, unshielded from the fluorescent lights, don't buy it there. It's better to shop for it in specialty groceries, where the oil is given proper care and the selection is usually better.

For sautéing and salads, use only extra virgin olive oil, the best you can afford. Lesser-grade oils are extracted from olive pulp that has already been pressed at least once, using chemicals and heat. They have little or no flavor and are of no gastronomical interest whatsoever. Like good wine, extra virgin oils differ in flavor and character from region to region—and even within regions. Experiment with the ones available to you, letting your own taste guide you in selecting one for your kitchen.

Peanut Oil: I once heard some patriotic Southern soul describe peanut oil as the olive oil of the South—an admirable bit of national loyalty but a thoroughly silly remark. That's not to say that peanut oil isn't important. Along with lard, it is unparalleled for deep-fat frying, lending a crispness of crust that no other vegetable fat can approach. Use a refined peanut oil. It should be clear but smell distinctly of fresh peanuts.

For sautéing without animal fat, a cold-pressed, unfiltered peanut oil is a great substitute for bacon drippings, lard, or butter. Of course, it does not taste like bacon, but it still provides a distinctive—and Southern—flavor. You'll find it only at natural-food and specialty groceries. The oil will be a little cloudy and may have residue on the bottom, but it should have a clean, fresh peanut aroma. If it smells like stale peanuts, the oil is rancid and shouldn't be used.

DAIRY PRODUCTS

BUTTERMILK AND YOGURT: Real buttermilk is the soured milk left over from making butter. What passes for buttermilk nowadays is skimmed milk treated with enzymes. Most commercial brands contain stabilizers, thickeners, and salt—and way too much of the latter. I use an all-natural, organically produced plain yogurt instead. Not only does it taste better, but it produces a much better result in my cooking. If the yogurt seems a bit too thick, I thin it out with a little plain milk. Look for organically produced (preferably from a biodynamic farm) yogurt at natural or health-food stores. Stonyfield Farm and Seven Stars are two dairies whose products are nationally marketed, and they are both excellent.

CHEESE: For the best results, use an all-natural product. So-called American cheese, that lurid orange vinyl stuff in the supermarket, is beneath discussion, and its imitations are even worse. Their only claim is that they melt into a smooth emulsion. So does plastic. Pass them by. Here's what you *do* want:

Cheddar: Use a sharp, all-natural Cheddar, ideally an imported English Cheddar. A good commercial Vermont or Canadian Cheddar is also acceptable. Where commercial Cheddar is concerned, there's a lot of hoopla about using "white" over the orange-dyed stuff; dyeing the Cheddar in part covers up a truncated curing process and has been done for two hundred years. If all you can find is orange-dyed Cheddar, don't worry. All-natural cheeses are colored with vegetable dyes that are harmless.

Blue: During the late War of Northern Aggression, on land that was to become my old alma mater in the foothills of Carolina, Confederate workmen busied themselves digging railway tunnels into the hills. Eventually the tunnels were abandoned, incomplete. It would be years before they were finally put to use—by the dairy school of Clemson University—as aging caves for an excellent, rich blue cheese. For many years, this cheese was available only through an outlet at the university and has always been as popular as it was scarce. Today it is being marketed commercially and has been picked up by a few national mail-order vendors, but production is still limited and it is sometimes hard to get.

Good-quality Roqueforts, Gorgonzolas, or Danish blues all make good substitutes. However, English Stilton, as good as it is in its way, is not an acceptable substitute.

Parmesan: If possible, use only imported Italian Parmesan, preferably Parmigiano-Reggiano. The reason that it is the best for use in Italian cooking applies equally to Southern cooking.

CREAM: Throughout this book, heavy cream is used. Look for cream with a minimum milkfat content of at least 36 percent, preferably not one that is "ultra-pasteurized." Sometimes you can find an all-natural cream with up to 40 percent milkfat in natural-food stores. If you do find one, close your eyes to the cost and buy it.

SOUR CREAM: All of the recipes in this book were tested with commercial sour cream—and it will work in any recipe calling for "sour cream," but it isn't the best choice. It is far better to make your own sour cream from cultured heavy cream, which usually goes by its romantic-sounding French name, *crème fraîche*.

CRÈME FRAÎCHE

MAKES 1 PINT

> *2 tablespoons all-natural yogurt*
> *1 pint heavy cream (minimum 36 percent milkfat)*

1. Line a wire sieve with a double layer of cheesecloth or an undyed microwave-quality paper towel over a bowl. Put the yogurt into it and let it drain for 30 minutes.

2. Put the drained yogurt and cream in a clean glass jar. Discard the whey in the bowl. Seal the jar tightly and shake until the yogurt is dissolved into the cream. Set the jar aside at room temperature until the cream clots, about 4 to 8 hours, depending on how warm the room is. If it's a sunny day, I usually put the jar in the sun for an hour to get it started. When the clotting is complete, store the cream in the refrigerator. It will keep for about 2 weeks.

THE UBIQUITOUS PIG

The best-known, and perhaps most infamous, flavoring in Southern vegetable cookery is the salt-cured flesh and fat of that much-maligned barnyard animal, the pig. Poor thing; he spends his life minding his own business—and the best that he gets is a wallow in mud and a dinner of swill. When this rather prosaic life is ended, he provides the farmer not only with dinner but all manner of beneficial products. In return for this blameless life and sacrifice, he has been posthumously charged with killing the farmer off by clogging his arteries.

Pork is not, however, by any means as universal in our cookery as is widely supposed. Nita Dixon, a traditional chef in Savannah, explains that the reason her vegetables are so good is because she learned to cook them without using meat. Her family—as was true of so many Lowcountry black families—was poor; they couldn't afford to have meat often, so, she says, "I had to learn to make vegetables taste good some other way." That other way was with herbs, garlic, and cayenne pepper.

All the same, if porcine husbandry were brought to a halt, and pigs were to be banned from the South altogether, the blow to what we think of as a Southern flavor would not be fatal, but it would nonetheless be severe. It's widely supposed that salt-cured pork was first added to the pot by African American cooks as a means of supplementing a meager, mostly vegetarian diet—and this is probably in part true, though there were families like Nita's that couldn't even afford that. What I've found, in fact, is that adding salt-cured pork to the pot was more a white thing than a black one, because the white settlers had long been using this seasoning in their native Europe, and pigs are not native to Africa.

Here are the pork products that every good Southern pantry is seldom without. For those who are not able to cook with them, I've suggested some alternatives, both here and in the applicable recipes. I only did this where it was possible to get at a recognizably Southern taste without using meat, and in looking for substitutes for pork, my aim was not to imitate meat by using another product, but to find another way of producing the same character and essential substance. My aim was not to find a substitute for the meat but rather, for what the meat did. So I won't coyly pretend that these suggestions are anything more than substitutes; naturally they will not taste the same as pork. However, they will still give you a taste of that traditional satisfying flavor.

COUNTRY OR DRY-CURED HAM: These are hams that are cured with dry salt and air or smoke. The hind leg is first rubbed with salt and left to lie for a week or so. Then it is wiped dry, rubbed with more salt and sometimes spices and sugar, and hung up to air-dry just like prosciutto. Usually, though not always, country ham is finished with smoke, after which it goes through a final hanging to age the meat. A good country ham that has been smoked will have a distinct flavor of smoke to it, but it is subtle and never as heavy and pervasive as commercial water-cured hams. The longer the ham hangs and ages, the more concentrated and richer the flavor will be.

Lean country-ham meat is used when a dish calls for its salty, dusky depth of flavor but does not also need fat. You can use a good-quality prosciutto instead of country ham, but for meatless cooking, the only satisfactory substitutes I've found for it (believe it or not) are salt-cured anchovy fillets, a dash of Thai fish sauce (an anchovy-based condiment), or for strict vegetarians, a small dash of good-quality soy sauce. The secret to these substitutes is to use them in very small quantities; too much anchovy will make the dish taste fishy, and too much soy will overpower the other flavors.

SALT-CURED PORK OR SALT PORK: This is the side or belly meat of the pig, which is heavily streaked with fat, pickled in dry salt but not smoked. When salt pork is called for in a recipe, never substitute a smoked product. It is used when a certain amount of fat is required in addition to flavor. Generally, you can use one of the substitutes suggested for country ham in conjunction with a mild-flavored fat (peanut oil or butter).

When a recipe calls for a piece of salt pork or ham to be stewed with the vegetables, a well-scraped Parmesan cheese rind (preferably from a piece of Parmigiano-Reggiano) is a very good substitute for either meat. It lends a body and richness to the broth that is similar to that lent by the salt-cured meat. Scrape the inner side of the rind well to remove any soft bits of cheese before using it.

BACON: When bacon is called for in this book, I mean smoked breakfast bacon. Historically, all salt-cured pork used to be called "bacon," regardless of the cut, and it was usually not smoked. In the historical recipes, I've used salt pork or ham in my version of the recipe and call for bacon only when the sweet-smoky taste of modern bacon is the desired flavor. I've never found a satisfactory substitute; smoked turkey and tofu are too harsh and smoky tasting, and the "bacons" made from soy products are even worse. Therefore, the suggested substitutions were not aimed at imitating bacon, but at producing a distinctly Southern, albeit different, taste.

Fatback: This is the layer of pure fat on the back of the hog. It is salt-cured in the same way as salt pork, but it is not the same thing. The cheapest and crudest of the pork seasonings used in Southern cooking, it is not used anywhere in this book. If the salt pork in your market does not have a generous streak of lean meat, it's probably fatback. Pass it by and use country ham, prosciutto, or one of the suggested substitutes.

Lard: Here we go: pure, rendered pig fat—full of flavor and browning properties that cannot be imitated. I believe that lard is healthier than a fat that has been hydrogenated and treated with chemical hardeners and emulsifiers. As long as you do not have a medical condition that is aggravated by ingesting saturated fat, using limited amounts of lard wisely will not jeopardize your health. If you are not able to use pork fat, butter can be substituted for lard in pastries or for sautéing. If you do not use any animal products, substitute a flavorful vegetable fat such as peanut or olive oil for sautéing and peanut oil for frying.

BROTH

A good broth or stock is often the sure foundation on which the flavors of so many vegetable dishes—and not only soups—are built. It is very little trouble to make, freezes beautifully, and adds a depth of flavor and body that makes the difference between a good dish and a great one. And yet so few cooks take this extra careful step. I tested many of the recipes in this book with canned broth, not because I prefer it or cook with it very often in my own kitchen, but because I wanted to be sure that the dish still tasted good when that shortcut was used. So when the ingredients list says "or canned broth," it will work in the recipe, but it is not, and never will be, a recommendation. My preference, in all instances, is broth that I've made myself.

If you choose to use canned or commercially frozen broth, look for a brand that does not contain monosodium glutamate (good luck), and if it is canned broth, dilute it with equal parts water, even if the package directions say to use it full strength.

The only caution I have about homemade broth is that it is addictive. Once you make your own and taste the difference that it makes, you'll never again be satisfied with anything else.

Meat Broth

This is a sort of master recipe that can be used to make any sort of meat broth, since the kind of bones used determines the broth. The most usual is beef, though occasionally veal and even pork broth are used in traditional Southern vegetable cookery. You can even mix up the bones for a more complex broth, but where pale color and subtlety of flavor are important, it's better if veal bones aren't mixed with those from beef or pork. If, on the other hand, you want a more intense color, brown the bones first in the oven. Position a rack in the upper third of the oven and preheat it to 400 degrees F. Put the bones in a roasting pan and toss them with just enough oil to coat them. Bake them until they are nicely browned and fragrant, about half an hour. Be careful not to scorch them.

When a clear broth is important, careful skimming is critical, but when all that matters is flavor, you can happily ignore the pot. If the simmer is kept imperceptible, the broth will still be clear enough for most of the recipes of this book. If you want crystalline aspic, though, take the time to skim the broth.

MAKES ABOUT 5 QUARTS

6 pounds meaty bones, shank, neck, tail, knuckles, or feet
1 large yellow onion, peeled and stuck with 3 whole cloves
1 large carrot, peeled and thickly sliced
1 rib celery with leaves attached, thickly sliced
1 leek, split and washed (or the green part only)
1 Bouquet Garni (page 36), made with 2 to 3 sprigs parsley, 2 to 3
*   sprigs thyme, and 2 bay leaves*
6–8 whole peppercorns
1 quarter-sized slice ginger
Salt

1.   Put the bones in a 10-quart soup kettle with 6 quarts of cold water. Place the kettle over a very low heat, as low as you can get it, and let it come slowly to a simmer, which will take about three-quarters of an hour. As the scum begins rising to the top, skim it carefully away, and continue to do so as more forms on the top of the liquid. Do not stir the kettle, now or hereafter.

2.   When the scum no longer forms, let the liquid simmer for half an hour. Raise the heat to medium low and add all the remaining ingredients and a large pinch of salt. Let the pot come back to a simmer, again carefully skimming off the scum as it rises to the surface.

3.   Reduce the heat, as low as you can get it, and cook the broth at a bare simmer, uncovered, for at least 1½ hours or even longer, checking it periodically. The longer the broth simmers, the more concentrated its flavor will be. Simmer it very slowly, the steam bubbles not quite breaking the surface; it should never boil. Turn off the heat and let the broth settle and cool. Carefully strain it from the solids into a lidded metal or ceramic container or glass jars. Let the broth cool, uncovered, then seal it with a tight lid and refrigerate. It

will keep like this for 4 or 5 days. To store it longer, chill it, skim off the fat, then spoon it into freezable containers, seal tightly, and freeze. It will keep indefinitely.

CHICKEN BROTH

Stewing hens or scrap chicken parts make excellent broth, and they are inexpensive.

MAKES ABOUT 5 QUARTS

1 whole stewing hen, about 6 pounds, or the same weight in necks,
backs, wings, and feet
1 large onion, peeled and stuck with 3 whole cloves
2–3 large carrots, peeled and thickly sliced
1 rib celery with leaves attached, thickly sliced
1 leek, split and washed (or the green part only)
1 Bouquet Garni (page 36), made with 2 to 3 sprigs parsley, 2 to 3
sprigs thyme, and 2 bay leaves
8–10 whole peppercorns
1 quarter-sized slice ginger
Salt

1.   Put the hen or chicken parts in a 10-quart soup kettle with 6 quarts of cold water. Place the kettle over a very low heat, as low as you can get it, and let it come slowly to a simmer, which will take about three-quarters of an hour. As the scum begins rising to the top, skim it carefully away, and continue to do so as more forms on the top of the liquid. Do not stir the kettle, now or hereafter.

2.   When the scum no longer forms, let the broth simmer for half an hour. Raise the heat to medium low and add all the remaining ingredients and a large pinch of salt. Let the pot come back to a simmer, again carefully skimming off the scum as it rises to the surface.

3.   Reduce the heat, as low as you can get it, and cook the broth at a bare simmer, uncovered, for at least 1½ hours or even longer, checking it periodically. The longer the broth simmers, the more concentrated its flavor will be. Simmer it very slowly, the steam bubbles not quite breaking the surface; it should never boil. Turn off the heat and let it settle and cool. Carefully strain it from the solids into a lidded metal or ceramic container or glass jars. Let the broth cool, uncovered, then seal it with a tight lid and refrigerate. It will keep like this for 4 or 5 days. To store it longer, chill it, skim off the fat, then spoon it into freezable containers, seal tightly, and freeze. It will keep indefinitely.

VEGETABLE BROTH ⤐

Now that very few Southerners observe meatless fast days, few of us use vegetable broth anymore. But if you are cooking without meat, this aromatic broth will provide a welcome depth of flavor without adding meat to the pot. The flavor secret is the whole garlic. When garlic is slow-simmered in one piece as it is here, its taste is not pronounced, and it adds a subtle, almost meaty flavor to the broth.

MAKES ABOUT 4 QUARTS

3 tablespoons butter or extra virgin olive oil
2 medium onions, peeled, 1 left whole and stuck with 3 cloves, the other
    thinly sliced
2 large carrots, peeled and thickly sliced
2 ribs celery with leafy tops, thickly sliced
2 leeks, white and green parts, split, thoroughly washed, and thickly
    sliced
6 quarts water
4 large cloves garlic, peeled but left whole
1 medium fresh tomato or one whole canned tomato
1 Bouquet Garni (page 36), made with 3 sprigs parsley, 3 sprigs thyme,
    1 sprig each oregano and sage, and 2 bay leaves
2 quarter-sized ginger slices
6–8 whole peppercorns
Salt

1. Put the butter or oil, the sliced onion, carrots, celery, and leeks in a large kettle that will hold all the ingredients. Turn on the heat to medium high and sauté, tossing frequently, until the vegetables are nicely browned but not scorched, about 10 minutes.

2. Add the remaining ingredients, a healthy pinch of salt, and reduce the heat to low. Bring the liquid slowly to a simmer, skimming it carefully of any scum that rises to the top.

3. Reduce the heat, as low as you can get it, and cook the broth at a bare simmer, uncovered, for at least 1½ hours or even longer, checking it periodically, or until the liquid is reduced by about a third. The longer the broth simmers, the more concentrated its flavor will be. It should simmer very slowly.

4. Turn off the heat and let the broth settle and cool. Carefully strain it from the solids into a lidded metal or ceramic container or glass jars. Let the broth cool completely, uncovered, then seal it with a tight lid and refrigerate. It will keep like this for 4 or 5 days. To store it longer, chill it, then spoon it into freezable containers, seal tightly, and freeze. It will keep indefinitely.

THE SOUTHERN SPICE CABINET

One crisp winter day I spent the better part of a morning hashing over Southern cooking with two visitors from England, describing the many different cuisines that make it up, discussing its many regional differences, enumerating its characteristic elements. A good bit of that time went into trying to describe the real essence of the Lowcountry kitchen. Finally, famished from all that talk of food, we went over to Nita Dixon's café for lunch. Nita is a dynamic cook who is doing a lot to wake people up to real Lowcountry food. It isn't a crusade with her; she just cooks the way she learned to cook from her mama and grandmama—making people fall in love with both the cuisine and her. They keep coming back for more. We walked in and took a deep breath of the rich aroma that met us. I turned to my visitors—"Do you smell that? That aroma of okra and spice? That's the smell; that's the essence of the Lowcountry kitchen." Suddenly, they understood. Nita's cooking had accomplished in one deep breath what I hadn't been able to do in more than an hour of babbling.

There are kitchens that you can walk into blindfolded, and though you may not have been told where you were going, you nonetheless know where you are. The aroma of a particular spice—or of a blending of spices and herbs—is a culinary hallmark, defining a place more clearly than a road sign. That smell of spice defines so many of the world's cuisines, setting each distinctly apart from its neighbors.

These are the ones that define ours:

CAYENNE, CHILES, AND OTHER HOT PEPPERS: The seedpods of the many varieties of *Capsicum frutescens*, what we know as hot or chile peppers, are perhaps the most pervasive of all spices in the Southern kitchen. They are a hallmark of all African-influenced cooking and are common in all the cuisines of the South—from Creole New Orleans to Tidewater Virginia. The reason that these peppers—which by the way are not even remotely related to true pepper—have become so commonplace is simply that they were so cheap and readily available. True pepper was imported and, in the early days at least, very expensive. Naturally, peppercorns did not figure in the home cooking of Southern African Americans during the days of slavery—or even for many years after slavery ended. Even white families of average means had to be frugal in their use of this spice. But capsicum pepper plants were easy to grow; they flourished in practically any soil and in the South's milder climate; so, it's easy to see how they became so common an element in Southern cooking.

The heat in capsicum peppers is generated by an oily acid that is contained in the inner flesh and (especially) the seeds of the pod. When you are working with the flesh and seeds, take care to protect your hands if you are especially sensitive to this acid, because it can actually cause blisters. And in all cases, always wash your hands well before touching anything else—especially your eyes or lips—after you've handled the cut pepper, or you will put yourself or someone else at risk of a cross-burn, which can cause a lot of discomfort at best and a serious blister at worst.

Cayenne is the most commonly used member of the vast family of capsicum peppers in our region, but any hot red pepper can be used in the recipes of this book. Be aware, however, that they can vary in pungency and in level of heat, from a relatively mild lightly-warm-your-tongue tingle to a blazing knock-the-top-of-your-head-off blister. If you are substituting a Scotch bonnet in a recipe that calls for a fresh pod of cayenne, for example, you will want to use substantially less of it than the recipe indicates.

And speaking of less, that's what you should keep in mind when using all hot peppers. The idea is to add flavor first and a warming lift second. I am so weary of the prodigal way that this spice is overused by modern cooks. They pour on the hot pepper to the point that you can no longer taste anything, least of all the intriguing flavor that these peppers can actually lend to a dish.

Throughout this book, a whole pod of hot pepper, either fresh or dried, is frequently added to the pot in one piece, then removed and discarded when the dish is finished. This is an old Southern cook's trick for adding the flavor of the pepper without releasing the heat-generating acid. When the pod is left whole, the acid stays inside, but the flavor of the pepper is infused into the pot. Don't add part of a pepper, since the cut edge will release the hot acid into the food, and if you must substitute ground cayenne for the whole pod, use the smallest dose, since the dish is not intended to be hot.

PEPPER VINEGAR

Pickled peppers and the vinegar in which they are cured are important fixtures in a Southern kitchen, both in cooking, where they are used as a flavoring in countless vegetable and meat dishes, and at the table, where they are a condiment that accompanies everything from turnip greens to baked chicken. When a recipe calls for pepper vinegar, it means the vinegar from this pickle, and *not* hot pepper sauce, so don't substitute the latter for it. You can, however, use a few drops of hot sauce diluted in regular cider vinegar.

In the South, pickled peppers can be found in most markets, either in the pickle or bottled-sauce sections. Elsewhere, they can sometimes be found in West Indian or specialty markets. Or you can make your own; it isn't difficult.

MAKES 1 PINT

6 ounces whole fresh hot peppers (see note)
About 1 cup cider vinegar

1. Sterilize a pint jar by boiling it in a water bath for 10 minutes. Wash the peppers well and dry them. Making sure that your hands are very clean, pack the peppers in the jar.
2. In a stainless or nonreactive pan, bring the vinegar to a boil. While it is still boiling hot, pour it over the peppers until they are completely covered. Seal the jar and store it in a cool, dark place (the fridge is okay) for 2 to 4 weeks before using. Use the peppers within 2 months.
3. For more prolonged storage, process the jar in a water bath for 10 minutes. Place the jar on a folded cloth so that it doesn't touch anything, and let it cool completely. If it doesn't seal, reprocess it. See pages 9–11 for more detailed canning instructions.

Note: *You can use any green or red hot peppers to make pepper vinegar. Cayenne, tiny round bird peppers, and jalapeños are the most popular in the South. Each has its own distinct character, and some are much hotter than others, so take this into account when you are adding the peppers or pepper vinegar to a recipe.*

Some Southern cooks put their pickled peppers up in condiment bottles so that they are convenient to use at the table. If you like, you can use an old commercial catsup or Worcestershire sauce bottle, but make sure it is thoroughly cleaned and sterilized first. Also, never use a commercial bottle for canning purposes. Commercial bottles are not designed for the home canning process.

GINGER: The root, or more accurately, the bulb or rhizome of the perennial *Zingiber officinale* is a spice that has been popular in most Western cookery and medicine since antiquity. Originally native to Southeast Asia, ginger has been used in the West at least since the days of the Roman Empire. It was also widely used in English cooking by the beginning of American colonization, and so naturally it figures prominently in Southern cookery as well.

Ginger's popularity in the South is owed in part to the fact that, like capsicum peppers, the plant flourishes in our climate and is easy to grow. At one time, ginger was a common fixture in most Southern gardens; the fragrant flowers of the plants made them as ornamental as they were useful. Modern Southerners use ginger mostly to flavor pickles, preserves, and baked goods. The spice is less commonly found in meat or vegetable dishes, though historically that has not always been true.

Ginger is sold in several forms: fresh bulbs (or roots), dried powder, and preserved and candied ginger. Fresh gingerroot can be found in many vegetable markets and in the produce section of almost all supermarkets. Powdered ginger is universally available. Preserved gingerroot and stems—usually packed in syrup—can be found in specialty markets, as can the candied or crystallized variety. These last two types are used mostly in sweets and can't be substituted for fresh ginger in a savory dish.

MUSTARD: I don't mean that jar of turmeric-yellow condiment in your refrigerator, but those little round seeds in the jar of pickles. This spice has long been an important element of Southern cooking—flavoring those pickles, giving kick to a barbecue, putting the "devil" in anything that was called "deviled." Mustard doesn't figure as prominently in Southern vegetable cookery as it does in the preparation of meat, poultry, or fish, or as a seasoning in pickles and catsups or in spicy chow-chows and chutneys, but it does figure.

Historically, Southern cooks kept two kinds of mustard in the pantry: whole seeds and powdered mustard—or, as they called it, mustard flour. It was from the latter that the prepared condiment was made as needed. Cookbooks indicate that they knew and used both English (very hot and pungent) and French (much milder) mustards, depending on how hot the prepared condiment needed to be.

Today, most Southerners use a prepared mustard of one sort or another, but we do still use mustard powder. For the recipes in this book, keep a stock of three basic types of mustard in your pantry: dry powder (my own preference is English, but any dry mustard will do), a prepared Dijon mustard, and whole seeds. Many Southerners prefer an American-style salad mustard—that bright turmeric-yellow variety, which one clever manufacturer has labeled "classic yellow" in order to give it cachet. I never use it myself, because I find that turmeric is a spice that you cannot dress up and take everywhere. If you prefer, however, you may substitute American-style salad mustard in any recipe that calls for a prepared mustard.

NUTMEG AND MACE: Once very common in the meat and vegetable cookery of the South, these spices have more recently been relegated mostly to the baker's pantry. Fortunately, however, they are making a comeback in the stewpot.

Nutmeg and mace are intimately related to one another, since they are different parts of the same fruit of a tropical evergreen tree, *Myristica fragrans*. The nutmeg is the kernel of the fruit, and mace is a lacy, netlike membrane that covers this kernel. Sometimes in Caribbean markets, whole nutmegs are sold with the mace still attached. Unfortunately, they are not sold this way in U.S. markets. While whole nutmegs are readily available, whole blade mace is hard to come by. Most of the mace available is preground.

Avoid preground nutmeg and mace like the plague. The flavor and aroma of these spices are due to the aromatic oils that they contain. As long as the spice is whole, these oils remain locked inside, but they are very volatile and evaporate rapidly once they are exposed to the air, which is why preground nutmeg and mace taste like old eraser dust. Most of the oils have evaporated and, with them, most of the flavor. Keep a stock of whole nutmegs on hand and grate them with a nutmeg mill or grater only as needed.

When I don't have whole mace on hand, I usually substitute freshly grated nutmeg rather than resort to powdered mace. The spices have a similar flavor, though mace is the stronger and more assertive of the two. If powdered mace is all you can get and you prefer to use it, buy it in very small quantities and keep it in a small, tightly sealed jar, well away from light, air, and heat.

PEPPER: True pepper—the black pepper that we use nowadays with such abandon—was once one of the rarest and most exotic of spices, the soul of the mysterious Eastern spice trade. Whether the peppercorns are the familiar black ones, or green, or white, all are the berries of a tropical vine native to India, *Piper nigrum*. Their color is determined by when they are harvested, and how they are treated after the fact.

When the berries first form, they are, like most fruit, bright green. If picked at this stage and dried or pickled, they retain their green color and have a more subtle, almost herbal flavor. Green peppercorns are seldom used in Southern cooking. As the berries ripen, the color develops, first becoming pale yellow, then orange, then bright red. It is at these varying stages of ripeness that most of the berries are harvested. Black peppercorns are the whole berries, harvested and dried before they are completely ripe. The outer flesh of the berry turns black and clings to the inner kernel as it dries, producing the most common variety of peppercorn, with the most developed and complex flavor. White peppercorns are the kernels of the berries harvested when fully ripe. The outer skin is removed from the berry, leaving only the creamy, tan inner kernel. White peppercorns have the most assertive flavor and are usually the hottest.

The whole berries keep their flavor indefinitely, but once they are ground, they lose everything but the heat in pretty short order. Preground pepper may be convenient, but once you are accustomed to the fuller flavor of the freshly ground spice, you will appreciate why serious cooks never touch the preground stuff. Get yourself a couple of peppermills, one for black and one for white pepper, and stock them with the best-quality whole peppercorns that you can find.

SPICE BLENDS:　In Southern kitchens, various blends of spices have long been used to flavor many different things, from the Sunday chicken to a seafood boil to the holiday fruitcake. Commercial versions of many of these blends are widely available and are very convenient. But for the best flavor, the blends that are the most satisfying to use are always those that you have made yourself. The blends that follow are those called for in the recipes in this book. Please note that they are by no means definitive; there are many others that I haven't included, and individual cooks have their own variations.

All spice blends should be stored in well-sealed jars or tins, away from light, air, and heat for the best shelf life. Also, the jars should be small, so that there is as little air left at the top of the jar as possible.

Curry:　There are cooks who think that "curry" is a single spice; and even those who know better are often not aware that in India, where this family of spice blends originated, there is no such thing as "curry powder." Each cook blends, toasts, and grinds the spices as needed, and the precise blend will vary from cook to cook and dish to dish. The Madras blends that are exported from India were all designed for the Western market.

Well, regardless of their deviation from their origins, and of each cook's technical knowledge of what curry is, the blend is an important element in the Southern kitchen. All the early cookbooks included recipes for curry powder, and the blend has been frequently used to flavor many Southern dishes at least since the eighteenth century.

For meatless cooking, curry powder is especially valuable to achieve a traditional Southern flavor without adding animal products to the pot. A small pinch added to a soup or pot of stewed vegetables lends a meaty richness and adds a fragrance and subtle flavor that is distinctively and satisfyingly Southern.

CURRY POWDER

This is not, by any stretch of the imagination, a Far Eastern blend, but a Southern adaptation, based on the traditional curries from early Southern and English cookbooks. Make curry powder in small quantities, since the spices don't hold their flavor once they are ground.

MAKES ABOUT 1 CUP

2 tablespoons whole allspice
2 tablespoons whole coriander
2 tablespoons powdered dried ginger
2 tablespoons whole white mustard seeds
2 tablespoons whole black peppercorns
2 tablespoons whole turmeric (or powdered turmeric)
1 tablespoon whole cumin seeds
1 tablespoon whole cardamom seeds
1 tablespoon whole fenugreek seeds

1. Grind the spices to a powder in a blender until they are finely ground and well blended, or in batches in a spice mill, combine them in a pint jar, and shake until they are evenly blended.

2. Spoon the powder into small containers (½-pint or ¼-pint canning jars or small spice jars), seal tightly, and store away from light, heat, and air.

Seafood Boiling Spice: This blend is so called because it is most often used to flavor the boiling liquid for crab, shrimp, or crawfish, or that wonderful one-pot feast—the Lowcountry boil. However, this blend need not be limited to the boiling pot, nor to seafood. It's also frequently used to flavor stews, baked fish, deviled crab, and casserole-baked dishes. Good commercial boiling-spice blends are widely available in the South— Zatarain's, Old Bay, McCormick's, and Savannah Spice Company are all good commercial blends. Even so, making your own boiling spice has distinct advantages. Not only will it be fresher and more flavorful, but you can tailor it to suit your and your family's individual tastes.

Hoppin' John's
Seafood Boiling Spice

This is my favorite recipe for boiling spice, from John Taylor's classic *Hoppin' John's Lowcountry Cooking*. Notice that it contains salt. John says that this helps preserve the flavor of the blend and also makes it easier to use, since you won't have to add salt separately. For boiling shellfish, allow ½ tablespoon of boiling spice and ½ a fresh lemon for every quart of water. For use in other dishes, refer to the individual recipes in this book. If a recipe calls for a commercial mix, keep in mind that it has added salt, and cut back on, or even omit, the salt called for in the recipe.

MAKES ABOUT 1 CUP

¼ cup whole mustard seeds
2 tablespoons whole black peppercorns
2 tablespoons hot red pepper flakes
6 bay leaves
1 tablespoon whole celery seeds
1 tablespoon coriander seeds
1 tablespoon ground dried ginger
A few blades of mace or ¼ teaspoon powdered mace
¼ cup salt

1.   Put all the ingredients except the salt into a blender, and process until they are evenly ground. Add the salt and pulse the blender until the salt is evenly mixed with the seasonings.

2.   Spoon the spice mix into a ½-pint jar, seal tightly, and store away from light, heat, or air.

Note: *After making and using a couple of batches, you will know what you like and don't like, and can balance the blend to suit your own tastes. For example, if you prefer a milder boil, cut back on the cayenne pepper, and add a little sweet paprika for color and a more subtle flavor.*

THE SOUTHERN HERB GARDEN

Every now and again, some folk historian pronounces with authority that Southerners have never had much use for herbs, and that—while the traditional cookery of the South may be aromatic with many spices—herbs, especially fresh ones, play only a nominal role in it. I wonder what South they are talking about, because it surely isn't this one. The old cookbooks and kitchen gardens of the South that I know tell a different—and compelling—story.

The fact is, herb gardens have always been important in the South, from the lush bed of mint that wreathed the front porch of countless plantations and farmhouses to the great laurel trees that still survive on Georgia's barrier islands. And if old cookbooks are any indication, those herbs weren't grown for their looks; they were used. It has only been during the last few generations—our living memory, in fact—that herbs, especially fresh ones, have fallen into disuse. Happily, they are being rediscovered all across the South. They figure prominently in the kitchens of our most notable regional chefs. And best of all, they have once again become important in home cooking.

Here are the herbs that are essential to a Southern garden and kitchen, with some notes on their use:

BASIL (OCIMUM BASILICUM): Though infrequently mentioned in historical Southern recipes, basil did turn up from time to time, especially as an ingredient for herb-scented vinegars. Today, it is widely used by Southern cooks.

Basil is a part of the large family of mints, and there are dozens of varieties within its own branch of the family, from the famous small-leaved Genoese basil to the spicy, purple Dark Opal variety. In between the exotic extremes is the common variety, usually labeled "sweet basil" at the nursery or garden shop.

Basil is of very little use once it is dried. I use it in my own herb blend (page 37), but that's about all. When the freeze kills off the last of the plants in my courtyard, I wait until the next basil season comes around and make use of other herbs that stand up better to drying in the meantime. The best plan is to grow your own; if you have a sunny, well-drained garden spot, or even a window that will accommodate a large pot, the plants are easy to grow and care for. Failing that, fresh basil is available in many markets. Look for firm leaves without any brown spots, especially at the center.

In vegetable cookery, basil has many uses. Pairing it with tomatoes is classic, and adding it to a pot of okra and tomatoes transforms something wonderful into something downright sublime. Basil is also lovely with squash, eggplant, and green beans.

BAY LAUREL (LAURUS NOBILIS): This is the herb of nobility in antiquity, revered by the ancient Greeks and used as a symbol of highest honor. The spicy aroma of bay laurel is a touchstone for all Southern cooking, from the Creole kitchen of New Orleans, to the rice kitchen of the Carolina and Georgia Lowcountry, to the soul kitchen of African Americans everywhere. Bay trees were imported into the Carolinas and Georgia very early on and still flourish in milder coastal climates.

Since the plants take to our climate so well, many Lowcountry cooks grow their own and use only fresh leaves. If you live in a temperate climate, you can grow your own in a sunny spot in the garden, or indoors in a pot. Dried bay leaves are, however, the most common form available. Buy them from a store that sells them in bulk. Look for whole, unbroken leaves with a clear, green color and a pungent scent. Keep the leaves in a tightly sealed jar away from light, air, and heat.

Bay, one of the essential herbs of a classic Bouquet Garni (page 36), is used to season most Southern soups and stews, especially gumbos.

CHIVES (ALLIUM SCHOENOPRASUM): This delicate herb is actually a member of the pungent garlic branch of the lily family. Many's the wily Southern cook who has put its cousin, the common wild onion, to use and called it "chives." Actually, chives hardly figure at all in Southern cooking per se, yet they are an important herb in flavoring Southern vegetables. The seeming paradox is easily explained: the herb is never actually cooked; its fresh leaves are chopped or snipped and added at the end of the cooking, off the heat, so that the bright flavor is not blunted.

Use only freshly cut chives; the dried variety is of no gastronomical interest whatsoever. Chives grow well in a mild climate but wilt under the intense heat of a Southern midsummer, especially in a place like Savannah. Consequently, they are more commonly paired with delicate spring and hearty autumn produce.

MARJORAM AND OREGANO (ORIGANUM, MINT FAMILY): These two closely related members of the enormous mint family are not commonly used in traditional Southern cooking. Oregano is frequently added to the pot if the cook is Creole, and marjoram is occasionally mentioned in some of the Anglo cooking of the eastern seaboard. Today, thanks in part to a national interest in all things Italian, a bottle of dried oregano can be found on most Southern pantry shelves. All members of the marjoram family stand up pretty well to drying. Oregano and marjoram are also fairly hearty perennials and are easy to grow in a sunny garden spot or in a pot on a sunny ledge.

Oregano is most often used to flavor gumbos, field peas, squash, and sometimes okra and tomatoes.

MINT (MENTHA FAMILY):   Along with sage and bay leaves, this family of herbs forms an herbal triumvirate, the foundation of all Southern herbal cookery. The most common member of the mint family in the South is spearmint *(Mentha spicata)*, which flourishes in our warm, humid climate. You can grow your own fresh mint in a sunny garden spot or in a pot on a sunny window ledge. Fresh mint is also widely available in the market. If you go that route and your market doesn't have spearmint, don't panic; simply substitute peppermint for it.

When dried, mint loses its warm, herbal quality and becomes more distinctly "minty." Dried mint is useful in certain stews and ragouts, but don't substitute it for fresh mint unless the recipe says that you can.

Mint is probably best known outside the South as the essential ingredient of a drink, but inside the South it is as frequently paired with lamb, mutton, and game as it is with bourbon. It is also used to season peas (both fresh green peas and field peas), new potatoes, fresh melons, and squash.

PARSLEY (PETROSELINUM CRISPUM):   Poor parsley: in every pot but seldom noticed—unless it happens to be sprinkled over the top of things as a garnish. Parsley may not have an assertive flavor, perhaps, but no other herb is as universally used or important. Its flavor does not dominate, but it is an important underpinning for virtually all soups, stews, and gumbos. Parsley is also one of the three essential herbs of a Bouquet Garni (page 36).

Throughout this book, I never use the adjective "fresh" before parsley in the ingredients list, because this is one herb that must be fresh to be of any use at all. When dried, parsley loses all its flavor and is of absolutely no gastronomical interest.

SAGE (SALVIA OFFICINALIS):   If I were asked to characterize, in a single smell or flavor, the essence of Southern cooking, my answer would probably be sage. Ever popular in English cookery, its universality in Southern cooking points straight back to Anglo roots.

Though better known in our region as a classic seasoning for poultry, pork, game, and dressing, sage has many uses in the vegetable pot. It is frequently paired with squash, both winter and summer varieties, okra and field peas, and is the flavoring of choice for onions.

THYME (THYMUS, MINT FAMILY): Another member of the mint family; there are many varieties of thyme plants that are commonly grown, but the most familiar is *Thymus vulgaris*, or "common" thyme. This herb is one of the defining aromas and flavors of both Creole and Lowcountry cookery.

Thyme is one of the essential ingredients of a classic Bouquet Garni and a pot of Creole gumbo almost isn't gumbo without it. Thyme is also frequently paired with field peas and with both yellow crookneck and hearty winter squashes.

*B*OUQUET GARNI

You might think that this little bundle of flavoring herbs is used mostly in Creole cooking, since it still goes by its French name, but bouquets garnis are a common element of all Southern cooking. They are as important in a stockpot or a Lowcountry pilau as they are in a pot of gumbo or étouffée.

The essential, classic core of a bouquet garni consists of a sprig of parsley, a sprig of thyme, and a bay leaf. Often the leafy part of a celery stalk is incorporated into it, and another herb may be used in addition to—or, depending on the dish, instead of—the thyme. When that's the case, I have so indicated in the individual recipe.

Make sure that the string you use to tie the bundle is cotton kitchen twine, and not a coated or synthetic material.

MAKES 1 BOUQUET GARNI

1 leafy celery-stalk top
1 large sprig parsley
1 3-inch sprig thyme
1 bay leaf (fresh, if possible)

Wash the celery top and herbs, and pat them dry. Gather the celery, sprigs of herbs, and bay leaf together. Tie them together at the bottom with a 4- to 6-inch piece of kitchen twine. If you use a dried bay leaf, tie the bundle gently so that the leaf doesn't crumble. Then, wrap the string up and around the bundle as you would the laces of a dancing slipper. Tie it securely at the top of the bundle. The bouquet garni is now ready to use.

Note: *If you find yourself without any fresh thyme, you can use dried thyme in the bouquet garni. First, tie it up in a bit of muslin or a triple layer of cheesecloth, or place it into a stainless-steel teaball. Tie it to the remaining ingredients so that you don't have to fish around for it at the end of the cooking.*

FINES HERBES

Another important herb combination with a French name, fines herbes is a classic potpourri of dried aromatic herbs that is a critical element in many cuisines. Use it to flavor a pot of okra and tomatoes, especially when the tomatoes are the canned variety, and your favorite vinaigrette; or fill a tea ball with it and put it in a stockpot or stewpot, or slip it into almost any stewed vegetable—from slow-cooked green beans to sweet potatoes.

I prefer to make this recipe in small batches, so that it stays fresh, but you can make it in larger quantities and either give away or freeze what you won't use right away.

FOR ABOUT 1 1/2 CUPS

3 tablespoons dried, crumbled basil
3 tablespoons dried, crumbled marjoram
3 tablespoons dried, crumbled rosemary
3 tablespoons dried, crumbled sage
3 tablespoons dried, crumbled savory (winter or summer)
3 tablespoons dried, crumbled thyme
1 tablespoon dried, crumbled bay leaves
1 tablespoon dried, crumbled lavender flowers

Put all the herbs in a pint jar with a tight-fitting lid. Shake it vigorously until all the herbs are well mixed. Keep the jar tightly covered and store it away from light, air, and heat.

Sources

Here are a few selected sources for some of the regional ingredients called for elsewhere in this book:

Stone-ground cornmeal and whole corn grits:

HOPPIN' JOHN'S
30 Pinckney Street
Charleston, South Carolina 29401
Tel.: (803) 577-6404

OLD MILL OF GUILFORD
1340 NC 68 North
Oak Ridge, North Carolina 27310

FIELDER'S OLD FASHION
Mike H. Buckner, Miller
Junction City, Georgia 31812

For cornmeal only:

FOWLER'S MILLING COMPANY
[No relation]
12500 Fowlers Mill Road
Chardon, Ohio 44024
Tel.: (800) 327-2024

KYMULGA GRIST MILL
Grist Mill Road
Childersburg, Alabama 35044

For soft wheat flour:

WHITE LILY FOODS
P.O. Box 871
Knoxville, Tennessee 37901
Tel.: (423) 546-5511

KING ARTHUR FLOUR COMPANY
Baker's Catalogue
P.O. Box 876
Norwich, Vermont 05055
Tel.: (800) 827-6836

For exceptional country ham, naturally cured bacon, sausages, and other pork products:

S. WALLACE EDWARDS
& SONS, INC.
P.O. Box 25
Surry, Virginia 23883
Tel.: (800) 222-4267

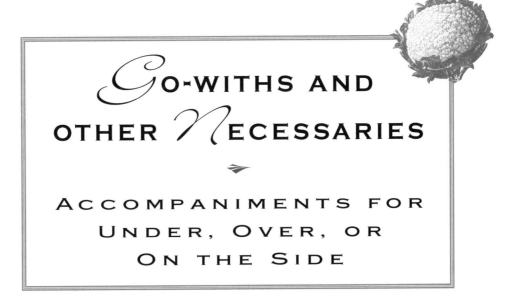

Go-withs and Other Necessaries

Accompaniments for Under, Over, or On the Side

---

*M*any Southern vegetable recipes are very simple, but they seldom find themselves going solo on the plate. There's always some kind of flavoring accompaniment, whether it's a splash of spicy Pepper Vinegar (page 27) or briny Old Sour (page 287), a dollop of sweet-sour relish or chutney or a garlicky okra pickle. And, more often than not, there's some kind of "go-with"—a bit of cornbread, a hoecake, or a bed of rice or grits. The following go-with recipes are some of the classics that round out a Southern meal. Also included are recipes for basics, such as pie crust, used elsewhere in this book.

Recipes for essential condiments such as pepper vinegar, seasoning spices, and spice and herb blends are discussed in the chapter entitled The Southern Kitchen (pages 7–38), while a few others are scattered throughout the book along with the main ingredient for other recipes: Bill Neal's Pickled Okra (page 109), Dilly Beans (page 134), St. John's Golden Mango Chutney (page 191), John Egerton's Lemon Curd (page 286), and Purefoy Cranberry Relish (page 289).

CORNBREAD, CORN STICKS, AND SKILLET BREAD

Many a Southern vegetable dish is not considered complete without cornbread, whether it comes to the table in the form of a hoecake, a wedge of skillet bread, a crispy corn stick, or a dumpling floating among the greens. Originally, Southern cornbread was a simple, rough batter of meal, water, and salt. The combination evolved over the years, becoming softer and richer. Most modern recipes include buttermilk, eggs, and some kind of enriching fat—bacon grease, butter, or cracklings. They might also include other enrichments, such as fresh corn kernels or jalapeño peppers. Here is the basic recipe, with the classic taste and texture that Southerners have come to prize:

MAKES 14 CORN STICKS OR MUFFINS, OR ONE 9-INCH ROUND

2 cups water stone-ground cornmeal
2 teaspoons baking powder, preferably single-acting
1 teaspoon salt
2 eggs
1½ cups buttermilk or yogurt
4 tablespoons rendered bacon fat, butter, or lard, melted

1. Position a rack in the center of the oven and preheat the oven to 450 degrees F. When it has reached that temperature, lightly but thoroughly grease the pan you plan to use and preheat it in the oven for at least 10 minutes.

2. Measure the cornmeal into a mixing bowl that is large enough to allow all the ingredients to be mixed together comfortably. Stir in baking powder and salt.

3. In a separate bowl, beat the eggs until smooth and stir in the buttermilk or yogurt and 2 tablespoons of the melted fat.

4. When the pan is well heated, make a well in the center of the cornmeal and then pour in the milk and egg mixture. Quickly stir in the liquid, using as few strokes as possible.

5. With a pot holder, remove the pan from the oven and add to it the remaining 2 tablespoons of melted fat. If you are using a corn-stick or muffin pan, drizzle the fat equally into each well. (When I use butter, I take a cold stick still wrapped in its paper and rub a little into each well. Butter will sizzle if the pan is hot enough. If it doesn't, put the pan back into the oven for about 5 more minutes.)

6.   Now, quickly pour the batter into the pan. Again, it must sizzle when it touches the pan. If you are using a corn-stick or muffin pan, fill each well level with the sides. Do it quickly so that each addition sizzles.

7.   Bake in the upper third of the oven until nicely browned and firm, about 25 minutes for corn sticks or muffins and 35 minutes for a skillet cake. As soon as the bread comes out of the oven, invert the pan over a plate (for the cake) or a linen towel (for the corn sticks or muffins). The bread should come right out of the pan.

Note: *If you are using a standard-sized muffin or corn-stick pan, this batter will make 2 batches. I keep two pans on hand for the purpose, but you can make the bread in batches. As soon as you have removed the first batch from the pan, add more fat to the pan and repeat as above. Roll the first batch up in a tea towel to keep them warm while the second batch cooks. Don't use paper towels, foil, or an insulated mat, as they will trap the steam in the bread and soften the crust. Serve the cornbread warm with plenty of good butter.*

SINGLE-ACTING BAKING POWDER

You can use commercial double-acting baking powder for the recipes in this book, but try to find one that is aluminum-free (such as Rumford). I prefer single-acting powder because many double-acting powders have a chemical aftertaste. Single-acting powder isn't made commercially, but making your own is easy.

MAKES ¹/₂ CUP

> *3 level tablespoons cream of tartar*
> *3 level tablespoons bicarbonate of soda*
> *3 level tablespoons rice flour or unbleached all-purpose flour*

Combine all ingredients in an airtight container and shake well. Shake the container well before each use, and use the powder up within a month.

*H*OECAKES ✐

Hoecakes are supposed to have been so named because they were originally cooked on the blade of a hoe that was held over an open hearth. They're basically just cornmeal pancakes. Many Southern cooks today add wheat flour and sugar to their cakes, but I prefer the older version. They are especially good to make on hot days when you want cornbread but don't want to heat up the oven.

Hoecakes are the perfect accompaniment for any vegetable but are especially suited to a pot of spicy gumbo or slow-cooked greens.

MAKES ABOUT A DOZEN CAKES

2 cups fine stone-ground cornmeal
2 teaspoons baking powder, preferably single-acting
1 teaspoon salt
2 large eggs, lightly beaten
2 cups whole milk, buttermilk, or yogurt
Oil, melted butter, or lard, for the griddle

1. Position a rack in the center of the oven and preheat it to 150 degrees F. Mix together the meal, baking powder, and salt in a bowl that will hold all the ingredients comfortably. In a separate bowl, combine the eggs and milk or yogurt, and beat until they are smooth. Stir this quickly into the dry ingredients, using as few strokes as possible.

2. Heat a griddle or cast-iron skillet over medium heat. When it is hot, brush it lightly with the fat. Using a large, pointed kitchen spoon, take up about 2 tablespoons of the batter and pour it onto the griddle from the pointed end of the spoon (this helps ensure that a round cake will form). Repeat until the griddle is full but not crowded.

3. Cook the cakes until the bottoms are nicely browned and airholes form in the tops, about 4 minutes. Turn, and cook until the second side is browned, about 3 to 4 minutes longer. Transfer the cakes to the warm oven and repeat with the remaining batter until all the cakes are cooked. Serve hot, with or without additional butter.

BUTTERED CROUTONS

These crispy, buttery morsels are the ideal accompaniment for just about any soup or salad. They are simple to make, much better than the store-bought variety, and are very economical, since they are best when made from stale bread. Freeze leftover baguettes and crusty rolls until you have enough. To cut them into croutons, use a serrated bread knife and cut the bread first into ½-inch slices and then cut the slices into cubes.

MAKES 2 CUPS

2 ounces (4 tablespoons or ½ stick) unsalted butter
2 cups crusty bread, cut into ½-inch cubes

1. Position a rack in the upper third of the oven and preheat the oven to 300 degrees F. Put the butter in a shallow pan (such as a rimmed cookie sheet or sheet cake pan) that will hold all the bread in a single layer. Put this into the oven to melt the butter.

2. As soon as the butter is melted, add the bread and toss until it is thoroughly coated. Return the pan to the upper third of the oven and bake, tossing the croutons from time to time, until they are delicately browned and crisp, about ½ hour.

Note: *Though it requires more attention, you can prepare the croutons on top of the stove if you prefer not to heat up the oven. Put the butter in a large sauté pan or skillet over medium heat. When it is melted, add the cubed bread and toss until it is evenly coated with the fat. Sauté, tossing frequently, until they are brown and crisp, about 10 to 15 minutes.*

CAROLINA-STYLE RICE

Every rice-based cuisine in the world has its own way of cooking this daily staple. Where chopsticks are the tableware of choice, the rice tends to be a bit sticky so that it holds together when picked up. In northern Italy, it is creamy. If either one of these is what you are accustomed to, Carolina-style rice, from the old rice-growing regions of South Carolina and Georgia, will take some getting used to. When properly done, it almost rattles when it hits the plate: each grain is distinct, firm, and yet tender and fluffy. The only time it gets creamy is when cream gravy is poured over it.

There are two basic rules to remember when cooking rice by the Carolina method.

First, the rice is always washed before it goes into the pot. Even if the package says it is pre-washed, give it a brief rinse. If the rinsing water is milky, wash the rice. Second, the rice should never be stirred while cooking. When it is cooked, fluff it with a fork that has widely spaced, narrow tines, such as a large dinner fork or carving fork.

MAKES 4 SERVINGS

1 cup raw, long-grain rice, preferably Basmati
2 cups water
Salt

1. Put the rice in a large bowl filled with water. Gently pick it up and rub it between your hands. Even prewashed rice will get milky. Let it soak for a few minutes, then pour the rice into a large, tightly woven wire sieve. Rinse it briefly under cold running water until the water running from it is clear, and set it aside in the sink to drain.

2. Put the water, a healthy pinch of salt, and the drained rice in a large kettle over medium-high heat and bring it to a good boil. Stir it to make sure that the salt is dissolved and the rice is not sticking, then put the spoon away.

3. Reduce the heat to low, and set the lid askew on the top. Let the rice simmer for 12 minutes. After that time, there should be clear, dry steam holes formed on the surface, and most if not all of the water should be absorbed. Gently fold the top rice under with a fork, "fluffing," not stirring it.

4. Put the lid on tight and let the pot sit over the heat for a minute more to rebuild the steam, then turn off the fire. Move the pot to a warm part of the stove (if you have an electric stove, leave it where it is; the residual heat in the burner should be just right). If the stove doesn't have a warm spot, put the pan in a larger pan of hot water.

5. Let it steam for 12 more minutes. It can be held like this for up to an hour without harm, but 12 minutes is the minimum. When you are ready to serve the rice, fluff it by picking it with a fork, then turn it out into a serving bowl. Serve at once.

GRITS AND HOMINY GRITS

Popularly known around here as "Georgia Ice Cream," grits is—with the possible exception of okra—perhaps the most infamous and misunderstood ingredient in all Southern cooking. (Now, let's just settle this singular/plural stuff right here: grits is singular and grits are plural—and that's that.) Once a staple on almost every Southern breakfast table, grits became a sort of culinary bogeyman in the South, equal to the nutty relative we kept hidden in the attic. We ate grits and still liked it, but some of us were pretty embarrassed about the whole thing. Grits began to disappear from breakfast menus, and hash-browned potatoes crept into their place. For grits-loving and otherwise patriotic Southerners who never did get embarrassed, it was a depressing state of affairs.

Then something even worse happened. Grits became trendy, the glitzy food star of every upscale Southern restaurant in the land. It went from unmentionable breakfast gruel to the one sure element of a nouvelle Southern menu. It got souffléed, caked and truffled, creamed and jalapeñoed, and infused with more garlic than a Genoa salami. It even got dumped into chocolate dessert. Today, grits is on the menu for practically every meal except, ironically, breakfast.

In short, it got nouvelled into culinary outer space.

However, there are those of us who haven't been impressed by all of this hoopla. Southern food preservationist Edna Lewis best summed up our take on the trend when she said, simply, "They need to leave grits *alone.*"

Basic Boiled Grits

Here's the basic recipe for preparing both whole-corn and plain hominy grits. Exact measurements for the proportion of grits to water are difficult. The usual ratio is four to one, but the amount of water needed can vary, depending on the grits. The safest thing is to keep a teakettle of water simmering close at hand in case the grits need more water before they get tender. You should never add cold water to the pot; it just confuses the poor grits.

MAKES 4 SERVINGS

1 quart (4 cups) water
1 cup raw corn grits
Salt

1.   Bring the water to a good boil in a stainless-steel or enameled kettle, and stir in the grits. Add a pinch of salt, but not too much; you can adjust it later. Bring the grits back to a boil, stirring frequently to prevent lumps from forming.
2.   Reduce the heat to a bare simmer and cover the kettle. Cook, stirring occasionally, until the grits absorb all the moisture and are the consistency of a thick cornmeal mush, about 1 hour. Taste and adjust the seasoning.

GRITS SQUARES

These semitraditional squares are from my friend Jackie Mills, a food editor at *Southern Living* magazine. Like her Grilled Okra Salad (page 104), this dish is at once rooted in Jackie's Kentucky childhood, where she was weaned on peas and grits, and enlivened by her forward-looking sensibility. Enriched with cream and cheese, the grits depart from tradition only in the way they are finished: instead of the usual frying, the cakes bake. "But," says Jackie, "it is a wonderful thing to coat each square in cornmeal and sauté them."

The grits squares can be topped with a fresh vegetable sauté in summer or a hearty stew in winter. Jackie likes to top them with a light, elegant ragout of field peas.

SERVES 9 WITH AN APPETIZER, 4 TO 6 AS A SIDE DISH

4 cups Chicken Broth (page 23) or canned broth
1 1/2 cups regular hominy grits (not quick-cooking or instant)
1/4 cup heavy cream
1 cup freshly grated Pecorino Romano
Black pepper in a peppermill

1. Bring the chicken broth to a boil in a stainless or enamel-lined pan (this helps keep the grits from sticking). Pour in the grits, stirring constantly to keep them from lumping. Cook 20 to 25 minutes, or until they are very thick and tender, stirring occasionally at first and more frequently as they get thick. Stir in the cream and cook 2 to 3 minutes more. Turn off the heat.

2. Add the cheese and a few grindings of black pepper (about 1/4 teaspoon) and stir until smooth. Rinse out an 8 × 8-inch baking dish with cold water and pour in the grits. Let cool and then refrigerate until the grits are very firm, about 4 hours.

3. Position a rack in the center of the oven and preheat the oven to 400 degrees F. Lightly grease a cookie sheet with butter or oil. Cut the grits into 9 squares and put them on the cookie sheet. Bake for 7 to 10 minutes until the grits are just heated through. Don't overcook them or, as Jackie puts it, "they'll squash."

BASIC PASTRY FOR PIES AND TARTS

This is my favorite all-purpose pie dough. It's perfect for just about any baked goods that need a pastry crust—from pecan pie to quiche. The secret to its flaky, tender crumb is lard, which helps tenderize the dough and lends a flakiness that even butter can't imitate. If you can't cook with lard, omit it and use an extra 2 tablespoons butter in its stead. An all-butter pastry is still pretty good.

A lot of people are afraid of making their own pastry, which for the life of me I can't figure out. We're talking here about less than a dollar's worth of ingredients and a technique that is virtually artless. All it takes is a little caution and practice. However, pastry is a cinch to make in the food processor; in fact, it's so easy that I seldom ever make it by hand. Alternate directions for the processor method are given at the end of the recipe.

MAKES TWO 9-INCH PIE SHELLS OR ONE 9-INCH PIE WITH TOP CRUST

10 ounces (about 2 cups) all-purpose, soft-wheat flour
1/2 teaspoon salt
1/4 pound (8 tablespoons, 1 stick) unsalted butter
1 ounce (2 tablespoons) lard
Ice water (1/3 cup or more)

1. Sift the flour and salt together into a metal or ceramic bowl. Cut the butter and lard into bits, and add them to the bowl, handling as little as possible to keep them from melting and becoming oily. If this happens, chill the butter and lard again before adding them.
2. Work the fat into the flour with a pastry blender or 2 knives (not your hands) until it has the texture of coarse meal.
3. Add the ice water, starting with 1/3 cup, and lightly stir it into the flour until it is moistened. Stir in additional water by the tablespoon until the dough is soft and smooth but not sticky. Lightly dust the dough and your hands with flour, and gather it into a ball. Wrap it well with plastic wrap and let it rest in the refrigerator for half an hour.
4. Lightly flour a cool work surface (marble is ideal, but plastic laminate works, too) and roll out the pastry for use as directed in the individual recipe.

Food Processor Pie Dough: If you own a food processor, once you learn to make pie dough with it, you'll never do it any other way. The only tricky part is keeping the dough from being overworked and therefore overheated. The blade's speed causes it to heat up quickly, which can make the fat oily. To prevent this, chill the blade in the refrigerator for about 5 minutes before using it.

Fit the processor with the steel blade and put in the flour and salt. Pulse it a few times to sift it, then add the butter and lard, cut into bits. Pulse the machine until the flour reaches the coarse meal stage. Add ⅓ cup of ice water and pulse again until it is mixed. Then add water in tablespoonfuls, pulsing to mix in each addition until the dough just gathers into a ball.

Sauces

Flavored Butters, Rich Creams, and Other Enhancements

udith Martin, better known as Miss Manners—the doyenne, not of food but of good behavior—reminds us that books on decorum from the past give away some pretty hair-raising things about what was going on in the parlors and dining rooms of yesterday. The very fact that they advised people *not* to do things like pick their teeth with a knife or blow their nose on the tablecloth suggests that there were a lot of people who were actually doing just those things.

Similarly, a perusal of cookbooks used in nineteenth-century Southern kitchens paints a dim picture of the state of sauce making in those days. They are full of all sorts of alarming indictments, which I think was partly because Southern cooks have never been much for using elaborate sauces on their vegetables. Particularly in the agrarian nineteenth century, vegetables were gathered the day they were meant to be served. They were very fresh, intensely flavorful, and didn't need much enhancement to make them taste good. This has remained true even in our own industrial age, thanks to the renewed popularity of farmers' markets and backyard gardening.

All the same, there are vegetable sauces that most Southern cooks, both then and now, would be hard-pressed to do without. From elegant pecan butter, reserved for state occasions, to the homey bowl of mayonnaise on the family table, these sauces are subtle; their aim is to enhance flavor, not cover it up. So don't let their simplicity fool you; they won't let a careless cook off the hook. Their preparation requires as much care as an elaborate sauce might, and their subtlety leaves nothing for a badly prepared vegetable to hide behind.

PECAN BROWN BUTTER

Nuts toasted in brown butter make a lovely sauce for all kinds of vegetables and fish. In Europe and other parts of the United States, almonds are the nut most usually put to use, but in the South, we prefer to use our locally grown pecans. Their rich flavor is very distinctive. Try this sauce with the season's first asparagus, tender young French beans, or broiled fish—especially catfish.

MAKES ABOUT 1 CUP

¹/₂ cup whole pecan halves
¹/₄ pound (1 stick or ¹/₂ cup) unsalted butter
Salt (optional)

1. Pick over the nuts and remove any lingering bits of shell from their grooves. Cut them lengthwise into thirds, using their grooves as guidelines, and set them aside.

2. Put the butter into a heavy-bottomed skillet and place it over medium-high heat. When it is melted, add the pecans and stir until they are coated. Cook, constantly but gently shaking the pan, until both nuts and butter are golden brown. Remove the pan from the heat, swirl in a pinch of salt if you like, and pour the pecan butter over the food that it is intended to sauce. Serve at once.

Note: In some areas, growers sell imperfect, broken pecan pieces that are culled from the premium whole nuts. While they are much more economical than whole nuts, they often have bits of broken shell in them. You can use them for this recipe, but be careful to remove all those stray bits of shell.

DRAWN BUTTER

There is no sauce for vegetables simpler or lovelier than this one, and yet it is seldom seen in modern American cookbooks. What usually turns up under the name nowadays is actually clarified butter, but in the nineteenth century, this thick sauce was what drawn butter originally described. Most old Southern versions followed eighteenth-century English practice, adding the smallest proportion of flour to aid in the thickening and lessen the risk of the butter separating. Later in the nineteenth century, the proportion of flour and liquid increased, and butter sauce degenerated into a pasty white sauce of flour and milk with hardly enough butter to justify the name.

The recipes that follow specify serving the butter sauce in a heated sauceboat. Don't warm the sauceboat too much or the residual heat could cause the sauce to separate. The sauceboat should be cool enough to handle with your bare hands.

It is important to have everything ready to serve before making this sauce; it won't wait while you finish cooking and cannot be reheated.

MAKES ABOUT ¹/₂ CUP

2 tablespoons water
Salt
4 ounces (1 stick or 8 tablespoons) unsalted butter, at room
   temperature

1. Half-fill a pan slightly larger than the saucepan you are using with water. Place it over a medium fire and let it come to a boil. Reduce the fire to a slow simmer.

2. While the water is coming to a boil, put 2 tablespoons of water into the smaller saucepan with a healthy pinch of salt to taste. Bring it to a boil over direct heat.

3. Remove the saucepan from the heat and add 1 tablespoon of the butter. Hold the saucepan just over the simmering water without letting it touch. Shake it gently in one direction in a swirling motion until the butter is almost melted. Add another tablespoon of butter and continue shaking the pan until it is melted. Continue until all the butter has been added and is melted but still quite thick. Pour into a heated sauceboat or directly over the food to be sauced, and serve at once.

LEMON BUTTER

Melted butter is, by itself, just about the best possible sauce for fresh vegetables, and the fragrance of lemon enlivens even the most lackluster. Here, butter and lemon are brought together in an especially nice sauce for asparagus, artichokes, or broccoli, or for dipping shrimp and steamed crab.

MAKES ABOUT ¹/₂ CUP

Salt
1 lemon
¹/₄ cup water
4 ounces (1 stick or 8 tablespoons) unsalted butter

1.   Prepare a pan of water as directed in the previous recipe. While it is coming to a simmer, peel the zest from the lemon, scrape off any white pith, and cut the zest into fine julienne. Put the zest into a saucepan with the water and bring it to a boil. Boil until it is reduced by half and turn off the heat.

2.   Cut the lemon in half and squeeze the juice from one of the halves into the saucepan with the zest and water mixture. Place it over the simmering water and, shaking the pan constantly, add the butter in bits until it is all melted and incorporated. Remove the pan from the heat and squeeze into it the juice from the remaining half of lemon. Pour the sauce into a heated sauceboat or directly over the food it is to sauce, and serve at once.

HOLLANDAISE, OR DUTCH SAUCE

Every now and again a magazine article or cookbook will credit Fanny Farmer's edition of *The Boston Cooking-School Cook Book* (1896) with the introduction of this popular sauce to American cooks. Actually, it was around long before Miss Farmer. Both Maria Parloa and Mary Lincoln, Miss Farmer's predecessors at the Boston Cooking School, gave recipes for it in their own cookbooks, and in the South it was already an integral part of *la cuisine Créole* when Miss Farmer was still in diapers. I suspect that some of the folk historians have forgotten that the word *Hollandaise* is just French for "Dutch." Recipes titled "Dutch sauce" were fairly common, and as for their being used in America, English writer

Eliza Acton (*Modern Cookery for Private Families,* 1845) even called a variation of this sauce "Cold Dutch, or *American* Sauce."

Still popular here in the South, Hollandaise is just about the best sauce imaginable for just about any vegetable—from the season's first asparagus shoots to artichokes, broccoli, young green beans, and cauliflower.

MAKES ABOUT 1 CUP

3 large egg yolks
1 tablespoon water
Juice of 1 lemon
4 ounces (1 stick or $^1\!/_2$ cup) unsalted butter, melted and kept hot (but
    not browned)
Salt and cayenne pepper

1. Have the bottom of a double boiler ready with simmering water. Combine the egg yolks and water in the top pan. Beat with a wire whisk until the mixture is smooth.

2. Place the upper pan on the lower half, over, but not touching, the simmering water. Stirring constantly with the whisk, cook until the eggs begin to thicken, about 2 or 3 minutes. Take the pan off the heat at once and beat in the lemon juice.

3. Slowly beat in the hot butter, a little at a time. The sauce should be quite thick, like a custard or soft mayonnaise. Taste and beat in a pinch or so of salt and a bit of cayenne. Serve warm or at room temperature.

$\mathcal{H}$OMEMADE MAYONNAISE

This sauce has become so commonplace in the South that it seems to be on—or in— virtually everything we eat. This ubiquitousness has, perhaps justifiably, made it the brunt of not a few jokes. Maybe this wouldn't happen if more Southern cooks made their own mayonnaise and showed a little more restraint in its use.

Classic mayonnaise is made by hand, working oil and vinegar a drop at a time, into raw egg yolks, and it's still the way to get the best texture. If all that work seems too much for you, the food processor makes perfectly respectable mayonnaise. You can also make it in a blender, though you do have to stop the machine and keep scraping the sides down.

Although other egg-thickened sauces are ruined if the eggs are cold, the opposite is the case with mayonnaise. The eggs should be very cold. And, of course, because it is made with raw eggs, the sauce must be stored in the refrigerator and should not sit out at room temperature for any length of time.

MAKES 1 1/2 CUPS

2 large egg yolks or 1 whole large egg
1 teaspoon dry mustard or 1 tablespoon Dijon mustard
Salt and cayenne pepper
1 cup olive oil
Juice of 1 lemon or 2 tablespoons wine vinegar

1. To make mayonnaise by the traditional hand method, put the egg yolks or egg in a mixing bowl with the mustard, a healthy pinch of salt, and a tiny pinch of cayenne, both to taste. With a wire whisk or pair of forks held together, beat everything together until the mixture is smooth.

2. Have the oil ready in a container that has a good pouring spout. Pour a teaspoon of oil into the yolk mixture and beat until it is incorporated. Begin adding the remaining oil a few drops at a time, beating until each addition is thoroughly incorporated before adding more. Keep at it until you have used about half the oil.

3. Add a little of the lemon juice or vinegar and beat it in, then alternate between adding vinegar and oil until both are completely incorporated into the sauce. Taste and adjust the seasonings. Keep the sauce cold until you are ready to serve it.

Food Processor Method

1. The sauce is less likely to break in this method if you use the whole egg instead of the yolks. Put the egg, mustard, a healthy pinch of salt, a tiny one of cayenne, and the lemon juice or vinegar in the bowl of a food processor fitted with a steel blade. Process until the mixture is smooth, about 1 minute.

2. With the processor motor running, add the oil in a thin, steady stream. This should take about 2 minutes; if it takes less time, you are pouring the oil in too fast. When the oil is incorporated, let the machine run for a few seconds more. Stop the machine, taste and adjust the seasonings, and pulse it a couple of times to mix them in.

Note: *If you are cooking for someone with an immune deficiency disease such as HIV, or for a young child or elderly person whose immune system may be otherwise impaired, do not use homemade mayonnaise.*

$\mathcal{H}$ERB MAYONNAISE

Jim King, a long-time Savannahian who was born and raised in Talledega, Alabama, is my best friend and long-suffering official recipe-testing guinea pig: he's been subjected to pretty much everything I cook—both the successes that make it into my books, and the failures that do not. Actually, he's a pretty good cook in his own right.

Jim has a serious addiction to mayonnaise. To feed it, he makes just about the best herb mayonnaise I ever tasted. You'll want to bury your face in it—it's that good. Use it with any cold cooked or raw vegetable, or with roasted meat or poultry, fish, boiled shrimp, or slather it on your next BLT.

MAKES ABOUT 2 CUPS

1 large egg
1$^1/_2$ tablespoons lemon juice
1 tablespoon Dijon mustard
1 clove garlic, crushed and peeled
1 teaspoon salt
1 large sprig each fresh parsley, rosemary, and basil (do not use dried
herbs), tough stems removed and discarded
$^1/_4$ cup extra virgin olive oil
1 cup vegetable oil

Put the egg, lemon juice, mustard, garlic, salt, herbs, and 1 tablespoon of the olive oil in the bowl of a food processor fitted with a steel blade. Turn on the machine and process for 1 minute. If your processor has a small feed-tube pusher with a pin hole, put the olive oil in it and, with the machine running, let the oil dribble into the egg mixture. If you don't have such a contraption, add the olive oil in a slow, very thin stream through the feed tube. Add the vegetable oil in a thin stream until it is all emulsified. Process for about 15 seconds more, or until the mayonnaise is quite stiff. Transfer the mayonnaise to a storage bowl, cover, and refrigerate it overnight, if possible, to allow the flavors to blend and mellow before using.

Savannah Sweet Red Pepper Sauce

Southerners use green peppers so frequently that ripe red and yellow peppers became rare in our markets until they were recently rediscovered. Consequently, ripe peppers may not seem particularly Southern, except perhaps when they appear in that ubiquitous Southern spread, pimiento cheese. So it may surprise you to know that the recipe dates back at least a hundred years. Adapted from Harriet Ross Colquitt's *Savannah Cook Book* (1933), it almost certainly predates that publication by a generation.

Mrs. Colquitt used this sauce to stew shrimp, but it is also excellent on green beans (page 130), Maryland Squash Croquettes (page 179), and even on a baked potato. I've made a couple of changes: Mrs. Colquitt precooked the peppers by stewing them in a little water; I roast them. It makes them easier to peel and concentrates their flavor. I've also added a bit of shallot to bring out the peppers' sweetness.

MAKES ABOUT 1 1/2 TO 2 CUPS

> 4 medium red bell peppers or 12 ounces commercially packed roasted
>   red peppers (not in vinegar; see note)
> 1/4 cup minced shallot or yellow onion
> 2 tablespoons unsalted butter
> Salt and ground cayenne pepper
> Water

1. If you are using the commercially packed peppers, skip to step 2. Position a rack in the upper third of the oven and preheat the oven to 400 degrees F. Wash the peppers, remove any sticky labels, and pat dry. Place them on an ungreased baking sheet and roast them in the upper third of the oven, turning them periodically, until the skin is evenly blackened, about half an hour. (If you have a gas range, you can do this over a burner; see note.) Put the peppers in a paper bag and let them stand for 10 minutes.

2. Skin the peppers, split them lengthwise, and remove the seeds and stems. If you are using commercially packed roasted peppers, they are already skinned, but you'll need to remove the seeds.

3. Put the shallot or onion and butter in a lidded skillet that will comfortably hold all the peppers, and turn on the heat to medium. Sauté, uncovered, tossing frequently, until the shallot or onion is softened but not colored, about 5 minutes.

4. Add the roasted peppers, a healthy pinch of salt (don't add salt with commercial peppers), a tiny pinch of cayenne, and about 2 tablespoons of water. Bring it to a boil, cover the pan, and reduce the heat to medium low. Simmer until the peppers are very tender, about 15 minutes. If it gets too dry, add a spoonful or so more water, but only as much as is absolutely necessary. When the peppers are tender, puree the sauce through a food mill or in a blender or food processor fitted with a steel blade. Taste and correct the seasonings.

5. Before serving the sauce, reheat it over medium-low heat, stirring frequently to prevent it from scorching or sticking.

Note: *To roast the peppers on a gas range, insert a carving fork into the stem end of a pepper and hold it 4 inches above a high flame, turning constantly, until the skin blisters and blackens.*

This sauce is at its best when made with fresh-roasted peppers, but commercially packed roasted peppers make a very nice sauce. Look for peppers that have been packed in their own juices. Goya is one very good brand, which is sold in 6$^{1}/_{2}$-ounce jars. Do not use peppers that have been packed in vinegar.

To make Mrs. Colquitt's Stewed Shrimp and Peppers, add 1$^{1}/_{2}$ pounds (headless weight) peeled raw shrimp in step 5 and simmer until the shrimp are just cooked through, about 4 minutes. Serve over Carolina-Style Rice (page 43).

Mint Butter

When I came home after a semester of studying architecture in Genoa, Italy, pesto, that classic, fragrant Genoese sauce of basil, garlic, pine nuts, olive oil, and cheese, was virtually unknown in this country. Since then, I have watched it become so popular that one would almost think Americans had invented it. I've seen it stirred into just about everything imaginable, including grits.

Dearly as I love it, pesto is to Southern cooking what grits is to Chinese cooking, a foreign entity that does not belong. Basil and pine nuts are not flavors that are even remotely Southern. I wish people would save pesto for pasta and Italian vegetables, and stop mucking up grits with it.

Having said all that, here's a similar idea that is right at home on a Southern table. It's based on a traditional English mint sauce, a blend of mint, vinegar, sugar and sometimes melted butter, that has long been a favorite sauce for lamb, mutton, and game in the

South. This one is a thicker, pestolike version of that classic combination. It's our house sauce for Easter lamb but is also slap wonderful melting over a grilled lamb, mutton, venison, or pork chop. Here, it makes fresh steamed vegetables such as whole green beans, spring peas, baby summer squash, and tiny new potatoes positively sing.

MAKES ABOUT 1 CUP

6 ounces (1¹/₂ sticks) unsalted butter
1 cup (loosely packed) fresh mint leaves, preferably spearmint
1 large clove garlic or 2 small ones, crushed and peeled
Juice of 2 lemons (about ¹/₄ cup)
Sugar
Salt

1. Melt the butter over low heat. When just melted, turn off the heat and set it aside to cool.

2. Place the mint leaves, garlic, lemon juice, a large pinch of sugar and a small one of salt in the bowl of a food processor or blender fitted with a steel blade. Pulse until the leaves and garlic are finely chopped. Then, with the motor running, slowly pour in the butter in a thin stream, as if you were making mayonnaise. When all the butter is added and the sauce is smooth, turn off the machine, taste, and adjust the amount of sugar and salt to suit your taste. The sauce should not be sweet but should have just enough sugar to enhance the natural sweetness of the mint. Pulse to incorporate the seasonings and let it stand for at least 10 minutes. The butter will begin to solidify.

3. Just before serving, turn on the machine again and whip until fluffy and smooth.

Note: *Mint butter can be made ahead, but it is at its best when fresh. The sauce will keep for up to a week in the refrigerator. Let it stand at room temperature until softened, then whip it briefly with a fork until fluffy before serving it.*

BOURBON CUSTARD SAUCE, OR SOUTHERN BOILED CUSTARD

Called, more elegantly, *crème anglaise* ("English cream") by the French, this classic sauce has long been a standard in the South, both as a dessert sauce and as a dessert on its own. It's also, believe it or not, served as a holiday beverage on Christmas morning. The Southern moniker is dangerously misleading, since custard cannot be allowed to boil, or it'll curdle and end up a horrific mess like watered-down, sweetened scrambled eggs.

You needn't confine the flavoring to bourbon (unless you are using it in one of the recipes in this book). Boiled custard can be flavored with almost any kind of spice or liqueur that you like.

MAKES 2 CUPS

2 cups half-and-half
⅔ cup sugar
6 large egg yolks, lightly beaten
2 tablespoons bourbon

1. Prepare the bottom of a double boiler with water, cover it, and bring it to a simmer over medium heat. Put the half-and-half and sugar in the top half of the double boiler and place it over direct medium heat. Stirring constantly, bring it almost to the boiling point.

2. Move the top half of the double boiler onto the bottom half and take up about ½ cup of the hot liquid. Beating constantly, slowly pour this liquid into the egg yolks to temper them. Pour the egg mixture into the remaining half-and-half and stir well. Cook the custard, stirring constantly, until it coats the back of a spoon. It will be only lightly thickened; so don't overcook it. It will continue to thicken as it cools.

3. Remove the top of the double boiler from the heat and stir until the custard is slightly cooled. Stir in the bourbon and continue stirring for another minute. Let the custard cool completely before serving. If you are making the custard sauce ahead, let it cool completely before you refrigerate it. Serve cold or at room temperature.

COLD CREAM SAUCE

Clotted with lemon juice, perfumed with nutmeg, this is one of the best all-purpose sweet sauces going. I can think of very few desserts or fruit dishes that it does not enhance. What makes it doubly appealing is that it is also very easy to make.

MAKES 2 CUPS

1 pint heavy cream (minimum 36 percent milkfat)
½ cup sugar
1 lemon
Whole nutmeg in a grater

1. Put the cream in a stainless, glass, or other nonreactive bowl. Add the sugar and stir until it is dissolved.

2. Grate the zest from the lemon and add it to the cream. Cut the lemon in half and squeeze the juice from one half through a strainer into the cream. Stir until the cream begins to clot and thicken, then season it generously with a few gratings of nutmeg. Refrigerate until fully thickened, about 2 hours. Serve cold.

Note: *This sauce benefits from being made at least 6 to 8 hours ahead of serving it. The longer it sits, the thicker it will be, up to a point. If you cannot make it ahead and it isn't thick enough when you are ready to serve it, whip it lightly with a wire whisk until it forms very soft peaks.*

SPRING

➤

SPROUTS,
NEW LEAVES, AND
FRESH STRAWBERRIES

n spite of a milder climate—and contrary to what a lot of people think—even the deepest part of the Deep South has four distinct seasons. Yet spring is the one that is probably the best known and certainly the most beloved. A Southern spring is an explosion of color, beginning with the purple-pink redbud and wild plum blossoms as early as mid-February and lasting until the late azaleas drop their blooms and the magnolias begin to open up in May. Visitors flock to our region, drawn by the spectacular floral displays of countless azalea, dogwood, cherry blossom, and magnolia festivals.

As spectacular as these ornamental plants are, they aren't the only ones getting the Southern gardener's attention at this time of year. Summer gardens have to be planned, tilled, and seeded. Even before the summer garden goes into the ground, as much as two months earlier than other parts of the country, there are already fresh new vegetables to eat. Asparagus and poke shoots poke their way up through winter mulch and the ruin of last year's plants. Vidalia sweet onions, just beginning to form their bulbs, are pulled while still slender and bright green. Close behind are fragrant strawberries, a profusion of tender young lettuces, and fresh green peas. Mint, lush and sweet, sprouts around countless porches, just in time to give its bright accent to peas, to the Easter lamb or ham, or to the year's first cooling juleps. Just as the earth renews itself, the sober colors and subtle smells of winter produce give way to fresh new greens and bright, herbal perfumes, making the

Southern table as bright and fragrant as the air outside. Often the table is actually moved outside. While parts of the country are still digging their way out of snowdrifts, we're already eating al fresco—and thanking God that we are lucky enough to live where we can do it.

ASPARAGUS

Asparagus, at least the species known to us in America *(Asparagus officinalis)*, is thought to be native to the Mediterranean region and has been enjoyed since antiquity. Imported into America by the early settlers, it was well established in the South by the time it began to appear in botanical records and cookbooks early in the eighteenth century. There are even places where it has established itself and gone wild.

People who have never had fresh-cut asparagus seem to think it is a great technological leap to have this quintessential whiff of spring shipped in from all parts of the globe and available in our markets year round, but I don't. And if you are ever lucky enough to find out how the freshly cut vegetable can taste, you won't, either. The asparagus that appears in vegetable stalls during midwinter comes from somewhere considerably south of us. Even with modern shipping, that means it has been on the road and under refrigeration for days, to the irreparable damage of its flavor. It'll never be more than a ghost of what it once was. So I'd much rather wait for spring, watching for the price drop that signals locally grown asparagus—or, better still, schedule a visit home and gather it from Mama's asparagus bed only moments before it goes into the pot. However, most of us don't have that kind of luxury, and, with care, market asparagus can still be quite good. Here are a few tips on selecting and preparing it.

Look for tight, plump buds at the tips, clear, unblemished stalks, and a distinct fragrance of asparagus when you sniff it. The cut ends will be scarred over, but they should still look moist and full. As soon as you get it home, trim off half an inch of the base and stand the spears in a vase or basin of water for a couple of hours. If you can't cook the asparagus the same day, refrigerate it standing in water or with the stems well wrapped in moist paper towels. Take it out of the refrigerator several hours before cooking, change the water, and let the asparagus stand at room temperature.

Every time I read an article advising people just to break off the tough parts of the asparagus, I come pretty close to violence. What a shame to waste as much as a third of this vegetable, when even the toughest stem can be made edible by peeling it. It only takes a few extra minutes and is worth the extra trouble.

Have ready a basin of cold water. If you haven't already done so, trim the cut ends.

Now, this isn't a complicated maneuver: arm yourself with a good, sharp vegetable peeler. Lay a stalk of asparagus on your work surface with the tip facing you. Put the peeler blade against the stalk just above the tough part, and using a light, quick stroke away from you, peel the base until the pale green center of the stalk is exposed, gradually rotating the stalk until all sides are evenly peeled. Drop it into the basin of water and repeat until all the asparagus is trimmed. Let the asparagus remain in the water until you are ready to cook it. It's preferable to wait until just before cooking the asparagus to peel it, but when this isn't feasible, you can prepare it up to 2 hours ahead. However, don't peel the asparagus a day ahead and then refrigerate it.

$\mathcal{B}$OILED ASPARAGUS

In all the old recipes, the asparagus was trimmed and peeled as directed above, then tied into bundles and dropped into a large kettle of rapidly boiling salted water. The bundles made it easier to remove the asparagus from the pot. Unfortunately, they also made it cook unevenly. Here is the way I cook asparagus; it takes less time and doesn't require a special pot.

SERVES 4

1½ pounds asparagus, refreshed, trimmed, and peeled as directed
    above
Salt

1.   Choose a large, lidded shallow pan such as a skillet that will hold the asparagus in no more than two layers. Put in the asparagus and add enough water to cover it completely. Lift the asparagus out of the pot and set it aside.

2.   Cover the pan, place it over high heat, and bring the water to a boil. Uncover the pan and throw in a small handful of salt. Let the water come back to a rapid boil and add the asparagus, placing the stem ends first into the side of the pot nearest you. Let the asparagus drop away from you. This way, if the hot water should splatter, it won't do it in your direction. Cover the pan once again and let the water come back to a boil. Uncover and cook until the asparagus is tender but still firm and bright green.

3.   Put on the lid slightly askew (to hold the asparagus in the pan) and carefully drain off all the water. Turn the asparagus out onto a serving platter and serve in any of the following ways.

Asparagus with Drawn Butter or Lemon Butter (pages 51 and 52): Have all the ingredients for the butter sauce ready before cooking the asparagus. As soon as you turn it out onto the platter, make the sauce. Pour a little of it over the asparagus and serve the remaining sauce separately.

Asparagus with Hollandaise Sauce (page 52): Make the sauce just before cooking the asparagus and have it ready in a heated sauceboat. Pass the sauce separately.

Asparagus with Pecan Brown Butter (page 50): This is an unusual but very happy combination. Have all the ingredients for the butter sauce ready, but don't make the sauce until after you have cooked the asparagus. Pour all the sauce over the asparagus, distributing the pecans evenly over the vegetables, and serve at once.

Asparagus with Mayonnaise (page 53): The asparagus can be either hot or cold, but in either case make the mayonnaise first. Pass the sauce in a separate bowl.

Asparagus Vinaigrette: Traditionally, this salad was once served hot, but today we prefer it at room temperature. Let the asparagus cool. Use the following dressing: Combine ¼ cup of freshly squeezed lemon juice or red wine vinegar with a teaspoon of prepared Dijon mustard and a healthy pinch of salt. Gradually beat in ½ cup extra virgin olive oil until it is emulsified. Stir in a tablespoon of chopped parsley or thyme and a liberal grinding of black pepper, and pour the sauce over the asparagus.

CREAM OF
ASPARAGUS SOUP

Here, leeks and asparagus are happily paired once again. When it comes to asparagus soup, there is none in the world to equal Lettice Bryan's (*The Kentucky Housewife*, 1839), a lovely and simple triad of asparagus, broth, and cream, which I included in *Classical Southern Cooking*—so long as the asparagus is very young and of impeccable freshness. When your asparagus is not quite so impeccable, adding a leek to the pot does wonders.

1 large leek

2 tablespoons unsalted butter

*1 quart Meat Broth (page 21), made with veal bones, or Chicken Broth
      (page 23)*

*2 pounds asparagus, washed, trimmed, and peeled as directed on pages
      62–63*

Salt and white pepper in a peppermill

*1 cup heavy cream (minimum 36 percent milkfat), at room
      temperature*

1 cup Buttered Croutons (page 43)

1 tablespoon chopped fresh chives

1.   Trim off the root end, the tough, outer leaves, and any yellowed or withered leaf tips of the leek and split it lengthwise. Wash it carefully under cold, running water, gently folding back the layers of the leek to make sure that there is no lingering soil between the leaves. Drain it well and slice it crosswise as thinly as possible.

2.   Put the leek and butter in a soup kettle that will comfortably hold all the ingredients and place it over medium heat. Cook, stirring frequently, until the leek is wilted, about 5 minutes. Add the broth, raise the heat to high, and bring it to a boil.

3.   Meanwhile, cut off the pointed tips of the asparagus, setting aside a dozen or so, and cut the stems crosswise into 1-inch long pieces. Drop the asparagus (except for the reserved tips) into the boiling broth. Cover the kettle and let the soup return to a boil. Reduce the heat to a simmer and cook until the asparagus is tender—about 5, and no more than 10, minutes. Season it to taste with the salt and pepper. While the soup simmers, coarsely chop the reserved tips and set them aside.

4.   With a slotted spoon, take out about a cup and a half of the greenest asparagus and leeks and set it aside. Puree the remaining solids with the broth, either by forcing them through a sieve or a food mill, or in batches in a blender or food processor.

5.   Pour the soup back into the kettle and heat it through over medium heat. Stir in the reserved pieces of stem and tips and the cream. Simmer just long enough to heat them through, stir well, and turn off the heat.

6.   Ladle out the soup into individual heated soup plates and garnish the top with the buttered croutons and a sprinkling of the reserved chopped raw asparagus tips and chives.

Note: There are no substitutes here for the butter and cream. However, a meatless version of the soup can be made using water instead of meat broth. Don't use vegetable broth; its flavor is too strong for this particular soup.

This soup is very good served cold. Substitute half-and-half for the cream in the recipe and omit the croutons. Let it cool to room temperature—uncovered—then cover and refrigerate until chilled. Let the soup sit for about 10 to 30 minutes at room temperature before serving it to knock off some of the tombstone chill of the refrigerator. Just before serving, whip 1 cup heavy cream until it holds soft peaks. Garnish each serving with a dollop of whipped cream and a sprinkling of reserved chopped tips and chives.

ASPARAGUS WITH LEEKS AND NEW POTATOES

When asparagus is very young and fresh, the only respectable way to cook it is quickly and simply, so that the fresh flavor and texture is allowed to shine. When it isn't so fresh, pairing asparagus with fresh leek greens and new potatoes and sautéing them both in butter is a lovely thing to do. The bright herbal flavor of the leeks revives the lagging flavor of older asparagus, and the pleasant hint of caramel adds another, subtle dimension that enhances rather than cloaks the dish.

SERVES 4

1¹/₂ pounds fresh asparagus, washed, peeled, and trimmed as directed
    on pages 62–63
Green tops of 2 large leeks, washed and trimmed
¹/₂ pound small red new potatoes, cooked as directed on page 68, but
    not peeled
4 tablespoons unsalted butter
Salt and black pepper in a peppermill

1. Cut the asparagus crosswise into 1-inch lengths, keeping the tips separate from the stems. Set them aside. Slice the leek leaves crosswise about ¼ inch thick. Slice the potatoes into ¼-inch thick rounds.

2. Put the butter in a skillet or sauté pan that will comfortably hold all the ingredients and turn on the heat to medium high. When the butter is melted, add the potatoes and asparagus stems. Sauté, tossing them frequently, until the potatoes are beginning to turn golden, about 3 minutes.

3. Add the leek greens and asparagus tips, a healthy pinch of salt, and a liberal grinding of pepper. Sauté, shaking the pan and tossing the ingredients frequently, until the asparagus is tender and beginning to brown a little. It should still be firm and bright green. Turn off the heat. Taste and correct the seasonings, and serve at once.

Note: *There is no substitute for butter here. No other fat will caramelize the asparagus or give the dish that rich, buttery-brown flavor. Though the flavor would in no way be the same, the only substitutes that I could suggest might be extra virgin olive oil or peanut oil.*

ASPARAGUS AND NEW POTATO SALAD WITH GREEN BELL PEPPER VINAIGRETTE

Here's another take on the asparagus and new potato theme from Savannah's award-winning chef, Elizabeth Terry. Since her restaurant, Elizabeth's on 37th, opened in 1981—in those days, a modest dessert café—its transformation and rise to regional and then international fame has made Elizabeth one of the South's most celebrated chefs.

Elizabeth and I are both ardent defenders of traditional Southern foodways, but we take slightly different approaches to them. This and the foregoing recipe demonstrate our similarities and differences. Both of us begin with an idea that is firmly rooted in Southern tradition. But while I stay pretty close to traditional flavor combinations, she likes to mix them up in unexpected ways.

FOR THE DRESSING:

1 green bell pepper, cored, seeded, and cut into $^1/_2$-inch dice

1 fresh poblano pepper, cored, seeded, and cut into $^1/_2$-inch dice

$^1/_4$ cup onion, cut into $^1/_2$-inch dice

2 teaspoons cider vinegar

$^1/_2$ teaspoon salt

$^1/_2$ teaspoon freshly cracked black pepper

$^1/_4$ cup extra virgin olive oil

FOR THE SALAD:

6 medium (about 1$^1/_2$ pounds) new potatoes, scrubbed and cut into
    1-inch dice

1 pound fresh asparagus, sliced crosswise into 1-inch lengths (tough
    stems peeled as directed on pages 62–63)

1 bunch (about 6 small) scallions or other green onions, thinly sliced

$^1/_2$ cup minced parsley (preferably Italian)

1.   To make the dressing: Combine the two peppers and the onion with $^1/_4$ cup water in a saucepan and place it over high heat. Bring it to a boil, cover, and lower the heat to medium low. Simmer until the peppers are quite soft, about 15 minutes. Transfer the pepper-onion mixture to a blender or food processor, and puree until smooth. Add the vinegar, salt, and pepper, and turn on the motor. With the machine running, slowly drizzle in the olive oil until it is incorporated and emulsified. Set the dressing aside.

2.   Bring enough water to cover the potatoes to a boil over high heat. Add the potatoes, bring it back to a boil, and reduce the heat to medium. Simmer until the potatoes are just tender, about 8 to 10 minutes. Drain and spread the potatoes on a platter to cool.

3.   Prepare a bowl of ice water that will hold all the asparagus at once. Bring another pot of water to a boil, drop in the asparagus, and blanch it for 30 seconds, or until it is bright green. Immediately drain and plunge it into the ice water to arrest the cooking. Drain at once and spread the asparagus on a platter to cool.

4.   Just before serving, combine the potatoes, asparagus, green onions, and parsley in a bowl or platter. Pour the dressing over the salad and toss until it is uniformly mixed. Taste and correct the seasoning, and toss until blended.

Note: *Elizabeth indicates that the entire salad can be made ahead up through step 4, but don't add the dressing to it until you are ready to serve it. The dressing is improved by allowing it to sit for an hour after being made, but don't make it more than an hour ahead and never refrigerate it.*

My own preference is for a milder dressing heatwise, and I like to up the proportion of sweet pepper to about 1½ peppers and cut back on the poblano pepper to about ½ pepper.

ARTICHOKES

The artichoke *(Cynara scolymus)* may not seem like an especially Southern vegetable, but if old cookbooks are any indication, it has been enjoyed by Southerners for a lot longer than is widely supposed. Artichokes originally came from the Mediterranean. Their migration into our continent was gradual and convoluted. First they were introduced to England, where they were grown as early as the sixteenth century and, by the early Colonial period, were popular enough in England to presume that the early settlers would have brought them along to America. At any rate, artichokes were growing in Virginia by the beginning of the eighteenth century. All the early Southern-cookery writers gave recipes for artichokes and talked about them in an offhand way that suggests that Southerners were familiar with them.

In spite of this history, modern Southerners treat artichokes as if they were a relative newcomer to our tables. This is a sad indicator of how changed and misunderstood Southern vegetable cookery has become. Fortunately, artichokes have been rediscovered and are becoming commonplace in our markets and on our tables. Southern chefs are doing some very interesting things with them, but most of the recipes that I offer here aren't new.

BASIC ARTICHOKE PREPARATION

The simplest and most effortless way (for the cook, at least) to serve artichokes is simply to wash them, trim off the dark discoloration, and boil them in well-salted water until tender. The artichoke is presented to each diner whole with a bowl of melted butter, Hollandaise Sauce (page 52), mayonnaise, or vinaigrette for dipping the leaves. The diner does all the work—and doesn't mind. For the recipes that follow, however, the artichoke must be trimmed before it goes into the pot. The cook is faced with a little extra work, but the diner is free to enjoy the dinner with no more effort than it takes to lift the fork.

Here is the Italian way of trimming artichokes, which I was lucky enough to learn firsthand from Marcella Hazan. It sounds like a lot of work, but after you've done it once or twice, the job goes quickly. When Marcella showed me, the whole operation took less than 5 minutes—even with the dull knives that she encountered in my kitchen.

For the job, you'll need a whole lemon, a sharp chef's knife, a small paring knife, and a scooping tool, such as a melon baller or a sharp-edged teaspoon.

Cut the lemon in half and have it close at hand on your work surface. Cover the work surface with newspaper. Don't cut off the stem of the artichoke; once peeled, it contains some of the sweetest and tenderest flesh. Pull off the small, tough leaves at the base of the artichoke (those close to the stem). Then begin snapping off the large outer leaves by bending them back until they snap. As you go, rub the cut surfaces well with the lemon to prevent them from turning brown. After a couple of rows of leaves, you'll find that they snap further and further away from the base. When this begins, put your thumb against the base of the leaf and pull down the top with your other hand so that the tough outer part strips away from the tender inner flesh. When you begin to see pale green about two-thirds of the way up the inner leaves, cut off the inner cone of leaves with a sharp knife. Rub the cut surface well with the lemon. Now pull back the leaves from the center and scoop out the fuzzy choke with the melon baller or spoon. Squeeze lemon juice into the cavity and rub it in with your fingers.

Finally, take a sharp paring knife and trim off any tough outer leaf parts that may be remaining on the base. Don't worry that you are wasting any of it; you'll be losing very little of the edible part of the vegetable. Rub all the cut surfaces well with the lemon. Then peel the stem, removing all the tough stringy skin, and again rub it well with the lemon. Set the artichoke aside and repeat the process with the remaining artichokes.

If you are preparing a lot of them, or are cutting them into quarters, fill a basin with enough cold water to cover them, squeeze half the lemon into it and drop in the spent rind. As you finish trimming an artichoke, drop it into the acidulated water to keep it from discoloring until you are finished with the others.

The artichokes are now ready to use in any of the following recipes.

ARTICHOKES IN CREAM

Artichokes take to cream like a duck to water, and I can think of no more luxurious or appropriate treatment for them than this recipe, which is adapted from Sarah Rutledge's classic, *The Carolina Housewife* (1847). It is just fine on its own but also is the foundation of a sauce for a wonderfully elegant veal main course given at the end of this recipe.

SERVES 4

1 lemon
4 medium artichokes
2 tablespoons unsalted butter
1 cup heavy cream (minimum 36 percent milkfat)
Salt
1 tablespoon chopped parsley

1.   Put enough water into a large stainless or glass bowl to cover the artichokes. Cut the lemon in half and squeeze the juice from one of the halves into the water. Drop in the spent rind. Trim the artichokes and remove the chokes as directed on the previous page. Cut them into quarters, rubbing well with the other half of the lemon. Drop the trimmed artichoke quarters into the acidulated water.

2.   When all the artichokes are trimmed and quartered, drain them and put them with the butter into a heavy-bottomed, lidded saucepan or skillet that will hold them in one layer. Turn on the heat to medium high and sauté, tossing frequently, until the artichokes are hot and bright green but not browned, about 5 minutes.

3.   Add a healthy pinch of salt to the artichokes and pour the cream over them. Bring it to a boil, then reduce the heat to low, cover the pan, and simmer, stirring occasionally, until the artichokes are tender, about half an hour.

4.   Remove the lid and, if the cream is not thickened, raise the heat to medium high and let it boil until it is thickened, stirring frequently to prevent scorching. Turn off the heat. Pour the artichokes into a warm serving bowl, sprinkle the parsley over them, and serve at once.

Note: Obviously, there is no substitute for cream in this recipe. The entire dish can be made ahead up through step 3. Turn off the heat, set the lid askew, and let it cool. If you are

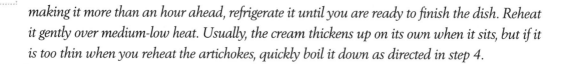

making it more than an hour ahead, refrigerate it until you are ready to finish the dish. Reheat it gently over medium-low heat. Usually, the cream thickens up on its own when it sits, but if it is too thin when you reheat the artichokes, quickly boil it down as directed in step 4.

Veal Scallops with Artichokes and Oysters, Creole Style: To serve 6, you'll need a pound of veal scallops, 2 additional tablespoons of butter, 1 cup of shucked, drained oysters, and 2 scallions, trimmed and thinly sliced. Make the artichokes through step 4. Sauté the veal scallops in a separate pan with the additional butter over medium-high heat—about a minute per side. Transfer them to a warm platter. Add the oysters to the artichokes, and simmer over low heat until the oysters plump, about 2 minutes. Pour the artichokes and oysters over the veal and sprinkle the scallions over them.

BRAISED ARTICHOKES
WITH ONIONS

I love to braise all kinds of vegetables; it's an especially happy way of cooking artichokes. It concentrates their subtle flavor and makes them meltingly tender without being mushy and textureless. Here, they are combined with little onions, which add a touch of sweetness and yet another dimension to their flavor.

SERVES 4

1 lemon
4 medium artichokes
8 very small boiling onions (about ¹/₂ pound)
3 tablespoons unsalted butter
Salt and black pepper in a peppermill
1 tablespoon chopped parsley
1 cup Chicken Broth (page 23) or water

1. Half-fill a kettle that will comfortably hold the onions with water, cover, and put it over medium-high heat to boil. Put enough water into a large stainless or glass bowl to cover the artichokes. Cut the lemon in half and squeeze the juice from one of the halves into the water. Drop in the spent rind. Trim the artichokes and remove the chokes as directed on page 70 and cut them into quarters, rubbing them well with the other half of the lemon as you go. Drop the trimmed artichoke quarters into the acidulated water.

2. When the kettle of water is boiling, drop the onions into the boiling water. Cover, and let the liquid return to the boiling point. Boil the onions for 1 minute, then drain them quickly and plunge them into cold water. Trim off the root and stem ends, peel them, and cut a deep "X" into the root end. Set them aside.

3. Thoroughly drain the artichoke quarters. Put them into a heavy-bottomed, lidded skillet that will hold all the ingredients in one layer. Add 2 tablespoons of the butter and turn on the heat to medium high. Sauté, tossing frequently, until they are bright green, about 3 minutes. Add the onions and continue sautéing until the onions are beginning to color, about 3 minutes more.

4. Add a healthy pinch of salt, a liberal grinding of black pepper, the parsley, and the broth or water. Bring the liquid to a boil, then reduce the heat to low, cover the pan, and braise until the artichokes and onions are tender, about half an hour. If the liquid gets reduced too much, add a few spoonfuls of water, but just enough to prevent scorching.

5. Uncover the pan. Raise the heat to medium high and boil away any remaining liquid. Add the remaining butter and shake the pan until it is melted. Serve at once.

Note: *A fine addition to this dish is a tablespoon of capers. Another one is 2 ounces of country ham, cut into julienne. Either should be added to the pan with the artichokes at the beginning of step 3.*

A completely vegetarian version of this dish can be made by substituting olive oil for the butter, but the flavor will be more Mediterranean than Southern.

CREOLE ARTICHOKE SALAD

When I was growing up, we didn't grow artichokes in our garden, and they were nowhere to be found in the markets of the sleepy, rural towns where we lived, so I never had a fresh artichoke until I went away to college. The first of any sort that I ever tasted came out of a jar—marinated artichoke hearts, which my grandmother bought by the case when she visited Aunt Alice in Florida. We used them to dress our salads and thought they were just wonderful, mainly I suppose because they seemed exotic.

In this salad, boiled fresh artichokes are marinated in a piquant lemon and olive oil dressing, enlivened with a little garlic and green onion. It makes a fine salad on its own, but you can do what my grandmother did and use it to dress a larger mixed vegetable salad.

SERVES 4

1 lemon
4 medium artichokes
Salt
1 clove garlic, crushed, peeled, and minced
Black pepper in a peppermill
$1/4$ cup extra virgin olive oil
1 tablespoon chopped parsley
2 scallions, trimmed and sliced thin (both white and green parts)
4 romaine or Boston lettuce leaves, washed and drained
1 large hard-cooked egg

1.   Put enough water in a kettle to cover the artichokes completely, cover, and put it over medium-high heat to boil. Meanwhile, cut the lemon in half. Trim the artichokes and remove the chokes as directed on page 70, rubbing the cut edges well with half of the lemon as you go.

2.   When the water is boiling, add a handful of salt. Let it come back to a boil and add the artichokes. Cover the kettle until the water is boiling again, then uncover and cook until the artichokes are just tender, about 25 to 30 minutes. Drain them thoroughly and let them cool slightly while you make the dressing.

3.   Squeeze the juice from the lemon through a strainer into a mixing bowl. Add a small pinch of salt, the garlic, and a liberal grinding of pepper. Beat well with a whisk until the

salt is dissolved. Slowly beat in the olive oil, a few drops at a time, until it is emulsified. Set aside.

4. While the artichokes are still warm, cut them into wedges. If there is still any choke in the center or if some of the outer leaves seem tough, remove them. Put the artichokes into a stainless or glass bowl, add the parsley and scallions, and pour the dressing over them. Toss until they are well coated, taste and adjust the seasonings, then set the bowl aside and let the artichokes cool completely.

5. When you are ready to serve the salad, arrange the lettuce leaves on a serving platter or individual salad plates. Peel the egg and force the white and yolk separately through a coarse sieve. Spoon the artichokes over the lettuce leaves and sprinkle them with the egg white and yolk. Serve at room temperature.

Note: *If you are cooking for a strict vegetarian, omit the egg garnish.*

If you are one of those people who think that Creole food has to have cayenne pepper in it, you can substitute it for the black pepper, but for heaven's sake don't overdo it. Artichokes have a delicate flavor that doesn't need a lot of heat.

FIDDLEHEADS, OR OSTRICH FERNS

The spring sprouts of our native ostrich fern *(Pteretis pensylvania)* can be found all over the eastern part of the country, from Maine to Georgia to the swamps of Louisiana. The common name, "fiddleheads," is peculiarly appropriate because that's precisely what the graceful, still-coiled fronds look like—the scroll head of a violin. They're not just pretty but also make very good eating. Popular with natural-food enthusiasts, they are usually gathered in the wild but in season can sometimes be found at farmers' markets or at natural-food and specialty groceries.

Fiddleheads can be eaten raw and make a fine addition to the salad bowl. When steamed, they may be served hot in any way that asparagus is, except for the cream soup (see page 64), or cooled and tossed in a salad with spring lettuce and chopped spring onions. Dress the salad with salt, olive oil, and lemon juice to taste.

CAMILLE GLENN'S
FIDDLEHEADS

Camille Glenn can arguably be called the "Grande Dame" of Southern cooking. A remarkable and irresistible lady, an incomparable cook, a generous and compulsive teacher—she personifies everything that is good about being both Southern and a cook. For decades, her graceful writing and lovely cooking enlivened the food pages of *The Louisville Courier*, and her grand opus, *The Heritage of Southern Cooking*, still sets a standard for youngsters like me to live up to.

No other recipe better encapsulates Mrs. Glenn's kitchen sensibility as does this one, in which local ingredients, selected at the peak of freshness, are handled with elegance, finesse, and forthright simplicity.

SERVES 4

¹/₂ pound fiddlehead fern shoots
3 tablespoons unsalted butter
Salt
1 lemon, cut in 4 wedges

1. Wash the fiddleheads in cold water and drain them well. Put the butter into a skillet that will comfortably hold the ferns in one layer and place it over medium-high heat.
2. When the butter is melted and bubbling, add the fiddleheads and sauté, tossing them constantly, until they are just crisp tender—about 1, and no more than 2, minutes. Do not overcook them or they will go limp and unravel. Season liberally with a healthy pinch of salt, toss to mix it in, and serve at once with wedges of lemon.

Note: *Mrs. Glenn suggests using a good-quality peanut oil as a substitute for the butter. For a variation, she also suggests the delicious addition of a pound of morels or other wild mushrooms. If you choose to add mushrooms, increase the amount of butter or other fat to 4 tablespoons.*

LEEKS

Leeks are available almost year round in the South and make a welcome addition to the winter table, but it's in the spring and fall—the transitional seasons—that they are really at their best. This heady member of the onion family is underappreciated and is seldom found on Southern tables by itself. Yet it is frequently used to flavor soups, stews, and, occasionally, other vegetable dishes. In the recipes that follow, however, leeks are allowed to shine all by themselves. For other recipes where leeks are a primary component, see also Asparagus with Leeks and New Potatoes (page 66) and Green Peas with Leeks (page 86).

BRAISED LEEKS

Braising is a lovely treatment for tender young leeks because it brings out and concentrates their natural sweetness. It is also an exceptional way to cook spring onions, especially the season's first green Vidalia sweet onions.

SERVES 4

4 medium leeks
$^1/_2$ cup water
Salt
2 tablespoons unsalted butter

1.   Trim the roots and tough upper outer leaves and upper parts of the inner leaves of the leeks and partially split the green part lengthwise, leaving the white part intact. Wash the leeks carefully under cold running water to remove all the grit and dirt.

2.   Put the leeks into a lidded skillet that will comfortably hold them in one layer. Add the water and a healthy pinch of salt. Place the pan over medium-high heat and bring the liquid to a boil. Reduce the heat to medium low and cover the pan. Simmer until the leeks are almost tender, about 8 to 10 minutes.

3.   Remove the lid and raise the heat to high, letting the liquid boil rapidly away until it is reduced to about 2 tablespoons. Turn off the fire and add the butter, swirling the pan until the butter has melted and thickened the juices. Serve at once.

$\mathcal{L}$EEK SPOONBREAD

North Carolina has been at the center of a renaissance of traditional Southern cooking in restaurants. One of the leaders and finest practitioners of the movement is Ben Barker, who, with his gifted pastry-chef wife, Karen, owns and operates Magnolia Grill in Durham. Ben's cooking, while solidly traditional, always seems fresh and new. Here, for example, he gives a fresh lift to spoonbread, a traditional cornmeal soufflé, by folding in a slightly unorthodox puree of leeks.

Ben says that the batter will stand up to just about any addition: "quince, apple, sweet potato, winter squash, or Vidalia onion puree, herbs, pork products, the kitchen sink."

SERVES 6 TO 8

2–3 leeks, split, washed, and with most of the green tops removed
2 1/2 cups whole milk
2 cups half-and-half
1 tablespoon salt
3 teaspoons sugar
1 cup cornmeal
1/2 cup all-purpose flour
4 ounces (8 tablespoons or 1 stick) unsalted butter
6 large eggs, separated
1/4 cup heavy cream

1.   Put the leeks in a heavy-bottomed, lidded skillet with enough water to half-cover them. Cover the pan and place it over medium-high heat. When the liquid begins to boil, reduce the heat and cook, tightly covered, until the leeks are wilted, about 8 to 10 minutes. Turn off the heat, drain, and puree the leeks in a food mill, blender, or food processor. You should have 3/4 cup of puree.

2.   Combine the milk, half-and-half, salt, and sugar in a heavy saucepan. Scald over medium heat. When small bubbles begin to appear around the edges, gradually stir in the cornmeal and flour with a wire whisk. Continue whisking the mixture until it thickens. When it is smooth and creamy, remove it from the heat and stir in the butter until it is completely absorbed.

3. Beat the egg yolks with the cream until light and smooth. Gradually add them to the cornmeal mixture. Fold in the leek puree until it is evenly distributed. Set aside. (You can make the batter ahead up to this point. Cover and refrigerate, but bring it back to room temperature before baking it.)

4. Position a rack in the center of the oven and preheat the oven to 350 degrees F. In a stainless, glass, or copper bowl, beat the egg whites until they are stiff but not dry. Fold them into the cornmeal batter. Lightly butter a large (4-quart) casserole dish and pour in the spoonbread batter, lightly smoothing the top with a spatula. Place the casserole in the center of the oven and bake until the spoonbread is puffy, golden brown on top, and just set, about 45 minutes. Serve at once from the dish in which it has baked.

MIRLITONS

Known also as chayotes (especially in the Southwest) and vegetable pears, mirlitons are actually a variety of American squash. Prized by Creole cooks, they are used in Louisiana more frequently than in any other part of the South. Creoles cook mirlitons in the same way that they do other squash and eggplants: they fry, braise, and bake them, and favor them as a vegetable casing for seafood fillings.

Mirlitons thrive year round in Louisiana but prefer a shady spot in the wilting heat of July and August. They make a welcome vegetable in spring, when other squash are not yet in season.

MIRLITONS ÉTOUFFÉES OR SMOTHERED MIRLITONS, CREOLE STYLE

One of the most famous of Creole dishes is crawfish étouffée, in which those quintessential crustaceans are cooked in a spicy, roux-based sauce. However, there are many other étoufféed Creole dishes, including this one.

Étouffée, in French, simply means smothered, and that is exactly what happens here. The mirlitons braise gently in a covered pan, bathed in a classic combination of Creole flavors.

SERVES 4

2 large or 3 small mirlitons
2 tablespoons extra virgin olive oil
1 medium yellow onion, split, peeled, and chopped
1 clove garlic, peeled and minced fine
1 tablespoon chopped parsley
1 tablespoon chopped fresh thyme or 1 teaspoon dried thyme
1 large bay leaf
$^{1}/_{2}$ cup dry white wine
4 medium tomatoes, blanched, peeled, and seeded as directed on page
     117, and chopped, or 1 cup canned Italian tomatoes, seeded and
     chopped
Salt and ground cayenne pepper or hot sauce such as Tabasco

1. Wash the mirlitons, peel them, then split them in half and remove the seeds. Cut them into bite-sized cubes and set aside.

2. Put the olive oil and onion in a lidded skillet that will comfortably hold all the ingredients. Turn on the heat to medium high. Sauté, tossing frequently, until the onion is translucent, about 4 minutes. Add the mirlitons and garlic, and sauté until the garlic is fragrant, about a minute more.

3. Add the parsley, thyme, bay leaf, and wine, let it come to a boil, and add the tomatoes, a healthy pinch of salt, a small pinch or so of cayenne, or a few dashes of hot sauce to taste. Stir, lower the heat to a slow simmer, and cover the pan. Simmer until the mirlitons are tender, about half an hour.

Seafood Stuffed Mirlitons: These are made in exactly the same way as Seafood Stuffed Eggplant (page 156). Prepare 4 mirlitons as follows: Put enough water to completely cover the mirlitons in a large kettle, bring it to a boil over high heat, and add the mirlitons. Cook until they are tender when pierced with a fork or knife, about 15 to 20 minutes. Drain and cool them, then carefully split them and remove their seeds. Proceed with step 1 of the recipe for Seafood Stuffed Eggplant.

$\mathscr{P}$ICKLED MIRLITONS

Spicy pickled squash are a popular condiment in the South, but while people who live outside Louisiana use yellow summer squash for pickling, Creole cooks prefer mirlitons.

Mike and Shelly Sackett, proprietors of Kitchen Affairs, a cooking school in Evansville, Indiana, have a very eclectic kitchen; they cook everything from Jewish to Southern to Italian. Mike has Louisiana roots, and this recipe came from those roots by way of his aunt, Dot Fischer.

MAKES 4 QUARTS OR 8 PINTS

8–10 mirlitons
1 quart cider vinegar
1 scant cup kosher or pickling salt
Pinch alum
1 green bell pepper, seeded and sliced into ¼-inch strips
2 carrots, peeled and sliced
8 cloves garlic, peeled
8 whole jalapeño peppers
2 cups cauliflower florets (about 1 large cauliflower)
4 teaspoons dill seed

1.   Wash, peel, split, and seed the mirlitons. Cut them into thin strips as you would potatoes for french fries. Put them in a stainless or glass bowl, cover with ice water, and refrigerate for 24 hours.

2.   The next day, drain the mirlitons and set them aside. Put the vinegar in a stainless kettle with 2 cups of water, a cup of salt, and a pinch of alum. Bring it to a boil over high heat and boil for 3 minutes. Turn off the heat.

3.   Divide the bell pepper, carrots, garlic, jalapeño peppers, cauliflower, and dill seeds among 4 sterilized quart jars or 8 pint jars. Add the mirlitons, leaving about ½ inch of headroom at the top of each jar. Pour the hot vinegar solution over the mirlitons until they are covered, leaving ¼ inch of headroom.

4.   Seal with new lids and process the jars for 10 minutes in a boiling water bath. Remove the jars with tongs and set them on folded towels so that they do not touch. Let them cool completely. Reprocess or refrigerate any that do not seal. (Refer to pages 9 through 11 for detailed canning instructions.) Age the pickles for at least 2 weeks before opening.

SORREL AND SPINACH

Sorrel is a sour herb that is not as widely used in this country as it is in France. But once it was common in Southern gardens, especially in the coastal regions of Carolina and Georgia. Spinach and sorrel are frequently mentioned together in the old cookbooks. Nowadays sorrel is rare in Southern markets and is expensive when you can find it at all. Unless you grow your own, using it in large quantities will be a luxury indeed. Consequently, the proportion of sorrel to spinach in the following recipes is smaller than was once possible.

Sautéed Sorrel and Spinach

The traditional proportion of sorrel to spinach in this dish is one to one, and if you grow your own sorrel, or can afford prodigal quantities of it, you can adjust the proportions of this recipe accordingly.

SERVES 4

1½ pounds fresh spinach (see note)
¾ pound fresh sorrel (about 3 bunches)
3 tablespoons unsalted butter
Salt and black pepper in a peppermill
4 buttered toast triangles, optional
1 lemon, sliced thin or cut into 4 wedges

1.   Wash the spinach and sorrel separately, and remove all the tough stems. Put the spinach in a large, lidded kettle without adding water. The water clinging to the leaves will be sufficient to wilt the spinach. Cover the kettle and place it over medium-high heat. Cook until the leaves begin to wilt, about 3 minutes. Add the sorrel, cover once more, and cook until the greens are wilted, about 2 minutes more. Quickly but thoroughly drain them.
2.   Put the butter in a skillet that will comfortably hold all the spinach and sorrel, and turn on the heat to medium high. When the butter is melted and hot but not browning, add the vegetables and sauté until they are tender and dry, about 3 to 4 minutes. Season lightly with a pinch of salt (the sorrel has a salty taste on its own and won't need much)

and a few grindings of pepper. If you like, you may arrange toast triangles on a platter or individual plates and top them with the spinach and sorrel, or you can serve this dish plain. Garnish with the lemon slices and serve at once.

Note: *Served over crisp buttered toast with its classic accompaniment of poached eggs, this makes a very nice main-course dish for supper or brunch.*

Spinach stands up fairly well to freezing, and two 10-ounce packages of frozen whole-leaf spinach can be substituted for the fresh spinach called for here, though it will not be as good.

LENTEN HERB, OR SPINACH AND SORREL SOUP

Nowadays Lent seems to be little more than an excuse for the weeklong drunken blowout that precedes it in New Orleans's infamous Mardi Gras celebration. Actually Lent is a Christian religious observance—a solemn, introspective season of practiced restraint and abstinence. Historically, the blowout began as a final feast designed to get all the fat (and booze) out of the house before the season began on Ash Wednesday—hence the name "Fat Tuesday."

This lovely soup is to help you behave yourself after the big party; it sure makes doing without seem like no real hardship.

SERVES 6

¼ pound sorrel leaves
¼ pound spinach
1 large leek
1 large yellow onion, split, peeled, and thinly sliced
2 tablespoons butter
1 clove garlic, peeled and minced
4 cups (1 quart) Vegetable Broth (page 24) or water
1 Bouquet Garni (page 36)
Salt and whole white peppercorns in a peppermill
4 large egg yolks
1 tablespoon freshly squeezed lemon juice
1 cup Buttered Croutons (page 43)

1.   Wash the sorrel and spinach leaves, and trim off their tough stems. Put them in a colander to drain and set aside. Remove the tough outer leaves of the leek and trim off the upper part of its green shoots. Split it lengthwise and wash it under cold running water, being careful to remove all the grit and dirt. Slice it thin.

2.   Put leek, onion, and butter in a kettle that will comfortably hold all the soup and place it over medium heat. Sauté until the vegetables are wilted, about 5 minutes. Add the garlic and sauté until it is fragrant, about a minute longer. Add the broth or water, the bouquet garni, a healthy pinch of salt, and a liberal grinding of white pepper. Let it come to a boil.

3.   Meanwhile, slice the sorrel and spinach into thin strips. Add them to the kettle as soon as the broth is boiling, let it come back to a boil, and reduce the heat to medium low. Simmer until the vegetables are tender, about 15 minutes. Remove and discard the bouquet garni.

4.   Puree the soup in batches in a blender or food processor (or, if you want to be authentic, through a sieve or food mill). Return the soup to the kettle and bring it back to a simmer.

5.   Beat the egg yolks and lemon juice together until the mixture is smooth. Beat a cup of the hot soup into it, then beat this mixture into the soup. Serve at once with the buttered croutons.

Note: *To make a strictly vegetarian soup, you can use olive oil to sauté the onion and leek at the beginning, or omit the sautéing step altogether and boil the onion and leek in the liquid until they are nearly tender before adding the other vegetables. To give the soup body without adding eggs, substitute a medium potato, peeled and sliced thin, in step 2.*

   If abstention isn't your goal, you can also omit the egg yolks and enrich the soup with a cup of heavy cream (minimum 36 percent milkfat) added before the final simmer in step 4.

ENGLISH, OR GREEN PEAS

Don't just ask for peas in the South unless you're in the mood for field peas—black-eyes, crowders, butter, or cowpeas—because that's what you'll get. If you want the green variety, you'd better ask for "English" peas. That's what we call them, though there's nothing exclusively English about them.

Like asparagus, fresh green peas were once a seasonal treat. Dried split peas were of course available year round, but only in the spring could one get tender, sweet fresh peas—so full of natural sugars that they are almost like candy. When I was growing up, the early peas were so sweet that we used to raid the garden and eat them raw. On the rare occasion that I get freshly gathered peas in late spring, I buy a lot more than I plan to serve because I know I'll eat more than my share while shelling them.

We've lost a lot of that sense of specialness. Canning and freezing have made green peas so commonplace (and ordinary) that the idea of this cafeteria standby as a rare treat seems perfectly ridiculous. Well, while nothing equals the sweetness and tenderness of freshly gathered peas, with care, even the frozen variety can be very satisfying to eat. They can be used in any of the recipes that follow.

MARY RANDOLPH'S FRESH ENGLISH PEAS

If you are lucky enough to find fresh peas in the market, or better yet, have a spot where you can gather your own, Mary Randolph's 1824 recipe is all you need—her instructions for gathering, keeping, and cooking the peas are lucid and still pertinent. Your only problem will be in finding peas that are really freshly gathered. Here's her recipe:

> "To have them in perfection, they must be quite young, gathered early in the morning, kept in a cool place, and not shelled until they are to be dressed; put salt in the water, and when it boils, put in the peas; boil them quick twenty or thirty minutes, according to their age; just before they are taken up, add a little mint chopped very fine, drain all the water from the peas, put in a bit of butter, and serve them up quite hot."
>
> —Mary Randolph, *The Virginia House-wife*, 1824

GREEN PEAS WITH LEEKS

Many recipes that contain leeks call for the white parts only, and yet the tender, pale green inner shoots are a lovely part of the vegetable. They can be set aside to add to the stockpot, but once you have tasted them, even that will seem like a waste. Here, their mild, fresh flavor is a perfect complement for the sweetness of the peas and gives the frozen variety back some of the freshness that they have lost.

SERVES 4

Inner, pale green parts of 3 large leek tops
2 pounds (unshelled weight; 1 pound if shelled) young green peas or 1
*   pound frozen peas*
2 tablespoons unsalted butter, divided
2 ounces lean salt pork, country ham, or prosciutto (about 3 thin slices
*   salt pork, 2 slices of either ham), sliced as thinly as possible and*
*   cut into julienne*
$1/2$ cup Chicken Broth (page 23)
Salt

1.   Carefully wash the leek leaves to remove any lingering dirt. Most of the dirt is in the outer, dark green leaves, but sometimes it may be in the inner shoot as well, so be thorough. Slice them crosswise as thinly as possible and set aside.

2.   If you are using fresh peas, shell and wash them briefly in a basin of cold water. Transfer them to a colander or sieve, and set them aside to drain.

3.   Put 1 tablespoon of the butter and the salt pork or ham in a shallow, lidded skillet that will comfortably hold the peas in no more than two layers. Turn on the heat to medium high and sauté until fat on the meat is beginning to color, about 2 minutes. Add the leeks and shake the pan until they are glossy and coated with the butter. Add the fresh or frozen peas, and continue shaking the pan until they are coated (and the frozen peas are thawed). Pour in the broth—it should cover the peas. If it doesn't, add enough water to barely cover them. Bring it quickly to a boil, then reduce the heat to medium low, cover the pan, and simmer until the peas are just tender, about 15 minutes for fresh peas, or 8 to 10 minutes for frozen ones.

4.   Remove the lid and raise the heat once more to medium high. Allow the liquid to boil away quickly until there are only a couple of tablespoons remaining in the pan. When

the liquid is evaporated, turn off the heat. Taste and adjust the salt, adding a pinch or so if needed. Add the remaining butter and shake the pan until it dissolves and coats the peas. Pour into a warm serving bowl and serve at once.

Note: *You may omit the salt pork or ham and use water instead of chicken broth, but there is no substitute for the butter. No other fat can enhance and complement the sweet flavor of the peas.*

Early English Pea Soup

This is an "early" recipe in both senses of the word. Not only is it best when made with the earliest and sweetest of green peas, the recipe itself is quite old, going back as far as the Middle Ages. The source of this soup's fine flavor is owed to first stewing the pea pods in the broth. This infuses the broth with a rich pea flavor while allowing the peas themselves to remain fresh and lightly cooked.

SERVES 6

> *1 quart (4 cups) Chicken Broth (page 23)*
> *3 cups (about 2 pounds) shelled young green peas, with hulls reserved*
> *1 tablespoon unsalted butter*
> *$^{1}/_{2}$ cup chopped onion*
> *1 leek, washed, trimmed, and chopped (page 65)*
> *4 large sprigs fresh mint*
> *$1^{1}/_{4}$ cups heavy cream (minimum 36 percent milkfat)*
> *Salt and whole white peppercorns in a peppermill*
> *A dozen or so chive leaves, chopped*

1.   Put the broth and the reserved pea hulls in a 2-quart kettle and place it over medium-high heat. Bring it to a boil, skim it carefully, and reduce the heat to a bare simmer. Cover loosely and let the broth simmer for about $^{1}/_{2}$ hour.

2.   Put the butter, onion, and leeks in a kettle large enough to hold all the ingredients, and turn on the heat to medium. Cook slowly until softened but not browned, about 10 minutes.

3. Strain the broth from the hulls and add it to the kettle with the onion and leeks. Discard the hulls. Let the broth come to a boil, add the peas and 2 sprigs of the mint, and reduce the heat to a simmer. Cook until the peas are tender, about 15 to 20 minutes.

4. Dip out a cup of the peas and set them aside. Puree the soup in a blender or food processor. Return the puree to the pot, stir in the reserved peas, 1 cup of the cream, and season to taste with the salt and pepper. Continue cooking just long enough to heat the cream through. While the soup is heating, whip the remaining ¼ cup cream until stiff and chop the remaining mint together with the chives.

5. When the soup is heated through, turn off the heat, remove the mint sprig, and serve at once, garnishing each serving with a dollop of whipped cream and a sprinkling of the chopped herbs.

Note: *This soup is equally good served hot or chilled. To chill it, put the kettle in a basin of ice water and stir until the soup is cooled, then chill it in the refrigerator. Don't cover the soup until it is cold, otherwise you are inviting spoilage. The soup will be thicker cold than hot. If you find it is too thick, thin it with a little water or half-and-half, but don't add more broth or heavy cream.*

Sugar Snap Pea Soup: If you can't get fresh young peas still in their shells, you can make a very nice soup with sugar snap peas, which are becoming commonplace in many markets. You'll need 1½ pounds of sugar snaps. Top and tail them and be sure that all their strings have been stripped away. Slice them crosswise about ¼ inch thick. Omit step 1. Set aside a cup of the peas and proceed as directed in step 2. In step 3, the sugar snaps will be tender in about 10 minutes. After the soup is pureed, add the reserved peas and cook until they are just tender, about 4 minutes.

POKE SALLET

"Sallet" is the old English word for all leafy greens—a term that is still used in some rural parts of the South, especially when the greens are from our native wild pokeweed.

Pokeweed *(Phytolacca americana)* has long been relished as a vegetable in the South but has never been cultivated. Those who eat it gather it in the wild. Fortunately, it's a hardy plant that can (and does) flourish nearly anywhere; I've even seen it growing in the median between street and sidewalk in downtown Savannah.

Poke is a seasonal vegetable, in part because only the young shoots and early leaves are tender enough to eat, and in part because youth is the only stage at which they are thought to be edible. Poke contains a mild toxin that becomes more concentrated as the plant matures. There is a time of the year when the berries are supposed to be safe as well, but the seeds, roots, and mature stems are all highly poisonous, so don't gather any poke leaves or shoots that are tinged with red, and don't take a chance with the berries. As added insurance, many cooks blanch the poke sallet, which is supposed to remove any poison that it may contain.

To prepare poke sallet, thoroughly wash the leaves in cold water, changing the water at least twice. Remove and discard any stems or red-tipped leaves. Half-fill a large kettle that will comfortably hold all the leaves with water. Bring this to a boil over high heat and add the leaves, pressing them below the surface of the water with a spoon. When they are wilted, but still bright green, drain them quickly and rinse under cold running water.

Ma Ma's Poke Sallet with Spring Onions

Ma Ma, my maternal grandmother, was passionate about greens of any sort, so much so that they were the only thing that we ever knew to interfere with her favorite hobbies—traveling and eating out. If there was a pot of greens on the stove, you could rest assured that she would sharply veto any suggestion that we go out, even if we were going to her favorite restaurant.

My happiest and earliest memories of my grandmother are of spring mornings spent in her old Chevrolet, driving down country roads with our eyes fixed on the shoulders, looking for signs of tender young poke shoots. Even when the trip wasn't a forage for greens, we'd throw a couple of grocery sacks in the backseat—just in case.

The best choice of green onions for this are spring shallots or very young, green Vidalia sweet onions, but even scallions will do nicely. If you can't get poke sallet where you live, Swiss chard makes an excellent substitute.

SERVES 4

2 pounds tender poke sallet leaves or young Swiss chard
2 ounces (about 2 thin slices) salt pork or country ham fat or 2
  tablespoons unsalted butter
4 large green onions (or 6, if they are small)
Salt
Pepper Vinegar (page 27) or 1 lemon, cut into wedges

1.   Wash the sallet or chard in at least two changes of water, making sure there is no lingering grit or dirt. Trim off any tough stems. (If you are using chard, remove all the stems and set them aside for another use. They make a delicious vegetable on their own.)

2.   If you are using poke sallet, blanch it as directed on page 89. If you use chard, put it in a large kettle without adding any water. The water clinging to the leaves will be enough to wilt them. Cover the kettle and place it over medium-high heat. Cook until the greens are just wilted, about 3 to 5 minutes.

3.   Drain the greens well and rinse them briefly under cold running water. Press them gently to remove the excess liquid and set aside.

4.   Trim off the roots and any tough or defective outer leaves from the onions. Wash and slice them crosswise as thinly as possible.

5.   If you are using salt pork or ham, put it in a heavy-bottomed skillet that will comfortably hold all the greens, and place it over medium heat. Sauté until the fat is rendered from it and the pork is crisp. Remove the pork and set it aside on absorbent paper to drain. Drain off all but 2 tablespoons of the fat. (If for some reason there isn't enough fat, supplement it with butter. If you wish to omit the pork altogether, put 2 tablespoons of butter in the pan and turn on the heat to medium high.) Add the sliced onions to the pan and sauté until they are softened but not colored, about 4 minutes. Add the greens and a pinch or so of salt. Sauté, stirring them frequently, until they are tender and nearly dry, about 5 to 8 minutes. Taste and correct the salt, then transfer the greens to a warm serving bowl. You may crumble the pork over them if you like. Serve at once, passing the pepper vinegar or lemon wedges separately.

Note: *Don't overcook the poke: after it has been blanched, it will only take a few minutes more cooking, and, as nineteenth-century author Lettice Bryan aptly noted, it isn't good when it has been boiled to mush. For a meatless version, substitute peanut oil for the salt pork or butter.*

NEW POTATOES

By "new" potatoes, I don't mean those small, red potatoes that one finds in all the super-markets—in the South, at least—next to the snap beans. I mean true new potatoes, freshly dug, smelling fragrantly of earth and tasting vaguely sweet, with waxy flesh and translucent, papery skins that are so thin and delicate that they rub right off when you roll the potato between the palms of your hands. At one time, they were the glory of every spring garden. Lightly steamed on top of the snap beans, or quickly boiled and shimmering with butter, they were also the glory of the spring dinner table. Sadly, few of us today have an opportunity to know such glories. The potatoes that are so frequently marketed as "new" seldom actually are. All that the name means now is that the potatoes were harvested before they were mature.

True new potatoes needn't be red. They can, in fact, be any variety of immature potato—round white, russet, or one of the yellow varieties such as Yukon Gold—though nowadays red ones are all that most of us are able to get. Look for very small, thin-skinned potatoes, and be wary of bright red ones; some producers actually dye them to make them look like new potatoes. Even if you suspect that the potatoes have been around a while, you can still use them successfully in any of the recipes that follow.

Two other excellent recipes for new potatoes are Asparagus with Leeks and New Potatoes (page 66) and Asparagus and New Potato Salad (page 67).

CREOLE DEVILED NEW POTATOES, OR *POMMES DE TERRE À LA DIABLE*

The legend behind the name of this dish may not be true but is typical of the Creole sense of humor. The story is that the dish was invented by a strong-willed Creole housewife to get back at her lazy no-count *mari* who spent most of his time—not to mention their limited income—on wine and cards. When he was especially surly and disobedient about being sent to the market for potatoes, and swore that the potatoes could go to the Devil, his wife in turn swore to make him eat potatoes *à la diable* for sure. In Creole and all Southern cooking, that means plenty of hot mustard: she dumped a healthy dose of it on the potatoes and added a big pinch of cayenne for good measure. She brought them angrily to the table and waited, arms folded, for her no-count *mari* to choke. But her revenge backfired: the potatoes were delicious; the lazy jerk actually liked them—and a new Creole dish was born.

Who cares if it's not true—how do you resist a story like that?

SERVES 4

1½ pounds very small new potatoes
5 tablespoons unsalted butter, softened
1 tablespoon Creole mustard (see note) or 2 tablespoons Dijon mustard
Salt and cayenne pepper
1 tablespoon chopped parsley

1. Put enough water to cover the potatoes in a pan that will hold them comfortably and place it over high heat. Wash the potatoes under cold running water, and when the water comes to a rapid boil, add them to the pot. Cover and let the water return to a boil. Reduce the heat to medium and cook until the potatoes are just tender, about 25 minutes. Drain them well and put the pan, covered, back on the heat for half a minute, then turn off the heat, uncover the pan, and let the potatoes sit until they are dry and cool enough to handle. Peel the potatoes and set them aside.

2. Mix 2 tablespoons of the butter with the mustard until it is smoothly blended and set it aside. Though this dish is best when the potatoes are finished right away, you may make it up to this point a couple of hours ahead. Keep the potatoes and butter-mustard mixture covered, but don't refrigerate them.

3. Put the remaining 3 tablespoons of butter in a skillet that will hold the potatoes comfortably in one layer and turn on the heat to medium high. When the butter is melted, add the potatoes, shaking the pan vigorously to coat them with the butter. Add a healthy pinch of salt and a small one of cayenne, and toss to distribute the seasonings. Sauté, tossing frequently, until the potatoes are lightly browned on all sides.

4. Add the butter-mustard mixture and shake the pan until the potatoes are coated with it and it browns. Turn off the heat. Add the parsley and shake the pan until the parsley is evenly distributed among the potatoes. Pour them out into a warm serving bowl and serve at once.

Note: Creole mustard is very à la diable *indeed; a little of it goes a long way. Exercise plenty of restraint if you use it. A larger amount of the milder Dijon mustard is necessary to give the potatoes their requisite kick.*

Sunday Dinner Herbed New Potatoes

Sook Faulk, Truman Capote's eccentric great-aunt who he portrayed so lovingly in *A Christmas Memory*, was one of many gifted cooks within the Faulk household, where Truman Capote spent much of his childhood. The cookery of that family was immortalized by another of its great cooks, Mr. Capote's aunt Marie Rudisill in her lovely culinary memoir *Sook's Cookbook*. Gifts for both cooking and writing seem to run in the Faulk family; Mrs. Rudisill inherited a goodly dose of each. *Sook's Cookbook* is a treasure.

These potatoes are just like one of Mrs. Rudisill's phone calls, which kept me sane while I was working on my first cookbook: they're light, fresh, and refined—yet homey and soul-nourishing all at once.

SERVES 6

1 1/2 pounds new potatoes
Salt
4 tablespoons unsalted butter, melted
1 tablespoon lemon juice
3 tablespoons parsley, snipped
1 tablespoon fresh chives, chopped
2 heads fresh dill, snipped (about 2 tablespoons)
Whole white peppercorns in a peppermill

1. Scrub the potatoes well with a coarse brush under cool running water. Pare a strip of the skin from around the middle of each potato, leaving the remaining skin intact.

2. Choose a kettle that will comfortably hold all the potatoes, put them in it, and add enough water to cover them. Remove the potatoes from the kettle, cover it, and place it over medium-high heat. When the water begins to boil, add a small handful of salt and let it return to a boil. Return the potatoes to the kettle and cover until the water begins to boil again. Uncover and cook until the potatoes are just tender, about 25 minutes. Drain them thoroughly and return them to the pan.

3. In a separate bowl, combine the melted butter, lemon juice, parsley, chives, and dill. Pour this mixture over the potatoes, add a light grinding of white pepper, and gently shake the kettle (or stir very gently) until the potatoes are evenly coated with the butter-herb mixture. Pour the potatoes into a warm serving bowl and serve at once.

STRAWBERRIES

Strawberries, that fragrant, luscious herald of springtime, have always figured prominently on the Southern table. Though commercially produced berries are available almost year round, the only ones really worth bothering about are the ones we pick ourselves, in season, from local fields, or from wild beds. For days afterward, our kitchens are fragrant with kettles of jam and preserves simmering on the back of the stove, but we always hold back some of the ripest and sweetest berries to smother with real cream or tuck into a rich, buttery shortcake.

You don't need a recipe to make the best strawberry dessert ever devised by men or gods: just pick the sweetest and ripest berries, wash and core them, and put them into individual serving bowls; put some good cane sugar into a caster for each person to sprinkle over them to taste, and pass with it a pitcher of thick, heavy cream or a bowl of Crème Fraîche (page 18).

STRAWBERRY SHORTCAKE

This quintessentially American dessert is usually made with shortcake, a biscuitlike quick cake, but here is another traditional version that uses a rich, buttery shortbread instead.

We Southern cooks are true believers in the power of pecans to lift a dish over the edge from good to incredible. They improve just about anything that they are added to. Here, they lend not only a crispy Southern twist, but nicely complement the subtle, tart-sweet flavor of the berries.

SERVES 4

1 pint ripe strawberries
Sugar
8 2½-inch Pecan Shortbread cookies (next page)
1 cup Cold Cream Sauce (page 60) or 1 cup lightly sweetened cream,
*   whipped to soft peaks*
Whole nutmeg in a grater
1 tablespoon finely julienned lemon zest

1. Wash the strawberries, then stem and core them. If you are not serving the shortcake right away, pat the berries dry and set them aside. Just before you plan to serve the short-

cake, thinly slice the strawberries and lightly sprinkle them with sugar. How much sugar you use will depend, of course, on how ripe and sweet the berries are.

2.   Place 4 of the shortbread cookies on individual serving plates. Spoon a thick layer of strawberries over each cookie, reserving about ¹/₂ cup of berries. Spoon about 2 table-spoons of the cold cream sauce (or whipped cream) over each and top with the remaining 4 cookies. Spoon the remaining strawberries over the top cookies, top this with another spoonful of cold cream sauce or whipped cream. Sprinkle the tops with a few gratings of nutmeg or julienned lemon zest (or both) and serve at once.

Note: You can make shortbread using any berries that are in season—raspberries, blackberries, or blueberries. In season, we Southerners love to make it with sliced ripe peaches, either by themselves or mixed with any of the above-mentioned berries.

PECAN SHORTBREAD

Scotch shortbread has long been a favorite Southern confection, but when we mix our native pecans into the dough, it loses its Scottish brogue and takes on a real drawl. Not only does it make a great base for Strawberry Shortcake (previous page), it's superb just on its own.

MAKES ABOUT 20 COOKIES

²/₃ cup demerara or turbinado sugar
10 ounces (2 cups) unbleached all-purpose flour
Salt
1 cup finely chopped pecans
¹/₂ pound (1 cup) unsalted butter, softened

1.   Position a rack in the center of the oven and preheat the oven to 325 degrees F. Pulverize the sugar until the granules are very fine, either in a mortar and pestle or in a blender or food processor fitted with a steel blade.

2.   Sift the sugar, flour, and a small pinch of salt together into a mixing bowl. Mix in the pecans and then work the butter into the dry ingredients until a smooth dough is formed. You can do this in a food processor, pulsing until the dough just forms, but be careful not to overprocess it.

3. Pinch off a small handful of the dough and lightly roll it into a ball between your hands. Place the ball on an ungreased cookie sheet and lightly press it flat into a 2-inch–diameter round, either with the palm of your hand or with a patterned cookie stamp. Repeat with the remaining dough, spacing the cookies about 1 inch apart, until all the cookies are shaped. Bake in the center of the oven until the cookies are lightly browned on the edges, about 25 minutes. Transfer the cookies to a rack to cool.

STRAWBERRY FOOL

This isn't what you're thinking it is: the word "fool" can actually mean several things other than one of your in-laws or a member of an opposing political party. In this case, it's an ancient English dessert—a simple, luscious confection of whipped cream and tart fruit, similar in concept to a classic Bavarian cream. It was once popular on this side of the Atlantic, too, and ought to be popular again.

SERVES 4

1 pint strawberries
Sugar
2 tablespoons bourbon
Freshly grated zest of one orange
1 cup heavy cream (minimum 36 percent milkfat)
4 sprigs fresh mint

1. Wash the berries and set aside 4 small, nicely shaped ones for garnish. Stem and core the remaining berries, and cut them into thick slices. Sprinkle lightly with sugar—how much will depend on how sweet the berries are already—the bourbon, and the orange zest. Cover and set them aside to macerate for half an hour.

2. Mash the berries to a pulp with a potato masher. (Don't use a blender or food processor; both machines do too good a job and liquify them.)

3. In a separate bowl, beat the cream until it forms soft peaks. Gently fold in the strawberries until the mixture is uniform. Spoon the fool into stemmed glasses. Thoroughly chill the fool for at least 1 hour. Just before serving them, garnish the tops with the sprigs of mint and reserved berries.

STRAWBERRY AMBROSIA

This is an old Florida twist on the classic Southern fruit salad that Florida oranges have helped to make famous. Many people don't realize that oranges are seasonal in Florida. As the orange season wanes, vast fields of strawberries begin to ripen. Here, the berries replace the oranges, though the salad is doused with fresh orange juice to give it sweetness and zip.

The berries go mushy if they sit in sugar and acidic juice for very long, so the salad can't be made more than an hour ahead.

SERVES 6

1 small fresh coconut (see note)
1 medium ripe pineapple (about 3 1/2 pounds)
2 quarts (about 2 pounds) ripe strawberries
Sugar
2 cups fresh orange juice
Orange liqueur, such as Cointreau or Grand Marnier

1.   Drain, crack open, and remove the meat from the coconut as directed on page 284. Reserve any juice. Grate the coconut meat with a box grater and set aside. Peel, core, and cut the pineapple into bite-sized pieces. Wash and core the strawberries.

2.   Put a layer of strawberries in the bottom of a glass bowl that will comfortably hold all the ingredients. Lightly dust them with sugar and a thick layer of grated coconut. Cover the coconut with a layer of pineapple. Repeat with the berries, sugar, coconut, and pineapple until all of them are in the bowl.

3.   Combine the orange juice and reserved coconut juice, if there is any. If you like, you may spike the juices with a few tablespoons of orange liqueur to taste—but don't overdo it; too much alcohol gives the salad a harsh aftertaste. Pour the juices over the ambrosia and let it macerate for 30 minutes to an hour. Serve cold.

Note: *You may use unsweetened frozen or unsulfured shredded coconut (available in natural-food stores), though the salad is at its optimum when you use fresh coconut. If the nut doesn't have any juice in it, make sure that it has a clean, fresh coconut smell before using it.*

SUMMER

TOMATOES, OKRA, AND RIPE GEORGIA PEACHES

*N*othing equals a Southern summer. It arrives early, while spring is lingering in the rest of the country, and stays late, like a visiting relative who won't go home. It comes to us full of fresh promise, so bright and bubbling with the happy memories of past fun that we forget its past indiscretions. But then it lingers, wearing out its welcome—and us in the process. Summer is our longest season, stretching from late April until well into October, and it is at once the South's blessing and curse.

For while the long stretch of warm, moist weather means a prolonged growing season and plenty of easy, outdoor living, it turns ruthless with boiling heat and cloying humidity. When at long last the weather breaks, the cool air of autumn is welcomed with the hope that summer will never happen again. Yet, even as the season passes, we're already looking forward to it coming back again.

In a Southern summer, everything explodes with the intensity of the heat; the colors, smells, and flavors of summer are as brilliant as the sun that beats down on us. The gentle greens and subtle, fresh flavors of spring give way to richer, more dazzling colors and more voluptuous and complex flavors. It is the season when the Southern table truly comes into its own, for while the flavors and colors intensify and become more complex, the recipes become simpler and more direct, not only in response to the heat, but to the fact that it does not take much in the way of art to make things taste good.

It's probably not surprising, then, that summer is the time when vegetables take the forefront on Southern tables. A summer vegetable garden is still a fixture in many Southern households, including urban ones. Even Savannahians and Charlestonians grow tomatoes, herbs, and often a few hot peppers or beans in their courtyard gardens. Where there's a patch of land, no matter how poor and unpromising that land may be, a Southerner will plant things in it.

Often we Southerners become what I call accidental vegetarians; though the vegetables may be seasoned with salt pork or accented with butter, cream, or bacon fat, we may go for days without actually having a meat main dish on the table. We don't usually miss it, either—Who would?—with all the sweet corn, fresh okra and tomatoes, succulent squash and eggplant, tender field peas and snap beans, spicy peppers, cooling cucumbers and mellow Vidalia onions, not to mention peaches, fresh blackberries and blueberries, watermelons, cantaloupes, and cherries.

The final ironic joke that summer plays on Southerners is that it is when the heat is its worst that we are forced inside to stand over steaming kettles, for when vegetables and fruit are most plentiful and flavorful is when they have to be put up for the winter—in relishes and pickles to give summer spice to winter meats, or in jams, jellies, and conserves to bring some of the taste and sunshine of summer to a cold, gray winter morning. It's a job we curse as the sweat rolls down our nose and back, but bless later on when we open that first jar of peach chutney or okra pickles.

TOMATOES AND OKRA

Perhaps nothing from Southern gardens speaks more of summer than does the union of fresh tomatoes with okra. The bright, sunny tartness of the tomatoes is at once underscored and mellowed by okra's more subtle, earthy musk. The combination is a classic and one of the essential pillars of Southern cooking; from it, dozens of dishes derive, from thick summer vegetable soups to Creole gumbos. However, the significance of the combination goes beyond its universality. It is an enduring symbol of the Southern culinary melting pot, in which okra, native to Africa, and tomatoes, to Central America, are brought together in an essentially European kitchen by an African cook.

That it was an African hand and imagination that first put the two together there can be little doubt; many historians believe that tomatoes were introduced to West Africa by the Portuguese and were already assimilated into African cookery when the slaves were brought to North America. Well, regardless of who or how, the result is pure genius.

STEWED TOMATOES AND OKRA

When okra and tomatoes are cooked together in the South, the okra is usually cut up into thick slices and stewed with the tomatoes for a very long time. The result is like a thick gumbo. Here, the tomatoes undergo a brief preliminary cooking, then young, tender okra pods are added whole to the pot and cooked briefly. Less of their mucilaginous juices escapes into the tomatoes, resulting in a lighter and fresher flavor and texture.

SERVES 4

2 tablespoons bacon drippings, unsalted butter, or extra virgin olive oil
1 small yellow onion, peeled and chopped
2 large cloves garlic, peeled and minced
2 pounds fresh tomatoes, blanched, peeled, and seeded as directed on
page 117, and coarsely chopped, about 2 cups, or 2 cups Italian
canned tomatoes, chopped
1 Bouquet Garni (page 36), made with thyme and parsley
1 pound whole young okra, each no more than 3 inches long
Salt, cayenne, and black pepper in a peppermill
6–8 fresh basil leaves
4 cups Carolina-Style Rice (page 43)

1. Put the fat and onion in a deep, lidded skillet, and turn on the stove to medium high. Sauté, tossing frequently, until the onion is translucent and softened, about 5 minutes. Add the garlic and continue cooking until it is fragrant, about a minute more. Add the tomatoes and bouquet garni, and bring to a boil. Reduce the heat to low, cover the pan, and simmer, stirring occasionally to prevent sticking and scorching, for 20 minutes.

2. Meanwhile, wash the okra under cold running water, rubbing the pods gently to remove their fuzz. When the tomatoes have simmered for 20 minutes, raise the heat to medium and add the okra. Season with a healthy pinch of salt, a small one of cayenne, and a liberal grinding of black pepper. Stir well and let it simmer, uncovered, until the tomatoes are thick and the okra tender, about 20 minutes more. Turn off the heat, and remove and discard the bouquet garni. Taste and correct the seasonings. Tear the basil into small pieces and stir them into the tomatoes and okra. Serve at once over cooked rice.

ℋ CREOLE GUMBO ⤜

Here is one spot where every Southern cook stakes out his or her own territory and dares anyone to cross it. Though the essential ingredients of a good gumbo are pretty universal, there are as many variations on the theme as there are Southern cooks.

This recipe is my own take, based mainly on *The Picayune's Creole Cook Book* (1901), which for most of this century has been the primary sourcebook for all things Creole. Nowadays, many Louisiana cooks use a spice mix to season their gumbo, and they usually add the so-called Trinity of the Creole kitchen—onion, celery, and bell pepper. I've included a healthy dose of the latter, but I find that the sausages provide all the spice the gumbo needs.

SERVES 8 AS A FIRST COURSE,
OR 4 AS A MAIN COURSE

1 stewing hen or roasting chicken (about 4 pounds)

2 tablespoons bacon drippings or unsalted butter

8 ounces andouille sausage or other spicy smoked sausage, such as
   kielbasa, sliced into $^1/_2$-inch rounds

1 small yellow onion, peeled and chopped

2 ribs celery, including the leafy green tops, washed, strung, and
   chopped

1 large green bell pepper, seeded and chopped

2 large cloves garlic, peeled and minced

2 pounds fresh tomatoes, blanched, peeled, and seeded as directed on
   page 117, and coarsely chopped (about 2 cups), or 2 cups Italian
   canned tomatoes, seeded and chopped

1 quart (4 cups) Chicken Broth (page 23) or water

1 Bouquet Garni (page 36), made with thyme, parsley, and 2 bay
   leaves

1 whole pod cayenne or other hot pepper

1 pound whole young okra, each no more than 3 inches long

Salt

4 cups Carolina-Style Rice (page 43)

1. Wash the chicken under cold running water and pat it dry. Disjoint it as you would for frying. Put the fat in a 5-quart, heavy-bottomed kettle or Dutch oven and place the kettle over medium-high heat. Add the chicken and brown it on all sides. Remove it and add the sausage. Sauté, tossing frequently, until the sausage is browned. Remove the sausage and spoon off all but 3 tablespoons of the fat. Add the onion, celery, and bell pepper. Sauté until they are translucent and softened, about 5 minutes. Add the garlic and sauté until fragrant, about a minute more.

2. Add the tomatoes, broth or water, the bouquet garni, and the whole hot pepper pod. Bring to the boiling point and return the chicken and sausage to the pot.

3. Meanwhile, wash the okra under cold running water, rubbing gently to remove their fuzz. Cut off the stem ends and discard them. Slice the pods crosswise into ¹/₂-inch rounds and add them to the pot. When the liquids begin boiling, add a healthy pinch of salt.

4. Reduce the heat to low, stir well, and loosely cover the kettle. Let the gumbo simmer until it is very thick and the chicken is tender, about 1¹/₂ to 2 hours.

5. Remove and discard the bouquet garni and whole pod of pepper. Remove the chicken, skin it, and take the meat off the bones. Roughly chop the chicken meat and return it to the kettle. Taste and correct the seasonings, and simmer until the chicken is heated through. Serve hot over cooked rice.

Note: *For meatless gumbo, omit the bacon fat, sausage, and chicken, and double the amount of onion, celery, and bell pepper. Begin by making a dark roux with ¹/₂ cup each flour and peanut oil. Put the oil and flour into a heavy-bottomed skillet (preferably cast iron) and place over medium heat. Cook, stirring constantly, until the flour turns a rich dark red-brown. Take care not to scorch it (it will smell burned if this happens). Add the onion, celery, and bell pepper to the roux and stir until they are wilted, then add the garlic off the heat. Transfer the mixture to a soup kettle and proceed with step 2, adding 1 tablespoon of Seafood Boiling Spice (page 31) and a shot of Worcestershire sauce. You can also make a seafood-sausage gumbo by substituting 1 pound (headless weight) of shrimp and 1 pound of crab for the chicken. Peel the shrimp and make a stock with the shells by simmering them in a quart of water for about 1 hour. Strain, discarding the shells, and use this stock instead of chicken broth. Add the shelled shrimp and crab just before serving the gumbo, and simmer until the shrimp are pink and just cooked through, about 5 minutes.*

Ma Ma's Vegetable Soup

When the first pot of vegetable soup filled my grandmother's kitchen with the heady, mingled perfume of freshly gathered tomatoes, okra, butter beans, and corn simmering together, I knew that summer was finally here. To this day, that smell brings on grateful memories of no school, bare feet, and lazy afternoons reading a good mystery.

If any one thing has marked my life as a cook, it has been the unfulfilled effort to reproduce that soup. My mother and I have both stood over Ma Ma as she cooked—and she has even done the same, telling us exactly what to do—and we still haven't been totally successful. Whatever it was that she brought to it—instinct, experience, or just vibrations—we never could imitate. My first printed attempt in *Classical Southern Cooking* only brought a smile to Ma Ma's lips and a gentle shake to her head. It was good; it was close even—but no, it wasn't right. Now that she is gone, the quest has become poignant.

SERVES 8 TO 10 (ABOUT 6 QUARTS)

4 ounces salt pork in 1 slice

2 pounds meaty beef shanks

3 quarts water

2 cups (about 2 medium) peeled, chopped onion

1 cup (about 3 ribs) thinly sliced celery

1 cup (about 2 large) peeled, chopped carrot

$2^1/_2$ pounds tomatoes, scalded, peeled, seeded, and chopped as directed on page 117, with their juice (about 4 cups)

2 cups fresh or frozen butter beans, preferably speckled

1 pound potatoes, peeled and diced (about 2 cups)

2 cups (tightly packed) thinly sliced green cabbage

$^1/_2$ pound (about 1 cup) trimmed, strung, and sliced pole beans

3 cups thinly sliced okra (about $1^1/_2$ pounds)

$^3/_4$ pound turnips, peeled and diced (about 2 cups)

$^3/_4$ pound yellow summer squash, washed and diced (about 2 cups)

Salt and black pepper in a peppermill

1 tablespoon sugar

2 cups corn kernels freshly cut from the cob (3 to 6 ears) or 2 cups good-quality frozen shoepeg corn

1. Put the salt pork in an 8-quart soup kettle and place the kettle over medium-high heat. Sauté until the pork is well browned and most of the fat is rendered from it. Remove the pork and add the beef shanks. Brown them well on all sides and then slowly pour the water over them. Bring the liquid to a boil and then reduce the heat to a slow, steady simmer. Simmer, uncovered, for 2 hours. The liquid should be somewhat reduced—by about a quarter of its original volume. (This can be done 2 to 3 days ahead. Cool, cover, and refrigerate the broth until you are ready to finish the soup.)

2. Remove the beef and set it aside to cool. Raise the heat under the kettle to medium high and bring the liquid to a boil. Add the onion and let the water return to the boiling point, then add the celery. Let the liquid come back to a boil, add the carrot, and let the water return to a boil again. Simmer for 10 minutes.

3. In the same manner add the tomatoes, butter beans, potatoes, cabbage, pole beans, okra, turnips, and squash, allowing the liquid to come back to a boil between each addition. When all the vegetables are in the pot, remove the meat from the shank bones, chop it, and add it back to the soup. Season with a couple of healthy pinches of salt and a few liberal grindings of black pepper to taste, and the sugar. Reduce the heat to a very slow simmer and let the soup simmer, uncovered, for 2 hours; even longer won't hurt it.

4. Twenty minutes before serving, add the corn, taste and correct the seasonings, and simmer until the corn is tender, about 20 minutes longer. Serve hot with Corn Sticks (page 40).

Note: *The soup can be made in stages. Simmer the meat for the broth one day, do the vegetables the next day, and serve the soup several days later. It's a wonderful standby to have in the fridge for quick suppers. If you are making it ahead, however, especially in hot weather, note that the soup should be cooled and refrigerated as quickly as possible. Let it stand for a few minutes, uncovered, after taking it off the heat, then fill the sink with ice and water, set the kettle in the sink, and stir until the soup is cooled. Cover and refrigerate promptly.*

GRILLED OKRA SALAD
WITH TOMATO VINAIGRETTE

If you are put off by the idea of eating okra, this salad is a good way to warm up to this vegetable. The salad is a great side dish for a grilled main course, since the grill will already be fired up. The recipe comes from Jackie Mills, one of the dynamic young food editors at *Southern Living* magazine.

Jackie brings to her work a forward-looking creativity that is tempered by a solid sense of tradition. Here, for example, the okra and tomato combination is given an unexpected and unconventional twist. First, each vegetable gets separate treatment: the okra is marinated and grilled; the uncooked tomato is tossed in a typically Southern mustardy and tart vinaigrette. Finally, the two are combined on a bed of mixed salad greens.

The tomato vinaigrette is good with other grilled vegetables, or cold boiled green beans, or asparagus. You can make it ahead, but don't add the basil until just before serving or it will turn dark and lose its fresh flavor.

SERVES 4

1 large lemon
1 teaspoon minced garlic (1 large or 2 small cloves)
1 teaspoon salt
Black pepper in a peppermill
2 teaspoons Dijon mustard
³/₄ cup extra virgin olive oil
2 dozen young pods of okra, each no more than 3 inches long
¹/₄ cup fresh basil
³/₄ cup (1 large) tomato, peeled, seeded, and diced
8 cups mixed salad greens, washed and torn into small pieces

1. Grate the zest from the lemon and put it in a bowl along with the garlic, salt and a few liberal grindings of black pepper (to taste), and the mustard. Halve the lemon and squeeze the juice into the bowl through a strainer. Whisk until smooth and then slowly whisk in the oil a few drops at a time.

2. Wash the okra under cold running water. Make a slit down two sides of each pod without cutting all the way through either end. Put the okra in a shallow dish that will hold it in one layer. Pour ¹/₄ cup of the vinaigrette over it, toss, and let it marinate for 1 hour.

3. Meanwhile, prepare a grill with coals. When they are ready, spread them and put the rack about 2 inches above the coals. Drain the okra and lay them on the rack. Grill them, turning frequently, until they are well browned on all sides, about 3 to 5 minutes.

4. While the okra is cooking, thinly slice the basil leaves and add them to the remaining vinaigrette base. If the emulsion has separated (this often happens), beat it until it is thick and smooth, then add the diced tomato. Remove the okra from the grill to a shallow bowl and toss it with ¹/₄ cup of the vinaigrette.

5. Put the mixed greens in a salad bowl and pour half the remaining vinaigrette over them. Toss until they are coated and then divide them among individual salad plates, mounding them to one side. Arrange the okra pods in a fan pattern on the other side of the plate, overlapping the greens with them, and pour the rest of the vinaigrette over the okra. Serve at once.

GUMBS—A WEST INDIAN EVOLUTION

Cooking is an ever-evolving process; recipes are never static, but undergo subtle changes as each cook takes ingredient and method into the kitchen and makes them his own. Nowhere was this pointed out to me better than when Karen Hess, the eminent culinary historian who is my teacher and mentor, gave me a recipe for okra for this book. It was her own version of a recipe from Mary Randolph's *The Virginia House-wife* (1824). Though faithful to the method and intent of Mrs. Randolph's recipe, it was marked by Mrs. Hess's distinctive touch. When I started to work with the recipe, I realized that I was doing the same thing. Mrs. Hess understood, and told me, "You may attribute it, as you please, to this Yankee interloper. Whatever. It is now yours." The only way to demonstrate this evolution is to give you all three versions.

GUMBS—A WEST INDIA DISH

"Gather young pods of ocra, wash them clean, and put them in a pan with little water, salt and pepper, stew them until tender, and serve them with melted butter. They are very nutricious and easy of digestion."—Mary Randolph, *The Virginia House-wife*, 1824.

Mrs. Hess elaborates: "There may be other ways of fixing okra, but none simpler and none better than that. Mrs. Randolph's name for the dish would seem to reflect what was thought to be its origin; perhaps her cook had come as a slave by way of the West Indies. That it calls for butter indicates that it had already been adapted for the gentry."

"I have very little to add, except to emphasize that the okra must be of impeccable freshness, just gathered, as she says. No amount of cooking will make overgrown okra tender. Neither top nor tail them. My only departure from her recipe is to add a good splash of best olive oil along with very little water, and, of course, sea salt and several twists of the pepper mill, both to taste. Cook them in a very heavy pot, covered, for *no more than four or five minutes* over a high flame. The result is lovely pods of okra that retain their shape and color, bathed in a light silken sauce of wonderfully subtle, haunting flavor, a flavor that is rarely permitted to star on its own.

"On no account should the sauce be allowed to dry up, although you do not want the okra to be swimming in it either. After a time or two, you will know exactly how you like it. Naturally, if you prefer, you may serve them with melted butter, as Mrs. Randolph suggests, but we prefer the olive oil, partly because we love them at room temperature the next day, when the flavor has deepened somewhat, and for that olive oil is best. Nicely presented, it is a very pretty dish that admirably illustrates what might be called the elegance of simplicity and would grace any buffet, or serve as a first course."—Karen Hess, 1996.

SERVES 4

1½ pounds very fresh okra pods, each no more than 2 inches long
1 large clove garlic, lightly crushed and peeled (optional)
2 tablespoons extra virgin olive oil
Salt and black pepper in a peppermill

1. Wash the okra under cold running water, gently rubbing it to remove the fuzz that coats the outside of the pod. Leave the pods whole; don't trim off the tops or tips.
2. Put them into a heavy, lidded skillet or shallow pan that will hold them all in one layer. Add ¼ cup of water, the optional clove of garlic, 1 tablespoon of the olive oil, a liberal pinch of salt, and a few grindings of black pepper. Cover the pan and turn on the heat to high. Cook for about 4, and no more than 5, minutes, until the okra pods are crisp-tender but still bright green. Do not let the sauce dry up or allow the okra to brown.
3. Pour the okra into a shallow serving bowl, remove and discard the garlic, drizzle the okra with the remaining olive oil, toss it well to coat it, and serve warm or at room temperature.

Note: *Garlic with okra is consistent with the dish's African roots. However, if garlic and olive oil bother you, don't use the former and substitute unsalted butter for the latter. Don't add the butter until the end of step 3, when you have taken the okra from the heat, shaking the pan until it is just melted into the sauce. Or you can leave out the fat altogether.*

FRIED WHOLE OKRA

If you want to make a homesick Southerner stop whining, put a dish of hot fried okra in front of him. This is a favorite in Savannah, not only at the dinner table but in the parlor during cocktail hour as well. There are many variations on the basic theme, but this version is still my all-time favorite. It will work only if the okra pods are very fresh, very young, and no more than 2 inches long.

SERVES 4 TO 5

5 dozen young okra pods, each no longer than 2 inches
2 eggs
Lard or vegetable oil, for frying
1 cup cornmeal or fine cracker crumbs
Salt and black pepper in a peppermill

1. Bring a large kettle of salted water to a boil over high heat. Rinse the okra pods, drain, and drop them into the boiling water. Let the water come back to a boil and cook for 2 minutes; the okra should still be crisp and bright green. Drain immediately and refresh it under cold running water.

2. Fit a wire cooling rack into a cookie sheet that is slightly larger than the rack. Put it in the upper third of the oven and preheat the oven to 150 degrees F. Break the eggs into a shallow, wide bowl, such as a soup plate, and beat them well. Put enough fat into a heavy iron skillet or a deep, nonstick pan to come up the sides by $1/2$ inch and turn on the fire to medium high. Spread the cornmeal or cracker crumbs out on a large plate or piece of waxed paper and put it, with the bowl of beaten eggs, right beside the skillet.

3. When the fat is very hot (about 375 degrees F), dip the okra pods in the beaten eggs, tossing until each is coated. Then lift out each pod one at a time, holding it over the bowl to allow the excess egg to flow back into the bowl. Quickly roll the okra in the cornmeal or crumbs, making sure that each piece is thoroughly coated. Shake off the excess and slip the pods into the fat.

4. Fry the okra quickly until golden on all sides, about 3 to 5 minutes. Drain well on absorbent paper and transfer to the wire rack in the oven. Repeat until all the okra is cooked. Sprinkle liberally with salt and a few grindings of black pepper, and serve at once.

BILL NEAL'S PICKLED OKRA

Pickled okra isn't an especially old dish, but it has become a standard hors d'oeuvre at virtually every Southern cocktail party (try one in your next martini instead of an olive) and picnic. This is Bill Neal's recipe (from *Bill Neal's Southern Cooking*), which is easy to make, as typical of most pickled okra, and virtually identical to my mother's, with its healthy dose of garlic and dill.

My eldest niece, Erica, was literally weaned on those okra pickles of Mama's and got addicted to them as a toddler. Mama never failed to bring a jar when she came to visit, and Erica's mother soon learned that this offering couldn't be put out of her daughter's reach. No matter where she hid it, Erica would find it and usually have the jar half-empty before she was caught. Expect to have the same problem with your own pickles.

MAKES 6 PINTS

2 1/2 pounds young okra pods, each no more than 3 inches long
6 cloves garlic
6 large sprigs fresh dill or 6 teaspoons dill seeds
12 whole small red pepper pods, preferably cayenne
3 teaspoons whole mustard seeds
48 black peppercorns
5 1/3 cups distilled white vinegar
3 3/4 cups water
3 tablespoons sea salt, kosher salt, or pure pickling salt

1. Sterilize 6 pint canning jars and new canning lids (page 10) and let them air-dry. Don't touch the insides of the jars after you have sterilized them. Wash the okra under cold running water, rubbing it gently to remove the fuzz. Trim off most of the stems but leave the tops of the pods intact. Using clean tongs, pack the okra pods into the jars, first stem down and then stem up, so that they mesh with one another. Add 1 clove garlic, 1 sprig of dill (or teaspoon of seeds), 2 pepper pods, 1/2 teaspoon of mustard seeds, and 8 peppercorns to each jar.

2. Combine the vinegar, water, and salt in a stainless pan, and bring it to a boil over high heat. Divide the pickling brine among the jars, leaving a full 1/2 inch of headroom at the top of each jar. Discard any leftover vinegar-water solution. Don't overfill the jars.

3. Seal the jars with the lids and rings, and process them, completely covered, in a boiling water bath for 5 minutes (see pages 9–11 for detailed canning instructions). Remove with tongs and set them—not touching—on folded kitchen towels. Cool completely and store for 6 to 8 weeks to allow the pickles to mature before using them. Store any jars that do not seal in the refrigerator and use them up within 2 months.

$\mathcal{T}$OMATO ASPIC WITH HERB MAYONNAISE

When my first cookbook, *Classical Southern Cooking*, was published, I began to get letters listing things that I'd "forgotten" to include. Tomato aspic, a velvety congealed salad that is very popular in the South, was on every one of those lists. One woman wanted to know how I could even have thought of publishing a book on Southern food with so egregious an omission. The explanation that I had run out of space and had left it out on purpose because it didn't need rescuing, since it is still popular in the South, fell on deaf ears.

Tomato aspic is generally made with canned tomatoes or tomato juice, and is most popular during that in-between season when the weather is warm but fresh tomatoes are not yet ripe. We serve it as a first course for formal meals—traditionally, ladies' luncheons and that long-gone Southern institution, the midday dinner. To this day I think it looks a little out of place on anything but old floral china. Well, old-fashioned though it may be, it's still a popular starter for luncheons, brunches, or even formal dinners.

SERVES 6

1 28-ounce can Italian tomatoes packed with basil or 4 cups canned
    tomato puree
2 tablespoons (2 envelopes) unflavored gelatine (see note)
$^{1}/_{2}$ cup boiling water
$^{1}/_{4}$ cup grated yellow or Vidalia onion
$^{1}/_{4}$ cup finely minced celery
$^{1}/_{4}$ cup chopped cucumber
1 tablespoon finely chopped celery leaves
1 tablespoon finely chopped fresh basil (do not use dried basil)
2 tablespoons fresh lemon juice or wine vinegar
Ground cayenne pepper or hot sauce

6 romaine or Boston lettuce leaves, washed and drained
½ cup Herb Mayonnaise (page 55)
2 tablespoons chopped fresh basil or chives, for garnish

1. If you are using whole tomatoes, seed them and strain their juice to catch any seeds that may be left behind. Put the strained juice and the tomatoes in the bowl of a blender or food processor fitted with a steel blade and puree them until smooth.

2. Put the gelatin in a bowl that will hold all the ingredients comfortably and pour the boiling water over it. Immediately start stirring and keep at it until the gelatin is completely dissolved. Stir in the tomato puree, making sure that the gelatin is completely mixed in. Stir in the onion, celery, cucumber, celery leaves, basil, and lemon juice or vinegar. Season to taste with a pinch or two of cayenne or a few shots of hot sauce and mix well.

3. Rinse out 6 small molds or ramekins or one 2-quart mold with cold water and pour in the aspic mixture. Cover the molds with plastic wrap and refrigerate until set, about 4 to 6 hours (keep in mind that the big mold will take longer) or overnight.

4. To serve the aspic, arrange the lettuce leaves on individual serving plates or, if you are using a large mold, a platter. Unmold the aspic by dipping the mold in hot water for a few seconds. Slip a knife around the edge to break the vacuum in the mold and invert it over the lettuce leaves. Give the mold a gentle tap. The aspic should slip right out. If it doesn't, dip it again in hot water. Top each serving with a dollop of mayonnaise and sprinkle with the chopped basil or chives, or if you've used a large mold, sprinkle the chopped herbs over the aspic and pass the mayonnaise separately.

Note: *Basil and tomatoes are a classic combination, but if you like, you can experiment with other herbs, or use chopped green onions, instead of yellow ones. In that case, use canned tomatoes that don't have basil in them. As to other seasonings, I've given you free rein with the hot pepper, but don't overdo it. The idea here is to keep cool.*

Though there is no meat here, this is not a vegetarian dish, since commercial gelatin is made from animal products. If you are cooking for a conscientious vegetarian, agar flakes (a gelatin made from seaweed, available at health food stores and Oriental markets) can be used instead of commercial gelatin, and, in fact, makes a more delicate aspic. Here's how: Place 3 tablespoons of agar flakes in a saucepan with the water and ½ cup of the tomato juice. Put the mixture over medium heat and, stirring constantly, bring it to a boil and cook until the flakes are completely dissolved, about 2 to 3 minutes.

TOMATO SHERBET IN AVOCADOS

Here are the ingredients of a classic tomato aspic again—but with a twist. Instead of setting the puree with gelatin, it is whirled together with seasonings and dressing and frozen into a luscious sherbet. It would be an appropriate first course for any meal but is especially nice with a fish or shellfish dish that doesn't contain tomatoes.

SERVES 6

2 cups tomato puree (see note)
¼ cup grated onion
¼ cup finely chopped celery, including a few leaves
2 cloves garlic, crushed, peeled, and finely minced
1 tablespoon finely chopped fresh basil, plus 6 whole sprigs for garnish
1 small cucumber, peeled and chopped fine
2 lemons, cut in half
Salt and cayenne pepper
1 tablespoon Worcestershire sauce
1 cup Homemade Mayonnaise (page 53)
3 ripe avocados

1.   In a large mixing bowl, mix together the tomato puree, onion, celery, garlic, basil, cucumber, and the juice of one of the lemons. Season with a healthy pinch or so of salt, a pinch of cayenne to taste, and the Worcestershire sauce. Stir in the mayonnaise and beat until smooth. Cover and refrigerate until chilled, at least 2 hours or overnight.

2.   You can freeze the sherbet in an ice-cream freezer, following the manufacturer's directions for your freezer. Or pour the mixture into a shallow pan, cover with plastic wrap, and put it in the freezer. When the mixture is frozen solid (about 4 hours), break it up and put it in the bowl of a food processor fitted with a steel blade. Whirl it until it is fluffy, but don't overprocess it and let it get slushy. Pour it back into the freezing container and freeze until solid, about 1 hour more.

3.   Chill individual serving plates for at least half an hour before you plan to serve the sherbet. Just before serving, split each avocado lengthwise and remove the pit. You can peel the avocados, if you like, but that isn't necessary. Slice off a little of the rounded side of each half avocado so that it lies flat. Squeeze a little lemon juice over them to prevent

discoloration, and place them on the chilled plates, pit side up. Fill the pit cavity of each with a scoop of the sherbet, garnish with basil leaves, and serve at once.

Note: *You can use fresh tomatoes for the puree, but only when they are really good and truly vine ripened. You'll need 2 pounds (3 to 4 large) of tomatoes for 2 cups puree. Scald and peel the tomatoes, split them crosswise, and squeeze out the seeds. Puree the tomatoes through a food mill or in a blender or food processor.*

TOMATO AND VIDALIA ONION SALAD

If you ask any Savannahian for a recipe using Vidalia sweet onions, chances are they will give you a variation on one of two dishes—whole onions baked in a microwave and this salad. Both have become summer standards.

Savannah has long had a large and influential Greek community, so it is no real surprise that this salad should have a distinctly Greek flavor. The salad is rather substantial, almost a meal in itself, especially when served with crisp buttered toast triangles or, for a really Southern flavor, with hot Corn Sticks (page 40).

SERVES 4

4 medium ripe tomatoes
2 medium Vidalia or other sweet onions
12 brine-cured black olives (Greek or Kalamata)
12–20 fresh basil leaves, depending on size
$^1\!/_2$ cup (2 ounces) crumbled feta cheese
Salt and black pepper in a peppermill
Wine vinegar or freshly squeezed lemon juice
Extra virgin olive oil
8 buttered toast triangles or Corn Sticks (page 40, optional)

1. Peel the tomatoes with a vegetable peeler, core them, and cut them into slices about $^1\!/_3$ inch thick. Spread them on a platter or divide them among 4 individual salad plates.
2. Trim off the root and stem ends of the onions and peel them. Cut them crosswise into the thinnest possible slices and separate them into rings. Spread the rings over the tomatoes.

3. Pit the olives and slice them into thin strips. Tear all but the smallest of the basil leaves into several pieces. Scatter the olives, basil, and feta over the tomatoes and onions. Season with a liberal pinch of salt and several generous grindings of pepper. Sprinkle sparingly with vinegar or lemon juice, and then drizzle olive oil generously over all. Serve at once with toast points or corn sticks, if you like.

BLT (AND O) SALAD

When I was a very small boy, my grandmother and I would get all dressed up—she in high-heeled pumps, hat, and gloves, I in Sunday shorts and oxfords—and go downtown to shop. An invariable part of these adventures was lunch at the Woolworth's lunch counter. I, who at the time lived in a place called Grassy Pond, thought we were being *so* sophisticated. I no longer remember what my grandmother ordered on those occasions, but my choice never varied: a BLT on toast. I loved it then and unapologetically love it now.

It's not without reason that the BLT became a diner standard: it's easy and good. Since basically a BLT is a salad between two slices of toast, I didn't see why my old favorite, with its classic combination of flavors and textures, would not be just as good on a salad plate, especially with a bit of Vidalia onion thrown in.

SERVES 4

4 medium ripe tomatoes
2 medium Vidalia or other sweet onions
8–12 romaine lettuce leaves, washed and well drained
1/2 cup Homemade Mayonnaise (page 53)
Salt and black pepper in a peppermill
8 slices bacon, fried crisp
1 tablespoon chopped fresh chives or parsley
1 cup Buttered Croutons (page 43)

1. Peel the tomatoes with a vegetable peeler, core them, and cut them into 1/2-inch slices. Cut the slices into dice and put them in a salad bowl. Split the onions lengthwise. Trim off the root and stem ends, peel them, split each half lengthwise, and then slice into thin strips. Cut 4 of the lettuce leaves into bite-sized pieces. Add the lettuce and onions to the tomatoes.

2. Add the mayonnaise to the salad bowl along with a generous pinch or so of salt and a few liberal grindings of pepper. Toss until the vegetables are evenly coated. Taste and correct the seasoning, but don't overdo the salt, as there's still a salty element that will be added by the bacon.

3. Line 4 individual salad plates with the remaining lettuce leaves and divide the tomato and onion mixture among them. Crumble the bacon evenly over the tops of the salads, sprinkle them with the chopped chives or parsley, and serve at once, passing the croutons separately.

Southern Minted Gazpacho

With an abundance of tomatoes and hot weather, it was inevitable that the South should heartily embrace this cool, uncooked Spanish salad-soup. It has been a summer standby at least since Mary Randolph published a recipe for it in *The Virginia House-wife* in 1824.

A good gazpacho should have plenty of texture. Those baby-food versions where everything is ground up in a blender are never as interesting as one in which the ingredients are cut by hand. It does take time, but you have to peel the vegetables anyway and cut them into manageable chunks before you can puree them in a machine. It's worth the extra few minutes to cut them up by hand.

This is a basic recipe; you can go in all kinds of directions from here. Dress it up with sour cream, spice it up with fresh hot pepper, or take it uptown with chopped boiled shrimp and crabmeat. What you can not do is used canned tomatoes.

SERVES 8

4 pounds fresh, ripe tomatoes
1 large yellow onion, preferably Vidalia sweet
2 medium cucumbers
2 medium green bell peppers
2 limes or lemons or 1/4 cup red wine vinegar
1/2 cup extra virgin olive oil
Salt and black pepper in a peppermill
Hot sauce or ground cayenne pepper or 1 fresh green hot pepper
1 cup firm white bread, cut into small cubes, or crumbled hard biscuits
*   such as Uneeda*
2 tablespoons chopped fresh mint or basil
1/2 cup sour cream, optional

1.   Holding a knife blade perpendicular to the skin of each tomato, scrape the entire surface of the fruit until the skin begins to wrinkle. Core the tomato and pull the skin off with your fingers. It should slip right off. Position a wire sieve over a bowl. Cut the tomatoes in half, holding them over the sieve to catch all their juices. Scoop out the seeds into the sieve and let the juice drain into the bowl. Roughly chop half the tomatoes and put them in a bowl that can hold all the ingredients. Put the remaining tomatoes and the reserved juice in a blender or food processor, fitted with a steel blade, and puree them until they are the consistency of bottled tomato juice. Add this mixture to the chopped tomatoes and set it aside.

2.   Cut off the root and stem ends of the onion, split it in half and skin it. Cut the onion into very small dice and add them to the chopped tomatoes. Lightly peel the cucumbers and cut them into dice the same size as the onion. Add them to the tomato and onion mixture. Slice off the top (stem end) and bottom of the green peppers, remove the core and seeds, and trim off the membranes. Cut the peppers in half and lay them flat on a cutting board, then slice them into thin strips and cross-cut the strips into dice. Add the diced peppers to the bowl.

3.   Squeeze the juice from the limes or lemons through a strainer and add it (or the vinegar) to the bowl along with the olive oil, a healthy pinch or so of salt, a few liberal grindings of pepper, and a shot or so of hot sauce (or a small pinch of cayenne or the fresh hot pepper, seeded, and chopped). Stir until the gazpacho is well blended. Cover the bowl and let it stand at room temperature for at least 2 hours, or better yet, refrigerate it overnight.

4.   Before serving the gazpacho, taste and correct the seasonings and if the soup has been refrigerated, let it sit at room temperature for about 1 hour before serving. To serve, put a few of the bread cubes or crumbled hard biscuits in each soup bowl. Ladle the soup over it and let it stand for a few minutes to allow the bread or biscuits to soften. Garnish each serving with the chopped herbs. If you like, you can also add a dollop of sour cream.

Note: *In Latin America, the traditional herb for gazpacho is cilantro, and you could substitute it for the mint, but add it to the mixture before marinating it.*

Stewed Tomatoes
à la Creole

Stewed tomatoes have been a Southern classic for more than two hundred years. Here, they get the Creole treatment—with lots of fragrant herbs and a healthy dose of garlic—but the recipe has not really changed much.

Southern stewed tomatoes are often thickened with soft bread crumbs, usually crumbled stale biscuits. In the Lowcountry, the tomatoes are often served over rice, so I've omitted the bread crumbs here. If, however, you prefer the bread-crumb approach, add 1/2 cup (about 2 small biscuits) crumbled stale biscuits or homemade-type white bread in step 3 after the tomatoes have simmered for 15 minutes.

SERVES 4 TO 6

2 pounds fresh, ripe tomatoes (don't use canned tomatoes)
2 tablespoons bacon drippings or unsalted butter (see note)
1 medium yellow onion, peeled and chopped
2 large cloves garlic, peeled and minced
1 tablespoon chopped fresh thyme or 1 teaspoon dried thyme
1 tablespoon chopped parsley
1 whole pod hot red pepper
Salt
8–10 whole fresh basil leaves

1. Fill a teakettle with water and put it on to boil. Put the tomatoes in a heat-resistant bowl and when the water begins to boil, pour it over the tomatoes until they are completely submerged. Let them stand for 30 seconds, drain off the hot water, and immediately rinse the tomatoes in cold water. Cut out the cores, pull off the peelings, and cut them into quarters. Over a sieve, set in a bowl to catch all the juices, seed the tomato quarters. Add them to the bowl with their juices and set aside.

2. Put the bacon drippings (or butter) and chopped onion in a deep, heavy-bottomed pan (preferably cast iron). Turn on the fire to medium. Sauté, tossing frequently, until the onion is translucent, about 5 to 8 minutes. Add the minced garlic and continue sautéing until it is fragrant, about a minute more.

3. Add the tomato quarters and their juices, the thyme, parsley, pod of hot pepper (left whole), and a healthy pinch of salt. Bring the tomatoes to a boil, reduce the heat to medium low, and loosely cover the pan. Simmer, stirring occasionally, until the tomatoes are tender and beginning to fall apart, about 30 minutes.

4.   If there is still a lot of liquid in the pan, uncover and raise the heat to medium high. Let it boil rapidly until the excess liquid has evaporated and the tomatoes are thick. This should take no more than 2 minutes, so don't turn up the heat and/or get distracted by something else. Turn off the heat and stir in the basil. Taste and correct the seasonings, and serve hot.

Note: *Bacon drippings lend this dish the most authentic taste, but many old recipes called for butter. So, you can substitute butter for the drippings, or even use an extra virgin olive oil (as I often do) if you are avoiding animal fats altogether.*

Savannah Stuffed Tomatoes

In our part of Georgia, late tomato plants are often producing fruit right into December, so our tomato recipes will sometimes have an autumnal touch, as does this one with its pairing of late tomatoes with the season's first pecans. It comes from *The Savannah Cook Book* (1909), an early charity cookbook produced by the ladies of Westminster Presbyterian Church.

SERVES 4

4 medium ripe tomatoes (about 2 pounds)
Salt
1/2 cup bread crumbs
1/2 cup chopped Toasted Pecans (page 219)
1 tablespoon chopped parsley
Black pepper in a peppermill
1 large egg
Unsalted butter, for greasing

1.   Position a rack in the center of the oven and preheat it to 350 degrees F. Wash the tomatoes and slice off the stem ends so that all the seed cavities are exposed. Set the stem

ends aside. Carefully scoop out the seeds and discard them. Lightly salt the tomatoes and invert them in a colander to drain.

2. Put the crumbs, pecans, and parsley in a mixing bowl. Season with a healthy pinch of salt, a few generous grindings of pepper, and toss until the ingredients are uniformly mixed. Break the egg into a separate bowl and lightly beat it until the yolk and white are well mixed. Add it to the crumb-and-nut mixture and stir until the egg has been absorbed into the crumbs.

3. Pat the tomatoes dry and fill the seed cavities with the crumb mixture (if there is a little excess, spread it over the top). Replace the reserved stem ends over the top of each tomato like a lid. Lightly butter a 9-inch square casserole or a pie plate and put the tomatoes into it. Put the dish on the center rack of the oven. Bake until the tomatoes are tender and their tops are beginning to wrinkle and brown, about 45 minutes.

Note: *This is an ideal accompaniment for any game dish that does not contain tomatoes and is also good with pork and roasted chicken or turkey. The whole secret is to use good tomatoes and fresh pecans. Unfortunately, the latter aren't universally available. If the pecans available where you live taste heavy and a touch rancid, don't use them. English walnuts or pine nuts make an acceptable substitute.*

Though the original recipe didn't call for it, ¼ cup chopped country ham is a welcome addition to the stuffing mixture.

FRIED GREEN TOMATOES

There was a time when a certain so-called progressive element of Southern society was embarrassed by the whole idea of fried green tomatoes. Breaded in cornmeal and fried in bacon drippings, they were considered too countrified, folksy, and unsophisticated, and were relegated to the backwoods. Mind you, smart Southerners weren't bothered by all that and kept right on eating them. But ever since Fanny Flagg's lovely *Fried Green Tomatoes at the Whistlestop Cafe* was made into a motion picture, fried green tomatoes are not only fashionable, they are the one Southern vegetable dish that everyone knows about. It's not a bad dish to be known by, either.

In some parts of the United States, fried green tomatoes are made only in the fall with the last of the crop, plucked from the vines before the first frost kills them off. However, throughout the South, we start frying as soon as the vines produce the first fruit.

SERVES 6

4–6 medium very green tomatoes
Sugar
Salt and black pepper in a peppermill
2 large eggs, lightly beaten in a shallow bowl
1 cup fine-ground white cornmeal
1 cup bacon drippings or a mixture of vegetable oil and drippings

1. Preheat the oven to 150 degrees F, and have ready a wire rack fitted on a cookie sheet. Cut out the stems of the tomatoes and cut them crosswise into slices at least ³/₈ inch thick. Don't peel them. Sprinkle them very lightly with sugar and salt, and lay them flat in one layer on a platter or cookie sheet for at least half an hour. Meanwhile, break the eggs into a shallow bowl and beat them lightly, spread the cornmeal on a dinner plate, and have both bowl and plate ready by the stove.

2. Wipe the tomatoes thoroughly with a cotton kitchen towel or paper towels. There should be no sugar remaining on them at all. Season them lightly with salt and a few grindings of pepper.

3. Put the fat into a well-seasoned iron (or nonstick) skillet and turn on the fire to medium. When it is hot but not smoking, dip the slices of tomato one at a time in the beaten eggs, letting the excess drain back into the bowl, roll them quickly in the breading, gently shake off the excess, and slip them into the pan. Fry the tomato slices until they are golden on the bottom, about 3 minutes, then gently turn them with a spatula and continue cooking until both sides are golden. Drain them briefly on butcher paper or paper towels, then transfer them to the wire rack in the oven while you cook the next batch. Repeat until all the slices are fried. The tomatoes cannot be reheated and must be served at once.

Note: *The classic taste can only be had with bacon drippings, but vegetarians can use peanut oil instead, as it comes closest to producing the right crispness, though the flavor is naturally in no way the same.*

The sugar is not intended to add sweetness to the tomatoes, but only to help remove the bitterness that some green tomatoes have. It should in no way interfere with the tartness of the tomatoes. So use only the very lightest sprinkling, and be sure you wipe it thoroughly from the slices before breading them.

GRILLED GREEN TOMATOES

Ripe tomatoes are an old favorite to put on the grill, and they are a classic accompaniment to grilled beef. Green tomatoes also take well to grilling, and their bright, tart flavor lends a pleasant accent to any grilled meat, poultry, or fish. You can also do this recipe under an oven broiler, though it will not have as much flavor.

SERVES 4

2 large green tomatoes
Salt and sugar
2 tablespoons bacon drippings, melted, or olive oil
Ground cayenne pepper and black pepper in a peppermill

1.   Wash the tomatoes and split them in half crosswise. Sprinkle them lightly with salt and the tiniest pinch of sugar. Invert them in a colander and let them stand in the sink for 30 minutes.

2.   Prepare a charcoal fire (preferably hardwood) or preheat the broiler. When the fire is ready, wipe the tomatoes thoroughly and brush them with the bacon drippings or oil. Sprinkle with a little more salt, a small pinch of cayenne, and a few grindings of black pepper.

3.   Put the tomatoes on the grill, cut side down (or under the broiler cut side up), and grill until the cut side begins to brown, about 5 to 8 minutes. Turn them cut side up and brush with more drippings or oil (if you are using the broiler, turning them won't be necessary, but watch to make sure they don't get too brown). Grill until tender, another 8 to 12 minutes, and serve hot.

GREEN TOMATO PIE

In the nineteenth century, when a tariff was levied on vegetables, a heated debate arose over whether tomatoes were a vegetable or a fruit—until a federal judge silenced the debate by ruling that they were a vegetable. Well, regardless, tomatoes are botanically speaking a fruit, and at one time they were frequently used as such in American cooking.

This typical, very old Southern favorite comes from a little-known, early postbellum Louisiana cookbook, *Verstille's Southern Cookery* (1866), by Mrs. Ellen J. Verstille. Green tomato pies could be as simple as this one, or as elaborate as a mincemeat pie.

MAKES ONE 9-INCH PIE (ABOUT 6 SERVINGS)

1 full recipe Basic Pastry (page 47)
4–6 medium green tomatoes
1 cup sugar
2 tablespoons cornstarch
1 lemon

1. Position a rack in the center of the oven and preheat the oven to 375 degrees F. Divide the pastry into two equal parts. Roll out one half to a thickness of about ⅛ inch. Line a 9-inch pie plate with the pastry, prick it in several places with a fork, and let it rest in the refrigerator for half an hour.

2. Meanwhile, thoroughly wash the tomatoes, core them, and cut them crosswise into thin slices. Set them aside in a colander for half an hour or so to drain. Combine the sugar and cornstarch, and mix until the starch is evenly distributed.

3. Grate the zest from the lemon, then cut the lemon in half and squeeze out the juice into a separate bowl through a strainer. Stir gently until the zest is evenly distributed. Gently press the tomatoes to remove their excess moisture; otherwise they will make a very soupy filling.

4. Sprinkle the prepared pastry shell generously with the sugar-cornstarch mixture and put a layer of tomatoes over it, completely covering the pastry. Sprinkle the tomatoes with sugar, lemon zest, and a little of the lemon juice. Repeat with another layer of tomatoes, sugar, zest, and juice until they are all used up.

5. Roll out the remaining pastry dough and lay it over the pie. Trim off the excess pastry, seal the edges by crimping or fluting them, and make several slashes in the top pastry. Bake in the center of the oven until the pastry is evenly browned and the filling bubbly, about 45 minutes.

THREE SOUTHERN TOMATO SAUCES

We tend to think of tomato sauce as Italian, but rare is the Southern kitchen without some variation of it. It's a common theme in all the different cuisines of the South—not just our South, but the whole geographical area, from here to the Southwest, the Caribbean, and the whole of Latin America.

*T*OMATO SAUCE

This sauce was originally intended mainly to dress up breaded veal or pork cutlets, though occasionally it was poured over poached eggs and omelets. Old cooks seldom used it to sauce vegetables, but modern Southern cooks know no such restrictions. This is a fine sauce for Quick-Cooked Young Green Beans (page 130), squash (page 170), or Braised Leeks (page 77). It's also spectacular over pasta or Carolina-Style Rice (page 43).

The whole point of this sauce is the mellow flavor and aroma of fresh tomatoes, but it is good even when made with canned Italian plum tomatoes. When choosing fresh tomatoes, the ones preferred for all sauces are the small, meaty Roma or plum tomatoes, but the heftier, juicier garden varieties, such as Beefsteaks or Better Boys, are fine, too.

MAKES ABOUT 2 CUPS

2 tablespoons unsalted butter

3–4 shallots or 1 medium yellow onion, peeled and chopped

1 small carrot, peeled and chopped

2 cloves garlic, peeled and minced

1³/₄ pounds fresh tomatoes, preferably Roma or plum, peeled and seeded as directed on page 117, and coarsely chopped, about 2 cups with their juices, or 2 cups canned Italian plum tomatoes, seeded and chopped

1 Bouquet Garni (page 36), made of celery, parsley, thyme, and 1 bay leaf

1 whole pod cayenne or chile pepper

Salt (optional, see step 2)

2 ounces salt lean pork or country ham in one piece (¹/₄-inch slice about 4 inches long, optional)

1.   Put the butter, shallots or onion, and carrot in a saucepan that will comfortably hold all the ingredients and turn on the heat to medium. Sauté until the vegetables are softened but not browned, about 5 minutes. Stir in the garlic and cook until it is fragrant but not the least colored, about a minute longer.

2.   Add the tomatoes, bouquet garni, the cayenne pepper pod, and a small pinch of salt, or the salt pork or ham (omit the salt if using either). Bring the tomatoes to a boil and reduce the heat to medium low. Simmer, uncovered, until the sauce is very thick, about 1 hour, stirring occasionally to be sure that the bottom doesn't scorch.

3.   Turn off the heat. Remove and discard the bouquet garni, pepper pod, and meat, if you have used it. If you like, you can puree the sauce through the food mill (or in the blender), as was done in the old recipes, or you can leave it as is. Serve warm.

Sauce Creole: Make tomato sauce as directed above, adding a medium green bell pepper, seeded and chopped, with the onions and carrots in step 1. After the sauce has simmered for about 1 hour you can, if you like, stir in ¼ cup sherry and simmer until the sauce thickens again, about 10 minutes more. Just before serving, thinly slice 2 scallions or green onions and stir them into the sauce. Let it simmer for about 2 minutes more.

Raw Creole Sauce
(Salsa Criolla Cruda)

There is a strong link between the old coastal cities of the American South and the islands of the Caribbean West Indies that goes back to the early days of the slave trade right through the slave uprisings of the late eighteenth century that led to an infusion of French Huguenot refugees into Charleston, Savannah, Mobile, and New Orleans. Perhaps nowhere is that link better felt than in the kitchen, and in none more so than in the Carolina and Georgia Lowcountry.

This sauce is just one of many suggestive elements that are common to the whole region. It is the ubiquitous *salsa cruda* of the Caribbean and of all Latin America, and a close cousin to the spicy *salsas* of our own Southwest. In the Deep South, we used to call it Creole sauce. But as Southwestern cooking spreads eastward from Texas, and as Cuban-Floridian cookery heads north, the Spanish name is nowadays falling from the most Southern of lips.

1 large or 2 small to medium ripe tomatoes (see step 1)
1 medium yellow onion
2 large cloves garlic
1 fresh hot green pepper (banana, jalapeño, or serrano)
1 tablespoon chopped fresh coriander (cilantro) or parsley
1/4 cup freshly squeezed lime juice or red wine vinegar
1/2 cup extra virgin olive oil
Salt

1. Peel the tomatoes with a vegetable peeler, core them, then split them in half crosswise. Remove and discard the seeds and chop the pulp. You should have 3/4 cup of pulp. Put the chopped tomatoes into a bowl that will hold all the ingredients comfortably.

2. Cut off the root and stem ends of the onion, split it lengthwise, and peel it. Chop it fine and add it to the tomatoes. Crush, peel, and mince the garlic. Cut off the stem end of the hot pepper and split it lengthwise. Remove and discard the seeds and connective membranes, and mince the hot pepper. Add it and the garlic to the tomato mixture. Add the coriander or parsley, the lime juice or vinegar, and the olive oil, and toss until well mixed.

3. Let the sauce stand at room temperature for at least 15 minutes (up to an hour, if possible). After the flavors have melded, taste the sauce and add a pinch of salt—not too much, just enough to bring up the flavor. Serve the Creole sauce at room temperature over fish, chicken, shrimp, or cold cooked green beans. It can also be used as a seasoning for cooked dishes. Spread it over raw vegetables (such as broccoli, leeks, squash, sliced sweet potatoes), or over fish steaks, filleted chicken breasts, or peeled raw shrimp, and steam them.

Note: The flavor of fresh coriander (cilantro) is an important element in Caribbean and Latin American cooking. Though less common in the South (at least, east of Texas and north of Florida), it is not completely unknown to traditional Southern cooking. Down here, people either love it a lot or think it tastes like soap. My advice is to use cilantro sparingly—too much really does taste like soap.

In spite of the presence of chiles, this is not an especially hot sauce. Still, if you or someone in your family can't tolerate hot pepper, it is probably because of an allergy to the acid that makes the heat. Substitute 1/2 green bell pepper. If, on the other hand, the hot stuff really turns you on, you can double the amount of chiles, or use one of the really hot chiles such as habañeros or Scotch bonnets.

BEETS

Beets are one of the nicest and loveliest of root vegetables. I love their earthy-sweet flavor and deep magenta color—though not as prepared in all too many Southern households, embalmed in heavy sweet-sour pickling or, worse yet, boiled and doused with sugar and vinegar or dumped into molded salads. With such indifferent treatment, the wonder isn't that they aren't better liked, but that they are liked at all.

The green, leafy tops of beets are regretfully neglected in America, but when cooked just as their cousins chard and spinach are, they make a delicious green and are plain wonderful when substituted for poke sallet in Ma Ma's Poke Sallet with Spring Onions (page 89).

$\mathcal{B}$AKED BEETS

When the new beets are just coming in and are at their sweetest and juiciest, this is the only recipe that you'll need. Baking concentrates their natural sweetness and keeps all the flavorful juices inside the vegetable, where they belong.

SERVES 4

4 medium beets, about 2 pounds
Unsalted butter
Salt and black pepper in a peppermill

1. Position a rack in the upper third of the oven and preheat the oven to 400 degrees F. If the greens are still attached to the beets, cut them off but leave a little of their stems on. Set the greens aside to cook separately either as a vegetable on their own as for spinach, or mixed with spinach (page 82). Scrub the beets well under cold running water, pat them dry, and trim off most of the taproot, leaving some of it attached to the beets. Do not peel them.

2. Rub each beet with a little butter and wrap each individually in foil. Place them on a cookie sheet or baking dish, and put them on the rack in the upper third of the oven. Bake, turning the beets occasionally, until they are tender, about 1 hour. They will yield slightly when pressed with your finger but will still be quite firm.

3.   Unwrap the beets and quickly trim off the remaining stem and root ends. You can also slip off the skins if you like, but the skins will be very tender and it isn't really necessary to peel them. Serve the beets at once, passing more butter, salt, and freshly ground black pepper separately. Or let them cool completely and use them to make the following salad.

$\mathcal{B}$EET SALAD

I'm not crazy about most beet salads, which are often too heavy with vinegar and sugar, but this one is excellent. The secret is to keep the dressing light; beets are sweet on their own and don't need a lot of help. The dressing should pick up their delicate flavor, not cloak it.

SERVES 4

4 Baked Beets (previous page)
1 large Vidalia or other sweet onion
1 large hard-cooked egg yolk
1 teaspoon Dijon mustard
2 tablespoons wine vinegar
Salt, sugar, and cayenne pepper
1/4 cup extra virgin olive oil
4–8 romaine or Boston lettuce leaves, washed and drained
1 tablespoon chopped parsley

1.   When the beets have cooled completely, cut them crosswise into 1/4-inch slices. Set them aside. Cut off the stem and root ends of the onion, peel it, and slice into the thinnest possible rings. Put the onion into a bowl of cold water with 2 or 3 ice cubes. Set aside.

2.   Put the hard-cooked egg yolk, mustard, vinegar, a large pinch of salt, and a small one of sugar into a small mixing bowl and beat with a whisk until everything is evenly mixed and smooth. Beat in the olive oil, a drop at a time, until it is incorporated and emulsified. Taste the dressing for salt and sugar—keeping in mind that its flavor alone is more assertive than it will be when spread over the salad. Adjust the seasonings and add a small pinch or so of cayenne pepper. Beat the dressing until it is smooth again. The salad can be made up to this point as much as an hour ahead.

3. Just before serving, drain the onion and squeeze it dry. Line a platter or individual salad plates with the lettuce leaves and scatter the sliced beets over them, then scatter the onions over the beets. Beat the dressing again until it is smooth and pour it over the salad. Sprinkle with the chopped parsley and serve at once.

GREEN BEANS

Now here's a generic name to make you take to the bourbon. So-called green beans are the immature green pods of any member of the large family of legumes *Phaseolus vulgaris*, commonly known as kidney beans. There are many varieties, from French *haricots* and Italian *cannellini* to ordinary supermarket snap beans. Even though each variety has a distinctly different color, flavor, and texture, just as do their matured seeds, these distinctions are seldom marked when the beans come to market, let alone in recipes. They're just called "green beans."

Unfortunately, they are too often treated with indifference in the kitchen. This leads predictably to equally indifferent results—like skinny little snap beans slow-cooked to tasteless mush in salt-pork broth, or, conversely, tough pole beans (the slow-cooking variety) so underdone that you couldn't cut them with a chainsaw. The problem does not lie in the method but in its misapplication. There's nothing wrong with beans simmered slowly in an aromatic salt-pork broth; properly cooked, they are one of the South's culinary glories and perhaps the most satisfying vegetable dish on Southern tables. There will, however, be a lot wrong with this dish if you use the wrong kind of green beans. To that end, what follows are recipes that give each variety its appropriate treatment.

SOUTHERN POLE BEANS

This recipe has been largely misunderstood both without and within the South, making it the brunt of way too many rude jokes about Southern vegetables. When Linda Negro, a Southern-born colleague in Evansville, Indiana, was asked by an eminent chef to design an ideal menu, she included these beans. The chef said that anyone who could down this slop had no palate. Far from being offended by such culinary snobbery, Linda roared with laughter. Had she called it a "ragout" (which it essentially is) and compared it with its French cousin *cassoulet*, he'd probably have had a different attitude.

The only important point for success with this recipe is that you cannot slow-cook just any green bean. Use only broad, flat, thick-skinned pole beans for this recipe.

SERVES 4 TO 6

3 pounds pole beans
1 country ham hock or ½ pound country ham in 1 piece
1 small yellow onion, finely chopped
Salt and freshly ground black pepper
1 small sweet onion, preferably Vidalia (optional)
Pepper Vinegar (page 27, optional)

1.   Wash the beans thoroughly in cold water and drain them. Have ready a fresh basin of cool water. Top and tail the beans and strip off the woody "strings" that run down the seams of the pods. Be careful to remove all traces of these strings—they won't ever get tender. Break or cut the beans into 1-inch lengths and drop them into the water.

2.   Put the ham hock or ham in a heavy-bottomed kettle that will hold all the beans comfortably, and turn on the heat to medium. Cook, turning frequently, until it has thrown off most of its fat. Add the onion and sauté until it is golden but not scorched, about 5 minutes. Add about a pint of water and let it come to a boil. Lower the heat, cover the pot, and simmer for 30 minutes.

3.   Raise the heat to high and bring the liquid back to a rolling boil. Add the pole beans, let the water again come back to a boil, then reduce the heat to a bare simmer. Loosely cover the pot and let the beans simmer for at least 1½ hours—longer won't hurt—until the beans are very tender. At this point, there should be very little liquid left. However, if there is, raise the heat to medium high and cook until most of the liquid has evaporated and been absorbed, stirring often to prevent scorching. Pour the beans into a warm vegetable dish.

4.   The beans are often served with condiments of chopped raw onion and pickled hot peppers. If this appeals to you, peel and chop a small sweet onion and pass it and the pepper vinegar separately.

QUICK-COOKED
YOUNG GREEN BEANS

Whether the beans are true French *haricots verts* or merely Blue Lakes (that ubiquitous supermarket variety), this is a good basic method of cooking them. Quick-boiled, young green beans can be served dozens of ways—from salads to savory gratins. The water must really boil—and hard—or the beans will lose their color and become flabby and uninteresting, especially if they are those generic supermarket beans.

SERVES 4

1½ pounds young, thin, "stringless" green beans
Salt
2 tablespoons unsalted butter, softened

1.   Wash the beans in several changes of water and drain them well. Snap off the stem ends, but unless the individual recipe calls for them to be broken up, leave the beans whole.

2.   Put 2 quarts of water into a 3- to 4-quart kettle, cover, and bring it to a boil over high heat. When the water is boiling, uncover the kettle, add a small handful of salt, and when it returns to a boil, add the beans. Cover until the water is boiling once again, then remove the lid and let the beans cook, uncovered, until barely tender, about 6 to 8 minutes. Drain and toss with butter or serve in one of the following ways:

Green Beans with Savannah Sweet Red Pepper Sauce: As soon as the beans are cooked and drained, transfer them to a serving platter or divide them among individual plates. Spoon Savannah Sweet Red Pepper Sauce (page 56) over the beans and serve at once.

Green Bean Salad: Plunge the cooked, drained beans in ice water to arrest the cooking. Drain and serve with your favorite vinaigrette or the one for asparagus on page 64.

GREEN BEANS IN CREOLE SAUCE ➤

In this recipe the beans and the sauce cook together briefly, so that the sauce is absorbed into the beans and infuses them with flavor.

SERVES 4

2 cups Raw Creole Sauce (1 full recipe, page 124)
1½ pounds Quick-Cooked Young Green Beans (previous page), cooked
    for 4 minutes (they should be very underdone)

Put the Creole sauce in a lidded skillet that will hold the beans in no more than two layers and turn on the heat to medium. When the sauce is bubbling, add the beans and toss well. Cover the pan and cook until the beans are just tender, about 4 minutes more. Remove the lid and raise the heat, allowing any excess liquid to boil quickly away. Turn off the heat, transfer the beans to a serving platter, and serve at once.

CREAMED GREEN BEANS ➤

This is a way of cooking green beans that gives new life to beans that are not as fresh as you would like them to be. Before cooking the beans for this recipe, you can break them into bite-sized lengths, which makes them easier to manage in the sautéing stage.

SERVES 4

1½ pounds Quick-Cooked Young Green Beans (previous page), cooked
    for 4 minutes (they should be very underdone)
1 large shallot or small yellow onion, peeled and chopped
1 tablespoon unsalted butter, softened
1 cup heavy cream (minimum 36 percent milkfat)
Salt and whole white peppercorns in a peppermill

1.   Rinse the cooked beans under cold running water to arrest the cooking, drain well, and set aside.

2. Put the shallot or onion and butter in a skillet that will comfortably hold the beans. Turn on the heat to medium high and sauté, tossing frequently, until the onion is golden and beginning to brown, about 5 minutes.

3. Add the beans and toss well. Pour the heavy cream over the beans, bring it to a simmer, and cook until the cream is thick and the beans are nicely coated with it, about 3 to 4 minutes more. Taste and add salt, if needed, and a few grindings of white pepper.

Young French Beans with Pecan Brown Butter

Pecans are nice to pair up with green beans. Not only French *haricots* but any young, tender beans respond well to this recipe—even the ubiquitous supermarket variety.

MAKES 4 SERVINGS

1¹/₂ pounds Quick-Cooked Young Green Beans (page 130), cooked for
5 to 8 minutes (they should still be underdone)
1 cup pecan halves
¹/₂ cup unsalted butter
Salt
2 tablespoons chopped parsley

1. The beans should still be underdone, so don't overcook them. Drain and plunge them in cold water to arrest the cooking.

2. Slice the pecans lengthwise into 3 slivers per nut, using the natural grooves as a guide. Set them aside.

3. Put the butter into a cast-iron or heavy-bottomed nonstick skillet that will hold all the beans comfortably in a single layer. Turn on the heat to medium. When the butter is melted, add the pecans and cook, swirling the pan constantly, until the pecans and butter have colored a uniform light brown, about 4 minutes.

4. Add the beans and toss them with the butter until they are heated through, about 1 minute. Turn off the heat, taste, and add a pinch or so of salt, if needed. Add the parsley and toss once more to mix. Pour into a serving platter and serve at once.

Note: There is no real substitute for the butter in this recipe, but if you are a strict vegetarian, try substituting ⅓ cup mild walnut or peanut oil for the butter.

A tablespoon of marjoram, sage, or thyme can be substituted for the parsley to give a brighter flavor, but be careful of strongly flavored herbs such as tarragon or rosemary, which would fight with the pecans. Basil goes well with pecans, though the taste isn't traditionally Southern.

New-Cut Plantation String Beans

This lovely recipe was first printed in the Charleston Junior League's now classic *Charleston Receipts* (1950). There is a bit of that notorious bacon here, yes, but the treatment the beans get is light and fresh—and delicious.

MAKES 4 SERVINGS

1 pound young "stringless" green beans
4 slices bacon
6 green onions
Salt and black pepper in a peppermill

1.   Wash the beans in several changes of water and snap off the stem ends but leave the beans whole.

2.   Choose a heavy-bottomed skillet with a lid that will hold the beans in one layer, put in the bacon, and place it over medium heat. Fry the bacon, uncovered, turning it frequently until it is crisp, about 10 minutes.

3.   Meanwhile, wash the green onions and thinly slice them. When the bacon is crisp, remove it from the pan and set it aside to drain on absorbent paper. Add the onions to the pan and stir until they are just wilted. Add the beans and toss until they are glossy. Cook for 1 minute, then add a large pinch of salt and ¼ cup of water. Tightly cover the pan and steam the beans for 3 minutes. Uncover and cook until the moisture is evaporated and the beans are just tender, about 2 to 3 minutes more. Turn off the heat, taste, adjust the salt, and add a few grindings of pepper. Transfer the beans to a warm serving plate and crumble the bacon over the top. Serve at once.

DILLY BEANS

This old Southern favorite is prepared the same way as Bill Neal's Pickled Okra (page 109) and contains virtually the same ingredients.

If you like to make your own pickles, you'll love these. They are shamefully easy to make and even easier to eat. Try them on the relish tray at your next cocktail party, pass them as a cold relish with dinner, or mix them into a green salad.

MAKES 6 PINTS

3 pounds very young green beans (no more than 3 inches long)
6 cloves garlic
6 large sprigs of fresh dill or 6 teaspoons dill seeds
6 whole pods dried red pepper, preferably cayenne
48 black peppercorns
3³/₄ cups distilled white vinegar
3³/₄ cups water
3 tablespoons sea salt, kosher salt, or pure pickling salt

1.   Prepare 6 pint canning jars and new canning lids by sterilizing them (page 10) and let them air-dry. Don't touch the insides of the jars after you have sterilized them. Wash the green beans in several changes of cold water. Trim off the stem ends but leave the beans whole. Using clean tongs, pack the beans vertically in the jars. Add 1 clove of garlic, 1 sprig of dill (or 1 teaspoon of seeds), 1 whole pepper pod, and 8 peppercorns to each jar.

2.   Combine the vinegar, water, and salt in a stainless pan and bring it to a boil over high heat. Divide the pickling brine between the jars, leaving a full ¹/₂ inch of headroom at the top of each.

3.   Seal with the lids and rings, and process the jars, completely covered, in a boiling water bath for 10 minutes (see pages 9–11 for detailed canning instructions). Remove with tongs and set them—not touching—on folded kitchen towels. Cool completely and store for 6 to 8 weeks to allow the pickles to mature before serving them. Store any jars that do not seal in the refrigerator and use them up within 2 months.

BUTTER BEANS

Though many Southerners will vigorously protest the point, butter beans, speckled butter beans, butter peas, and the like are all varieties of lima beans, *Phaseolus limensis*, which are native to the Americas. The peculiarly Southern name for them—"butter" bean—appears to be a recent one; all the old cookbooks and reference books referred to them as either limas, civets, sievas, or occasionally, Carolina beans.

The most Southern of all the many varieties are speckled butter beans, so called because their creamy-white skin is beautifully marbled with red and purple. The bright colors fade when they are exposed to heat, and the beans turn a rich coppery brown when cooked. Though once commonplace (they have been found growing wild in Florida), nowadays speckled butter beans are not as easy to come by in the South, and they are almost unheard of in other parts of the country. Color isn't their only distinction; speckled butter beans have a unique flavor for which there is no substitute. If you can't find them, any fresh or frozen lima beans can be used in any recipe calling for speckled butter beans in this book.

$\mathcal{B}$UTTER BEAN RAGOUT

Though not technically related, lima beans are similar to European fava or Windsor beans. Here, they receive a treatment similar to an Italian classic, *fave al guanciale* (or *alla romana*), simmered with an aromatic combination of onion and salt-cured pork—in this instance, lean country ham.

SERVES 4

1 small yellow onion, peeled and chopped
3 tablespoons butter, divided
4 ounces (one $^1\!/_8$-inch slice) country ham or prosciutto, cut into julienne
    strips
16 ounces (3 cups) fresh shelled butter beans (preferably speckled), or
    frozen limas such as Fordhooks, thawed
Black pepper in a peppermill
Salt
1 tablespoon chopped parsley

1.   Put the onion and 2 tablespoons of the butter in a lidded skillet that will hold all the ingredients and place it, uncovered, over medium-high heat. Sauté, tossing frequently, until the onion is softened but not colored, about 3 minutes. Add the ham and continue sautéing, tossing constantly, for half a minute more.

2.   Add the beans and toss well with the onion and ham. Season with a few liberal grindings of black pepper, but do not add salt. Pour in just enough water to barely cover the beans and bring it to a boil. Let it boil for about 1 minute, then reduce the heat to a bare simmer, cover the pan, and simmer until the beans are tender. Depending on the type of bean and its freshness, this could take as little as 20 minutes and as much as 45 minutes. Check the beans from time to time to make sure they are not getting too dry. If the beans don't simmer in sufficient water, they become mealy and tough.

3.   When the beans are tender, remove the lid and raise the heat to medium high. Rapidly boil until the cooking juices are reduced to a lightly thickened glaze. Turn off the heat. Taste for salt and correct the seasoning, and swirl in the parsley and the remaining 1 tablespoon of butter. Pour the beans into a warm serving bowl and serve at once.

Note: *Like most stews, this ragout can not only be made ahead, but actually benefits from it. Omit the final reduction, butter glaze, and parsley in step 3, and do this step after reheating the beans.*

A traditional meatless version can be made by omitting the ham and adding ¼ cup of heavy cream (minimum 36 percent milkfat) before reducing the liquid in step 3. For strict vegetarians, omit the ham and substitute the same amount of peanut oil for the butter. Add 5 or 6 fresh chopped (or crumbled dry) sage leaves. The flavor won't be the same, but it will still taste Southern.

BUTTERY BUTTER BEANS

It is usually supposed that the name "butter bean" derives from their distinctly buttery flavor, but my friend Clara Eschmann, a fine Southern lady who was for many years the food editor of the *Macon Telegraph*, says that when she was growing up, she thought they were called butter beans because they were always cooked with butter. As far as she is concerned, they ought never to be cooked any other way. Once you've tasted them done this way, you'll agree.

SERVES 4

3 cups (about 1 pound shelled weight) fresh or good-quality frozen
    green butter beans or butter peas
Salt
4 tablespoons unsalted butter, cut into small pieces

1. Put the beans in a colander and rinse them under cold running water. Put them in a pan with enough cold water to just cover them, and place the pan over medium-high heat. Bring the liquid to a boil and reduce the heat to medium low. Loosely cover the pan and simmer, stirring frequently, until the beans are nearly tender, about 15 to 20 minutes.
2. Add a healthy pinch of salt, stir, and let the beans cook, uncovered, until they are tender, about 5 minutes more.
3. Raise the heat to medium high and quickly reduce the cooking liquid until it is beginning to get thick, about 2 to 3 minutes more. Turn off the heat and stir in the butter. The cooking liquid should be thick and creamy and coat the beans. Serve at once.

Note: *You can make this several hours or even a day or two ahead and reheat them, but don't reduce the cooking liquid (it thickens as it sits) or add the butter until you are ready to serve the beans.*

Needless to say, there's no substitute for the butter here. No other fat—not even olive oil—will work. Don't even think about using margarine.

$\mathcal{S}$ UCCOTASH

This lovely vegetable combination, which is usually credited to Native American cookery, has suffered much in the hands of the canned-food industry and lunchroom steam tables. Many people think they hate it, and small wonder: the fine flavor of fresh butter beans and corn is killed when succotash is canned or is made from canned vegetables. Being allowed to sit indifferently on a steam table only nails the lid on its coffin.

The classic proportions are two parts beans to one part corn, though there are Southern cooks who mix the vegetables in equal portions. However, the real secret to achieving the best flavor is seldom used nowadays, and that's the old practice of simmering the corn cobs with the beans.

SERVES 6

3–6 large ears fresh corn (2 cups cut from the cob)
1 medium yellow onion, peeled and chopped
5 tablespoons unsalted butter, cut into small pieces
4 cups fresh butter beans
Salt and whole white peppercorns in a peppermill

1. Cut 2 cups of corn kernels as close to the cob as possible, cover, and set aside. Break the cobs in half and set them aside.

2. Put the onion and 1 tablespoon of the butter in a deep lidded skillet and turn on the heat to medium. Sauté, tossing frequently, until the onion is translucent and softened, about 5 minutes. Add the cobs and 2 cups of water, raise the heat to medium high, and bring it to a boil.

3. Add the beans, let the liquids come back to a boil, reduce the heat to a slow simmer, and cover the pan. Simmer until the beans are just tender, about 20 minutes.

4. Remove and discard the cobs, and stir in the corn kernels. Add a healthy pinch of salt and a few liberal grindings of white pepper. Raise the heat long enough to bring it back to a simmer, then lower it once again to maintain a slow simmer. Cook, uncovered, until the corn is just tender, about 10 minutes.

5. By this time the liquid should be somewhat reduced and creamy. If it isn't, raise the heat to medium high and quickly boil until it is nearly evaporated, about 2 to 3 minutes.

Turn off the heat. Stir in the remaining butter, taste and correct the seasonings, then pour the succotash into a warm serving bowl. Serve hot.

Note: *You can get away with using good-quality frozen butter beans in this recipe, but don't use frozen corn. Not only does fresh corn taste better, but the cob provides an important flavoring agent.*

CORN

It would be hard to imagine any American table without corn, but most especially a Southern one. From grits at breakfast to pecan pie at supper, from a luncheon corn pudding to a creamy corn bisque on the formal dinner table, from a hunk of cornbread with a bowl of greens to the crackling-crisp crust of a fried green tomato, corn plays an important role. Used both as a grain and a vegetable, nothing has been as wholly integrated into our foodways as has this native American grass. Even our national alcoholic beverage is corn whiskey.

The weather may be hot and the trees may have been in full leaf for a month, but summer in the South really begins when the first sweet ears of corn appear in the market. In the very deep South, that may be as early as mid-June. In the northern reaches, it will not begin until July. Regardless, at the beginning of the season we consider that eating corn any other way than straight off the cob is almost a sacrilege. However, as summer comes on full force, fresh corn begins to appear in dozens of different forms—from soup to salad. Here are a few classics.

CORN BISQUE

This lovely soup was once very popular, but unfortunately it's seldom served anymore. Its fall from grace may have something to do with the fact that what was once a lovely balance of sweet fresh corn and cream had, by the middle of this century, degenerated into a conglomeration of several cans of things indifferently dumped together.

This recipe is the original delicate soup in which the fresh flavor of sweet corn is enriched with real cream and underscored by a suggestion of nutmeg and sherry.

SERVES 4

3–6 ears fresh corn (2 cups cut from the cob) or 2 cups good-quality
    frozen cream-style corn
1 medium yellow onion, peeled and chopped fine
2 tablespoons unsalted butter
2 cups light cream
1 whole pod cayenne or other hot red pepper
Salt and whole nutmeg in a grater
1/4 cup dry sherry
2 tablespoons chopped fresh chives (do not use dried chives)

1. Shuck the husks from the corn, rub off all the silk, and cut the kernels from the cob as follows: Over a large bowl, cut the outer half of the kernels from the ear with a sharp knife, leaving the other half of the kernels still attached to the cob. Thoroughly scrape the cob with the knife to force out all the milk into the bowl. Repeat with the remaining ears until all the corn is cut and scraped. Break one of the cobs into about 3 pieces and put it and the kernels aside. Discard the remaining cobs.

2. Put the onion and butter in a soup kettle that will easily hold all the ingredients and turn on the heat to medium. Sauté, tossing frequently, until the onion is translucent but not in the least colored, about 5 to 8 minutes.

3. Add the corn to the kettle and stir until it is heated through. Slowly add the cream, stirring constantly. Add the pod of cayenne, a small pinch of salt, and a few gratings of nutmeg and the reserved cob. Bring to a simmer and cook, stirring frequently, until the soup is thick, about 20 minutes.

4. Stir in the sherry and let the soup heat through. If you find that the soup is too thick, thin it with a little milk—don't add more cream—and let it heat through. Remove and discard the cob and pod of hot pepper. Ladle the soup into individual soup plates and garnish with a light grating of nutmeg and sprinkling of the chopped chives.

GRILL·ROASTED CORN

This is my favorite way of preparing fresh corn on the cob. It is practically effortless, since the ears need no preliminary cleaning and cook in their husks. The process also causes the pesky, sticky silks to loosen up and come right off with the husk when you shuck them.

The best way to do this is on the grill, but if you can't grill, the oven does a pretty good job of it. I've given both methods here.

SERVES 4 HEALTHY PEOPLE OR 8 DAINTY ONES

8 large, fresh ears of corn
Unsalted butter, salt, and freshly ground black pepper

1.   Prepare a grill with charcoal, light it, and when the coals are ready, spread them and position the grill rack about 3 to 4 inches above the coals. (Or position a rack in the upper third of the oven and preheat the oven to 400 degrees F.) Meanwhile, put the corn in a basin filled with enough cold water to cover it and let it soak for 10 minutes. Lift it out and let it drain.

2.   Put the whole ears on the grill and roast, turning them frequently, until the outer leaves of the husk begin to brown and char and the kernels are tender, about 15 to 20 minutes, depending on the heat of your grill. (If you are using the oven, roast the corn—again turning it frequently—until it is just cooked through and tender when gently pressed, about 20 minutes.)

3.   Wearing a pair of insulated kitchen mitts, take the corn off the grill (or out of the oven), and quickly shuck it. The silks will pull right off along with the husks. Brush off any silks that remain, cut out any brown spots, and pile the ears onto a warm platter or serving bowl. Serve at once with fresh butter, salt, and freshly ground black pepper passed separately.

GRILL-ROASTED
CORN SALAD

When I'm roasting corn on the grill, I usually throw on a couple of extra ears which will later be made into salad or relish.

SERVES 4

3–6 large ears Grill-Roasted Corn (page 141), or 2 cups of kernels cut
  from the cob (see step 1)
4 green onions or scallions, sliced thin, or 1 medium Vidalia or other
  sweet onion, peeled and diced
1 green bell pepper, seeded and diced
¼ cup red wine vinegar
Salt, ground cayenne, and black pepper in a peppermill
½ cup extra virgin olive oil
1 tablespoon each chopped parsley and fresh basil
2 medium ripe tomatoes
1 bunch watercress

1. Cut the kernels from the corn as close to the cob as possible. You will need 2 cups. Put the corn, green onions, and bell pepper in a mixing bowl and toss until they are well mixed.

2. In a separate bowl, combine the vinegar, a large pinch of salt, a tiny one of cayenne, and a few liberal grindings of black pepper. Gradually whisk in the olive oil until it is emulsified. Whisk in the parsley and basil, and pour the dressing over the corn mixture. Cover and refrigerate for at least an hour. You can make the salad to this point up to 2 days ahead.

3. When you are ready to serve the salad, core, seed, and cut the tomatoes into ½-inch dice. Break the watercress into bite-sized pieces and add it with the tomatoes to the corn mixture. Toss until the tomato and cress are coated with the dressing. Taste and correct the seasonings and serve at once.

Miss Ruby's Fresh Corn Relish

Ruth Adams Bronz—Miss Ruby to her friends—is an expatriate Texan living in Berkshire County, Massachusetts. Eccentric, funny, and generous to a fault, Miss Ruby is living proof that you can plant Southerners anywhere in the world and they won't change: they'll just keep right on being Southern—whether they like it or not.

Nowhere is this tendency more evident than in Miss Ruby's kitchen, where her palate always wanders southward to the cooking of her native Texas. This corn relish is a case in point, exemplifying the almost schizophrenic character of Texas cookery—which is one part Deep South, one part Southwest, and one part Mexico.

This relish can stand alone as a salad, with thick slices of ripe tomato on the side, or can be served as a relish over grilled tuna steaks, pork chops, or chicken.

MAKES ABOUT 3 1/2 CUPS,
OR 4 TO 6 SERVINGS

3–6 ears fresh corn (2 cups when cut from the cob)
1/2 cup red bell pepper, diced small
1/2 cup green bell pepper, diced small
1 small red onion, diced small
1/4 cup celery, diced small
2 teaspoons cumin seeds, toasted and ground fine
1 tablespoon fresh chopped coriander (cilantro)
Salt
Tabasco or other hot red pepper sauce
1 lime

1. Shuck the corn and remove the silks. Cut the kernels from the ears as close to the cob as possible until you have 2 cups. Toss together the corn, two bell peppers, onion, and celery until they are well mixed. Add the cumin, coriander, a large pinch of salt, and about 2 long dashes of hot pepper sauce.

2. Grate the zest from the lime, then cut the lime in half and squeeze the juice over the relish. Add the zest and toss until the seasonings are well blended. Cover and let stand in a cool place for at least 2 hours. Taste and correct the seasonings, and toss again before serving.

FRIED CORN ✦

Fried corn is a standard in the repertory of all Southern cooks. It isn't actually "fried" as we usually think of frying, but comes closer to stewing in its own milk and a little fat. The result is rich and creamy—not brown and crispy—and the natural sugars are marvelously concentrated and intensified.

My preferred choice of corn for this recipe is sweet white corn, such as Silver Queen, because that's what I was raised on, but you can use any sweet corn that is available.

SERVES 4

8 young, tender ears sweet corn
2 tablespoons rendered bacon fat or unsalted butter
1 small yellow onion, peeled and minced (optional)
Salt and pepper in a peppermill to taste

1. Shuck the corn and carefully brush away all the silks. Over a large bowl, with a sharp knife cut the outer half of the kernels from an ear, leaving the inner half of the kernels still attached to the cob. Thoroughly scrape the cob with the knife to force out all the milk from the cut kernels into the bowl. Repeat this with the remaining ears until all the corn is cut and scraped.

2. Put the bacon fat or butter and optional onion in a large, well-seasoned iron skillet and turn on the fire to medium high. If you use the onion, sauté it until it is colored gold, about 4 minutes. Add the corn and all its milk. Bring this onion-corn mixture to a boil, stirring and scraping the pan to keep it from sticking. Turn the heat down to medium, and continue cooking and stirring until the milk begins to thicken.

3. Reduce the heat to a slow simmer. Cook, stirring constantly and carefully scraping the bottom to keep it from scorching, until very thick and tender, about 5 minutes more. Turn off the fire, season to taste with a pinch of salt and a few grindings of pepper, and serve at once.

Note: *Bacon fat can lend the taste that most Southerners are accustomed to today, but it's not necessarily the most traditional, as most of the old recipes called for butter. If you are not able to use either bacon fat or butter, an acceptable substitute is corn oil—preferably an unrefined, cold-pressed oil that really tastes of corn. If you are omitting the animal fat, though, don't omit the onion.*

CREOLE CORN AND TOMATOES

Here is another traditional Southern favorite that takes full advantage of the full-blown summer flavors of vine-ripened tomatoes and fresh-picked corn.

SERVES 4

1 medium yellow onion, peeled and chopped
2 tablespoons rendered bacon fat
4 large ripe tomatoes, scalded, peeled, seeded, and chopped as directed
*   for Stewed Tomatoes à la Creole (page 117)*
1 tablespoon chopped parsley
1 tablespoon fresh thyme or 1 teaspoon dried thyme
1 bay leaf
3–6 ears fresh corn (2 cups when cut from the cob)
Salt, ground cayenne, and black pepper in a peppermill

1. Put the onion and bacon fat in a deep cast-iron skillet or stewing pan that will hold all the ingredients and turn on the heat to medium. Sauté, tossing frequently, until translucent but not colored, about 5 minutes. Add the tomatoes, parsley, thyme, and bay leaf, and bring it to a simmer. Cook, uncovered, for 10 minutes.

2. Meanwhile, cut the kernels from the corn as close to the cob as possible until you have 2 cups. Stir the corn into the tomatoes, add a healthy pinch of salt, a small one of cayenne, and a few grindings of black pepper. Let it come back to a simmer, cover, and reduce the heat to medium low. Cook, stirring occasionally, until the corn is tender, about 20 minutes. Uncover the pan, raise the heat to medium, and cook until thick, about 5 minutes more. Turn off the heat. Remove and discard the bay leaf, taste and correct the seasonings, and serve hot.

Note: The smoky flavor of the bacon fat is essential to the character of this dish, but if you are unable to use it, butter or corn oil would still make a reasonably good dish, though it will by no means taste the same. I would use sage instead of thyme, add a minced clove of garlic, and let the onion brown a little to compensate for the absence of the bacon flavor.

SHRIMP AND CORN PUDDING

This traditional Lowcountry supper dish is an especially happy pairing of two summer staples of coastal Georgia and the Carolinas. The natural sweetness of fresh shrimp is both complemented and enhanced by the equal sweetness of freshly gathered corn. It is by no means an accident that in midsummer, when both shrimp and corn are at their peak, they frequently appear together on the table.

SERVES 4

4 green onions or scallions or 1 medium yellow onion
2 tablespoons unsalted butter
2 cups sweet corn, freshly cut as for Fried Corn (page 144)
2 large eggs, lightly beaten
½ cup light cream or half-and-half
1 tablespoon each chopped fresh thyme and parsley
Salt, ground cayenne, and whole white peppercorns in a peppermill
Whole nutmeg in a grater
1½ pounds (headless weight) peeled small shrimp

1. Position a rack in the center of the oven and preheat the oven to 350 degrees F. Put on a teakettle of water to boil. Wash the green onions, trim off any discolored leaves, and thinly slice them, or if you use yellow onion, peel it and chop it fine. Put the onions and butter in a sauté pan and place it over medium-high heat. Sauté, tossing frequently, until the onions are softened but not colored, about 3 to 4 minutes. Turn off the heat.

2. Combine the sautéed onion, corn, eggs, cream, and chopped herbs in a mixing bowl. Season with a generous pinch or so of salt, a stingy one of cayenne, a few grindings of white pepper, and a liberal grating of nutmeg. Mix well until all is thoroughly combined, then stir in the shrimp.

3. Lightly butter a 9-inch square or round ceramic casserole or soufflé dish and pour in the corn batter. Place the casserole in the center of a wide, deep pan (such as a sheet-cake pan) and put it on the center rack of the oven. Pour the boiling water carefully into the larger pan until it comes about halfway up the sides of the casserole dish.

4. Bake until the pudding is set and the shrimp cooked through. Depending on the shape of your casserole dish, it will take about 1 hour. The wider and shallower the pan, the quicker the pudding will cook, so keep an eye on it and be careful not to overcook it, or the eggs will separate and the shrimp will be tough. Serve hot or at room temperature.

Corn and Mushroom Pudding: The whole point of the preceding recipe is the flavor combination of shrimp and corn. However, a perfectly good corn pudding can be made without the shellfish by adding a seeded and chopped red bell pepper and ½ pound sliced wild or cremini mushrooms to the mixture. Sauté the bell pepper with the onions in step 1, and when both are wilted, add the mushrooms and sauté until softened, and proceed with step 2, omitting the shrimp. Of course, if shellfish really turns you on, you can stretch the pudding to serve 6 by adding ½ pound (1 cup) of crabmeat.

CUCUMBERS

Two kinds of cucumbers, both native gherkins *(Cucumis anquria)* and imported European cucumbers *(Cucumis sativus)*—which one record says Columbus planted in Haiti as early as 1494—have played a part in Southern food. The record of their cultivation, and exactly what type was used by who and when, is very confused. For our purposes, however, it's sufficient to say that cucumbers have always been on Southern tables.

In the summer they have, until recently, been practically a permanent fixture, plucked from the garden that morning, cooled on ice, and bathed in a simple marinade of vinegar, salt, and black pepper. They were naturally cooling and refreshing—a sort of culinary air-conditioning—and that's still how we like them best; indeed, *The Picayune's Creole Cook Book* (1901) asserted that this was the only way of serving them that the Creoles would tolerate. But cooked cucumbers do turn up, from time to time, in other Southern kitchens.

FRIED CUCUMBERS

Yes, Southerners will fry just about anything. As a matter of fact, a few years ago there was even a craze for—I am not making this up—fried *dill pickles*. Actually, fried cucumbers are an old European idea that the colonials brought with them to this country, but it gets a peculiarly Southern twist with cornmeal breading.

The cucumbers that you want for frying should be very young so that the seeds are still tender. Choose small to medium cucumbers that are quite green, not too fat, and very firm. If even after taking that precaution you find that the seeds have turned brown and woody, split the cucumbers, remove the seeds, and slice them lengthwise into strips instead of rounds before cooking them.

SERVES 4

1 pound young cucumbers (see headnote)
Salt
1 large egg
1 cup cornmeal, spread on a dinner plate
Lard or peanut oil for frying
Black pepper in a peppermill
1 lemon, cut into 8 wedges

1. Wash the cucumbers under cold running water. Lightly peel them with a vegetable peeler and cut them crosswise into rounds about ¼ inch thick. Spread the rounds on a platter, sprinkle them liberally with salt, and set them aside for half an hour.
2. Break the egg into a shallow bowl and beat it until it is smooth. Place the bowl and the plate of cornmeal within easy reach of the frying pan. Put enough lard or oil into the pan to come halfway up the sides. Turn on the heat to medium high.
3. Pat the excess moisture from the cucumbers and sprinkle them lightly with a few grindings of black pepper. Dip the slices one at a time into the beaten egg, let the excess flow back into the bowl, and then roll them in the cornmeal. When the fat is hot but not smoking (about 375 degrees F), add enough of the cucumbers to the pan to fill it without crowding. Fry until the bottoms are brown, about 3 minutes, turn them, and continue frying until they are evenly browned, about 3 minutes more. Remove them to drain on absorbent paper and transfer them to a wire rack. Repeat with the remaining cucumber slices until they are all fried. Serve hot with lemon wedges.

CUCUMBERS IN SOUR CREAM DRESSING ◢

Here, the cool, mild flavor of cucumbers makes an inviting contrast to the sharp tang of soured cream. The luscious sour cream dressing is an old one, dating back well into the nineteenth century, but it still makes a great salad for any modern summer meal, tastes superb paired with barbecue when the meat is lamb or goat, and is tailor-made to serve with any kind of fish.

SERVES 4

¹/₂ cup homemade Crème Fraîche (page 18) or sour cream
1 tablespoon freshly squeezed lemon juice
1 teaspoon Dijon mustard
2 tablespoons extra virgin olive oil
Salt, ground cayenne, and black pepper in a peppermill
2 pounds (2 large or 4 small) cucumbers
1 small Vidalia or other sweet onion
4 large lettuce leaves, such as romaine or Boston
1 tablespoon chopped dill or chives and paprika (optional)

1. In a mixing bowl that will hold all the ingredients, combine the crème fraîche or sour cream, lemon juice and Dijon mustard, mixing until smooth. Beat in the olive oil a little at a time until it is incorporated. Season the dressing with a pinch or so of salt, a small pinch of cayenne, and a few liberal grindings of black pepper, and mix them in. Set the dressing aside.

2. Split the onion in half lengthwise. Peel it and slice each half as thinly as possible. Wash the cucumbers and if they have been waxed, lightly peel them with a vegetable peeler so that there is still a blush of bright green on them. Slice the cucumbers crosswise into rounds a little less than ¹/₄ inch thick.

3. Add the onion and cucumbers to the dressing, and toss until everything is thoroughly coated. Put the lettuce leaves on individual salad plates and divide the cucumbers among them. If you like, you can sprinkle the top with chopped dill or chives and a light dusting of paprika. Serve at once, or the cucumbers will begin to throw off liquid and make the salad watery.

CUCUMBER AND FENNEL SALAD

Fennel—that lovely vegetable that looks like a cross between celery and dill and tastes vaguely of licorice and sweet celery—is thankfully becoming commonplace in markets down South, though a lot of Southern cooks still look at it with wonder and puzzlement. Wonder no more.

This is a refreshing salad that goes nicely with all fish and shellfish dishes. It also perks up any roasted poultry or game.

SERVES 4 TO 6

1 large head fennel
1 large or 2 medium cucumbers
1 large sweet onion, preferably Vidalia
2 hard-cooked large egg yolks
1 tablespoon Dijon mustard
Salt, sugar, and black pepper in a peppermill
2 tablespoons fresh lemon juice
1/3 cup extra virgin olive oil

1.   Wash the fennel well, trim the root end, and cut off the stalks. Clip enough of the feathery leaves to make about 1/2 cup and set them aside. Discard the stalks. Cut the fennel bulb crosswise into the thinnest slices you can manage and put them in a salad bowl.

2.   Wash the cucumbers and, only if they have been waxed, lightly peel them; otherwise, peeling isn't necessary. Cut the cucumbers crosswise into thin rounds and add them to the salad bowl with the fennel. Trim the root and stem ends from the onion, peel it, and slice it into the thinnest possible rings. Add the onion rings to the fennel and cucumber. Chop the reserved fennel leaves and add them to the mixture, then toss until the vegetables are uniformly mixed.

3.   In a separate bowl, combine the egg yolks, mustard, a pinch of salt, a small pinch of sugar, and a few grindings of black pepper, mashing everything with a fork until it is a

smooth paste. Gradually stir the lemon juice into the paste, then, a few drops at a time, beat in the olive oil until the dressing is emulsified.

4.   Pour the dressing over the salad and toss until the vegetables are evenly coated. Taste and correct the seasonings, and toss again to distribute them evenly. Serve at once.

EGGPLANT

What a strange name we have given this vegetable, or so it always seemed to me, having grown up with the type of large, deep-purple, pear-shaped eggplant that resembles a chicken egg about as much as it does an artichoke. There are many varieties of eggplant, one of which is a small white oval, the variety from which the name is derived. This type was eventually eclipsed by its purple-skinned cousins, but it hasn't altogether disappeared; occasionally white and even yellow eggplants turn up in the markets. Still, in the South we continue to prefer the purple ones.

Originally native to the Far East, eggplant gradually migrated westward and was well known in the Mediterranean and Africa by the time the Americas were colonized. In some parts of the South, eggplants were once also known as "Guinea melons" or "Guinea squash," after the West African nation of that name, which suggests that they were probably introduced to our continent by way of the African slave trade. At any rate, from the late eighteenth century forward, eggplant has been enjoyed on Southern tables. The recipes that follow have a long tradition.

SMOTHERED EGGPLANT
À LA CREOLE

A close cousin to the Provençal classic *ratatouille*, this Creole dish is usually served hot, but like *ratatouille* it is equally as good eaten cold the next day when the flavors have had time to settle in and marry with one another. It is an excellent side accompaniment to any shrimp, crab, chicken, or lamb dish that does not contain tomato or cream.

SERVES 6

1½ pounds eggplant (about 2 medium)
Salt
2 tablespoons unsalted butter or extra virgin olive oil
2 medium onions, peeled and chopped
2 ribs celery, washed, strung, and chopped
2 green bell peppers, stemmed, seeded, and diced
2 large cloves garlic, minced
1¾ pounds ripe tomatoes (preferably plum), scalded, peeled, seeded,
    and chopped as directed on page 117, or 2 cups (28-ounce can)
    Italian canned tomatoes, seeded and chopped
2 ounces (a ⅛-inch-thick slice) country ham or prosciutto, chopped
Ground cayenne pepper and black pepper in a peppermill
1 tablespoon chopped fresh thyme or 1 teaspoon dried thyme
1 tablespoon chopped parsley

1. Peel the eggplants and cut them into 1-inch dice. Place them in a colander, sprinkle liberally with salt, and toss to coat them evenly. Let them stand in the sink for 30 minutes.

2. Meanwhile, put the butter or olive oil, onions, celery, and green peppers in a lidded skillet that will comfortably hold all the ingredients. Turn on the heat to medium high and sauté until the vegetables are softened and beginning to color, about 4 to 6 minutes. Add the garlic and continue cooking until it is fragrant, about 1 minute more. Add the chopped tomatoes and their juices, the ham or prosciutto, a pinch of cayenne, a few liberal grindings of black pepper, and the chopped thyme. Bring it to a boil.

3. Wipe the eggplant dry, pressing it gently, and add it to the pan. Bring the liquids back to a boil, then reduce the heat to low, cover the pan, and simmer slowly, stirring frequently to prevent scorching, until the eggplant is tender, about 30 minutes. If, at the end of this time, there is a lot of excess liquid in the pan, raise the heat briefly and boil it away. Turn off the heat, stir in the parsley, taste and correct the seasonings, adding salt, if needed, and serve hot. You can also let the eggplant cool to room temperature, cover it, and refrigerate it overnight or for up to 3 days. Take it out of the refrigerator an hour before serving and serve at room temperature.

SCALLOPED EGGPLANT ◄

With not even a hint of the Mediterranean, the ingredients of this sumptuous casserole are not what one would expect to have paired with eggplant—cream, pecans, butter, and cheese. It is ridiculously rich and pure Deep South. It's also some kind of wonderful.

SERVES 4

1½ pounds eggplant (about 2 medium)
1 large yellow onion, peeled and chopped
6 tablespoons unsalted butter
¼ cup all-purpose flour, spread on a dinner plate
1 cup heavy cream (minimum 36 percent milkfat)
1 cup grated Parmigiano-Reggiano or sharp Cheddar
Salt and black pepper in a peppermill
¾ cup dry bread crumbs
1 cup chopped raw pecans

1. Peel the eggplants, cut them into 1-inch dice, and put them in a colander. Sprinkle them liberally with salt and toss to coat them evenly. Let them sit in the sink for 30 minutes. Position a rack in the upper third of the oven and preheat the oven to 375 degrees F.

2. When the eggplant has drained for half an hour, gently squeeze it against the sides of the colander and wipe it dry. Put the onion and 4 tablespoons of the butter in a sauté pan that will hold all the eggplant and turn on the heat to medium high. Sauté, tossing frequently, until the onion is translucent and softened but not browned, about 4 minutes.

3. Quickly roll the eggplant in the flour, shake off the excess, and add it to the pan. Sauté, tossing frequently, until it is beginning to color, about 3 minutes. Turn off the heat.

4. Lightly butter a 2-quart casserole and put the eggplant mixture into it. Pour over it the cream, add the cheese, a pinch of salt, a few grindings of pepper, and toss until well mixed.

5. Wipe out the pan in which the vegetables were sautéed. Put in the remaining 2 tablespoons of butter and place the pan over medium heat until the butter is just melted. Turn off the heat. Add the bread crumbs and pecans, and toss until the butter is evenly absorbed into the crumbs. Spread this mixture over the top of the eggplant, place the casserole in the center of the oven, and bake until bubbling hot and the top is golden brown, about 40 minutes. Serve hot.

A PAIR OF
STUFFED EGGPLANT DISHES

Stuffing eggplants with savory fillings is a wonderful way to cook and serve them. They make neat individual portions and—what's more important for most of us—can be assembled ahead of time to suit your schedule. Then all you will have to do is take them from the refrigerator, pop them in the oven, make a salad, and relax—dinner's ready.

TO PREPARE EGGPLANTS FOR STUFFING: In the recipes that follow, the eggplants are parboiled before being stuffed. While this makes the pulp easier to scoop out, it also makes the shell a lot more fragile, so be careful not to break the skin or cut through it when you are removing the inner pulp.

Half-fill a kettle that will hold all the eggplants with water and place it over high heat. Wash the eggplants under cold running water. When the water in the kettle is boiling briskly, add a small handful of salt and slip the eggplants into it. Cover and let it come back to a boil, then skew the lid so that the kettle is only partially covered and cook the eggplants, turning them over in the water frequently, until softened, about 15 minutes. Drain and set aside to cool. They are now ready to use in any of the following recipes.

STUFFED EGGPLANT
À LA CREOLE

This fine meatless stuffed eggplant can be served as a side dish but is also substantial enough to stand on its own as a main course. The recipe is an old Creole one, though you don't have to be told that; the perfume of tomato, garlic, and thyme gives its origin away.

For a completely vegetarian version, substitute extra virgin olive oil for the butter.

SERVES 4

1 medium yellow onion, peeled and chopped fine
4 tablespoons unsalted butter
1 large clove garlic
2 medium eggplants (about ³/₄ pound each), prepared as directed above
1 cup soft bread crumbs

1 medium ripe tomato, blanched, peeled, seeded, and chopped (page
117) or 2 canned tomatoes, drained, seeded, and chopped
1 tablespoon chopped fresh thyme or 1 teaspoon dried thyme
1 tablespoon chopped parsley
Salt, cayenne pepper, and black pepper in a peppermill
³/₄ cup dry bread crumbs

1. Position a rack in the upper third of the oven and preheat the oven to 375 degrees F. Put the onion and 2 tablespoons of the butter in a skillet and turn on the heat to medium high. Sauté, tossing and stirring frequently, until the onion is translucent and softened, about 5 minutes. Add the garlic and continue cooking until it is fragrant but not in the least colored, about 1 minute more. Turn off the heat.

2. Split the eggplants lengthwise and scoop out the inner flesh, leaving a shell about ¹/₂ inch thick on all sides. Chop the pulp and add it to the skillet with the onion and garlic. Add the crumbs, tomato, thyme, and parsley. Season liberally with a healthy pinch of salt, a small one of cayenne, and a few grindings of black pepper. Stir until well mixed.

3. Lightly butter a casserole that will hold the eggplant halves in one layer. Put in the shells and divide the stuffing among them.

4. Wipe out the pan in which the onions cooked and put in the remaining 2 tablespoons of butter. Place it over medium heat. When the butter is just melted, turn off the heat and add the bread crumbs. Stir until the butter is evenly absorbed into the crumbs. Sprinkle the crumbs over the eggplants until they are evenly coated, and place the casserole in the upper third of the oven. Bake until the crumbs are browned and the filling is heated through and bubbly, about half an hour.

Seafood Stuffed Eggplant

Shellfish has a happy affinity for eggplant, and their union in a dish is almost always a good idea. Here, fresh seafood is stuffed into eggplant shells and gently baked. This makes an especially nice luncheon dish but can be served as a first course for 6 persons at a formal dinner: use 3 small eggplants (about ½ pound each) in place of the larger ones called for here.

SERVES 4

*2 medium eggplants (about ¾ pound each), prepared as directed on
   page 154*
4 tablespoons unsalted butter
1 large onion, peeled and chopped
2 ribs celery, strung and diced
1 ripe red or green bell pepper, stemmed, seeded, and diced
2 large cloves garlic, lightly crushed, peeled, and minced
2 tablespoons chopped parsley
4 ½-inch slices firm white bread, soaked in milk and squeezed dry
½ pound (1 cup) fresh crabmeat
½ pound (headless weight) small shrimp, peeled
Salt, cayenne pepper, and black pepper in a peppermill
Whole nutmeg in a grater
¾ cup dry bread crumbs

1. Position a rack in the center of the oven and preheat the oven to 350 degrees F. Split the eggplants lengthwise and scoop out the inner pulp, leaving a shell about ½ inch thick on all sides. Chop the pulp and set it aside.

2. Put 2 tablespoons of the butter in a skillet with the onion, celery, and bell pepper, and turn on the heat to medium high. Sauté, tossing frequently, until the vegetables are wilted but not browned, about 5 minutes. Add the garlic and continue cooking until it is fragrant, about a minute more. Turn off the heat.

3. Add the parsley and chopped eggplant pulp. Crumble in the soaked bread and set aside.

4.   Pick through the crabmeat and remove any lingering bits of shell and cartilage. Cut all but the tiniest shrimp in half crosswise. Add the crab and shrimp to the stuffing mixture. Season liberally with a healthy pinch or so of salt, a small pinch of cayenne, a few grindings of black pepper, and a generous grating of nutmeg. Thoroughly mix the stuffing ingredients together.

5.   Lightly butter a casserole that will hold the eggplant shells in one layer and put them in it. Divide the stuffing among the shells, mounding it up in the center. Wipe out the pan in which the vegetables were sautéed and put in the remaining 2 tablespoons of butter. Place the pan over medium heat until the butter is melted. Turn off the heat and mix in the bread crumbs until the butter is evenly absorbed. Sprinkle the crumbs evenly over the eggplants and bake them in the center of the oven until the shrimp is cooked through, about 40 minutes.

VIDALIA SWEET ONIONS

By now, most people know the history of Georgia's famous onion—how many years ago the farmers around the little central Georgia community of Vidalia discovered that their soil produced exceptionally sweet onions. Since that time, those onions have become so popular that a flood of pretenders and outright fakes prompted local growers to petition for legal protection. Today, the name "Vidalia Sweet Onion" is one of only a few regional American product names to be protected by law as French wines are.

The secret of the Vidalia onion's legendary sweetness lies in the region's soil—or, rather, in what isn't in the soil. A reporter from Atlanta, unfamiliar with the local dialect, was completely bemused when one of the growers tried to explain this secret, telling her, "Ain gah no suffer inna soll." Sure that he was reciting some weird Druid incantation, she backed away and asked him to repeat it. Finally the light dawned—it was no curse; he was only explaining that there was no sulfur in the soil.

Chemicals and incantations aside, the onions do tend to be milder than most, though the claim that they can be eaten raw—like an apple—is only carried out by people who want to prove the point. There are better ways of enjoying them. Patriotism and a sense of self-preservation dictates that I tell you to cook only Vidalias, but there are other Southern sweet onions that will work as well in these recipes: Texas 1015s (so called because they are planted on October 15), Walla-Wallas, and Wadmalaw Sweets (from South Carolina's Wadmalaw Island) among them. I know, I'm in trouble now.

BAKED VIDALIA ONIONS

No wonder this way of cooking Vidalias has become a regional classic. It's easy to do, and no other way concentrates the natural sweetness of Vidalias as does slow baking. In the dead of summer, many local cooks bake them in a microwave to avoid the oven heat. Though I tend to view "microwave cooking" as an oxymoron, this is one of the few times that my own microwave sees any action beyond melting butter or heating water. Still, these onions are best when slow-baked.

SERVES 4

4 large Vidalia or other sweet onions
4 tablespoons unsalted butter, plus more for greasing
1/2 cup freshly grated Parmesan, preferably Parmigiano-Reggiano

1. Position a rack in the upper third of the oven and preheat the oven to 375 degrees F. Trim off the root tendrils of the onions, leaving all the layers attached to the root end, and cut out the stem ends, leaving a shallow, cone-shaped well in the top of each. Peel off the brown, papery outer skins and lightly rub the outsides of the onions with a little butter. Put them, stem side up, in a shallow baking dish that will just hold them and top each one with a tablespoon of butter.

2. Bake in the upper third of the oven, basting frequently with the pan juices, until nearly tender, about 45 minutes.

3. Take the onions out of the oven, mound the grated Parmesan in the cut well of each, baste with the pan juices, and return them to the oven. Bake until the cheese is melted and golden brown, about 15 to 20 minutes more. Remove them from the oven and let them sit for 5 minutes or so to disperse some of the intense heat. Put the onions on individual serving plates or, if they are intended as a first course, on soup plates, pour their pan juices over them, and serve at once.

Note: *To cook the onions in a microwave oven, prepare them as directed in step 1, using a microwave-safe baking dish. Cook on full power for 7 minutes. Baste them, top with the cheese, and cook at full power until the cheese melts (it will never get as brown as it would in a regular oven) and the onions are tender, about 3 to 5 minutes more. Exact cooking times may vary depending on your oven and the size of the onions, so keep an eye on them.*

Vidalia Onions with Sausage and Pecans

Onions filled with sausage meat and then baked are an old classic. Here, pecans enrich and give added depth to the filling, making for an especially luxurious—and wholly Southern tasting—dish. They're comfortable in any social situation, as a first course at a formal dinner or luncheon, or as a main course, along with a green salad, at a casual family supper.

Though Vidalias stuffed with sausage can be found on many Georgia tables during the summer, the dish is also popular in early fall, before the last of the sweet onion crop disappears from the market.

SERVES 4

4 large Vidalia or other sweet onions
1/2 pound bulk sausage meat
1/2 cup soft bread crumbs
1/2 cup chopped Toasted Pecans (page 219)
Salt
1 tablespoon chopped parsley
1 tablespoon chopped fresh sage (use only if your sausage meat does not
  contain an herb)
1 large egg
1/2 cup freshly grated Gruyère or sharp Cheddar

1.   Position a rack in the center of the oven and preheat the oven to 375 degrees F. Put enough water to completely cover the onions in a large kettle that will comfortably hold them. Place the kettle over high heat and bring the water to a boil. Add a small handful of salt and the onions, and let it come back to a boil. Reduce the heat to low and simmer for 20 minutes. The onions will still be a little underdone. Drain them and let them cool enough to handle.

2.   Trim off the root tendrils of the onions, leaving all the layers attached to the root ends, and cut out the stem ends, leaving a shallow, cone-shaped well in the top of each onion. Peel off the brown outer skins. With a melon baller or similar sharp instrument, carefully scoop out the center of each onion, without breaking the root end, leaving a shell 1/2 inch thick (about 3 layers). Set the shells aside and chop the pulp fine.

3. Crumble the sausage meat into a skillet and place it over medium heat. Sauté until the sausage is browned, about 5 minutes. Spoon off the excess fat, leaving about 1 tablespoon in the pan, and add the chopped onion pulp. Sauté until the onion is beginning to color, about 4 minutes more. Turn off the heat.

4. Add the bread crumbs and pecans, a light pinch of salt, the parsley, and optional chopped sage. Toss well. Break the egg into a separate bowl and beat until the yolk and white are well mixed. Add it to the sausage mixture and stir until it is absorbed.

5. Lightly grease a baking dish and put the onion shells into it. Spoon the stuffing mixture into the shells, mounding it up on top, and sprinkle the grated cheese over them. Bake in the center of the oven until the filling is set and the cheese is golden brown, about 40 minutes. Let the onions stand for a few minutes to allow some of the intense heat to subside, and serve warm.

$\mathcal{S}$CALLOPED
VIDALIA ONIONS

Here, pecans and onions are paired together again. Easy, rich, and oh-so-wonderful to eat, this dish is a fine accompaniment for just about any meat or fish dish that doesn't contain cream, and it can even stand on its own as a meatless main course. It makes a perfect addition to a buffet table, as it is simple to put together and forgiving of having been made ahead and reheated.

SERVES 6 TO 8

6 medium Vidalia or other sweet onions (about 3 pounds)
1 cup soft bread crumbs
Salt and whole white peppercorns in a peppermill
Nutmeg in a grater
2 cups heavy cream (minimum 36 percent milkfat)
3 tablespoons unsalted butter
1 cup dry bread crumbs
1 cup Toasted Pecans (page 219), cut into slivers

1. Position a rack in the upper third of the oven and preheat the oven to 350 degrees F. Cut off the root and stem ends of the onions, peel them, and cut them crosswise into ¼-inch rounds.

2. Lightly butter a 9 × 13-inch baking dish. Sprinkle the bottom lightly with soft bread crumbs. Place a row of onion rounds at one end of the dish, sprinkle more soft crumbs over them, and season them lightly with a sprinkling of salt. Add another row of onion rounds, overlapping the first one. Sprinkle this row with more soft crumbs and a bit of salt, and continue until all the onions are in the dish in one layer of overlapping rows. Sprinkle with a few generous grindings of white pepper and gratings of nutmeg, and pour the cream evenly over all.

3. Put the butter in a skillet and turn on the heat to medium. When it is just melted, turn off the heat and add the dry bread crumbs and pecans. Stir until the butter is evenly absorbed, and then spread the crumbs and pecans over the onions. Bake in the upper third of the oven until the onions are tender, the juices thick, and the crumbs nicely browned, about 1 hour.

FRESH FIELD PEAS

One of the great glories of a Southern summer is something that depressingly few people (including Southerners) are exposed to nowadays—fresh field peas. These peas get their name because they are grown in a field, instead of the kitchen garden, as a rotation crop to refresh the soil with nitrogen and other nutrients after being planted with more demanding crops such as corn or cotton. From those ubiquitous black-eyes, to pink-eyes, white acres, cowpeas, lady peas, to nearly extinct types like seminole peas, there are literally dozens of varieties, all with a wonderful subtlety of flavor that is largely lost when the peas are dried or even frozen.

Part of the charm and flavor of fresh field peas comes from mixing them with snaps—that is, whole, immature pea pods. These literally snap in two when you bend them. Because the peas are fresh and the snaps are already pretty tender, they cook quickly and require very little additional seasoning to bring up their flavor.

One pound of any variety of whole peas will yield 2 cups of peas when shelled. Though many markets sell fresh field peas already shelled, it is worth the extra effort to seek out whole peas and shell them yourself, not only for those lovely snaps, but because their flavor is better preserved when they are left in their pods until they are ready to be cooked.

FRESH FIELD PEAS
WITH SNAPS

When field peas are really fresh, just shelled, and have plenty of tender green pods mixed into them, there is no better way to cook them than quickly in plain water. Just season them with salt, pepper, and perhaps a lump of butter; they need nothing else. As the peas mature, their flavor diminishes and the complexity of the recipe's added flavorings increase proportionately.

Any fresh field peas are appropriate for this recipe: crowders, lady peas, white acres, pink-eyes, or even black-eyes, but crowder peas are my favorite.

Field peas are traditionally served with hot Cornbread (page 40) and finely chopped raw sweet onions passed separately.

SERVES 4

1¹/₂ pounds (unshelled weight) fresh field peas with snaps (3 cups
      shelled fresh peas)
2 ounces salt pork, well rinsed and patted dry
1 medium yellow onion, peeled and chopped
1 whole pod hot red pepper
Salt
1 small yellow onion, peeled and chopped fine (optional)

1. Shell the peas and break the snaps into 1-inch lengths. Half-fill the sink or a large basin with water and wash the peas in it, drain them well, and set them aside.

2. Choose a pot that will comfortably hold the peas and water, put in the salt pork, and turn on the heat to medium. Cook the pork, turning frequently, until the fat is rendered from it. Remove the pork and drain it on absorbent paper. Add the onion to the pot and sauté, tossing frequently, until it is softened and translucent, about 5 to 8 minutes.

3. Add the peas, 2 cups of water, the pepper pod, and the drained salt pork, raise the heat to medium high, and bring the liquid to a boil. Do not add salt yet. Reduce the heat to a slow simmer, loosely cover the pot (leaving the lid slightly askew), and simmer until the peas are tender, about 20 minutes. Don't overcook the peas, or the snaps will be mushy and uninteresting. Taste and adjust the salt, adding a pinch or so if needed, and sim-

mer until the peas have absorbed it, about 3 minutes more. Serve hot, passing the chopped raw onion separately, if you like.

Note: *Though the peas should be as fresh as possible and kept in their pods until just before you cook them, they can be cooked up to 3 days ahead. They are even better warmed over the next day.*

For a meatless version, omit the salt pork and sauté the onion in 1 tablespoon of extra virgin olive oil. Add a clove or two of garlic, finely chopped, to boost the flavor, and pass a cruet of olive oil at the table so that each person can drizzle some over his or her portion to taste.

PEANUTS

Peanuts have long been an important crop in Georgia, but until a Georgia peanut farmer—James Earl Carter—was elected president in 1976, they were more often associated with Virginia. It took President Carter's high profile to make the country aware that the state has a venerable and thriving peanut industry.

Although peanuts are native to our hemisphere, specifically to South America, they most likely came into the South by way of Africa. Introduced to Africa by the Portuguese early in the sixteenth century, peanuts were so quickly and thoroughly assimilated into the African diet that by the time of the slave trade, many Europeans thought that peanuts were native to that continent.

Peanuts are really neither pea nor nut, but are, rather, subterranean legumes *(Arachis hypogaea leguminosae)*, or beans that develop underground. The lion's share of peanuts are today used as nuts—toasted and salted or ground up into nut butter, they seldom see more than the top of a bar or the insides of two slices of white bread. Yet there was a time when they were better known as a vegetable.

Some of the recipes that follow call for "green" peanuts. That has nothing to do with color, but instead indicates immature peanuts that are freshly dug. Unfortunately, green peanuts are full of moisture and don't store or travel well, so they are only available within a short distance of their growing area. In some cases, cured peanuts can be used in place of green ones, though the cooking time will of course be longer, but where a recipe says to use only green peanuts, don't substitute cured peanuts. The best source for raw peanuts outside the South is vegetable markets that cater to African Americans.

ℬOILED PEANUTS

Boiled peanuts are a strictly regional specialty. When the weather turns warm, the roadsides all over Georgia, North Florida, Alabama, and the Carolinas sprout with vendors and produce stands selling this hot, salty confection out of steaming oil-barrel–sized kettles. They are the one sure appetizer at any Southern outdoor event, from ballgames to barbecues and Lowcountry boils (where shrimp and sometimes crab are cooked with smoked sausages, fresh corn on the cob, new potatoes, and spices), and "peanut boilings," parties that center around great vats of this salty treat, are still the way that the farmers around Americus and Plains celebrate the harvest.

Boiled peanuts are alleged to be an acquired taste, but if so, the people I serve them to acquire the taste quickly. When I put a bowl of boiled peanuts in front of fellow food writer and vegetable lover Faith Willinger and her very Italian husband, I did so with reservation, not being at all sure how their palates—conditioned as they were by Italian food—would react to them. I needn't have worried: they dug in with enthusiasm, and my only worry was whether or not I would have enough.

MAKES ABOUT 8 CUPS

3 pounds whole (unshelled) green peanuts
3 quarts water (approximately, see step 1)
3 rounded tablespoons salt (approximately, see step 1)

1. Wash the peanuts briefly and drain them well. Put them into a 6-quart kettle. Add the water in 1-quart batches until it covers them by about 1 inch: the nuts will float, so test the depth of the water by pressing them down. It will take about 3 quarts of water to cover them. Sprinkle in 1 rounded tablespoon of salt for each quart of water and stir until it is dissolved.

2. Turn on the fire to medium high and bring the water to a good boil. Reduce it to a simmer and cook until the peanuts are tender. This will take at least 1 1/2 hours, and maybe as long as 2 hours, depending on the freshness of the peanuts and your own taste. Some people like them very soft, while some like them to fight back a little. Start tasting them after an hour and a half, and continue simmering until they achieve the level of softness desired.

3. Turn off the heat and let the peanuts soak in the brine until they are salty enough for you, about 15 to 30 minutes. Let your own taste be your guide. When they reach the right stage of saltiness, drain off and discard the brine. (If you like your peanuts very salty, do not drain off the brine.)

4. Serve the peanuts either warm or cold, providing a large bowl for castoff shells. If you accidentally serve them to a bunch of unrefined palates that hate them and you actually have leftovers, store them in the refrigerator. They'll keep for 4 or 5 days.

Note: Southerners consider boiled peanuts a snack food, but you can shell them and eat them as a vegetable; either serve them plain with a little butter or olive oil or in a Peanut Ragout (page 169). Make sure that they don't sit in the brine and get salty if you plan to use them in these ways.

ℛOASTED PEANUTS

Traditionally, peanuts are commercially toasted by frying them in deep fat, but Southerners often toast or parch them at home by roasting them in their shells. The latter method produces nuts that are a lot less fattening, but they can be messy to serve. This method falls somewhere in between.

MAKES 4 TO 4¹/₂ CUPS, ABOUT 8 SERVINGS

1 pound (4–4¹/₂ cups) shelled, raw peanuts
2 tablespoons peanut oil, preferably cold-pressed
Salt

1. Position a rack in the upper third of the oven and preheat the oven to 275 degrees F. Spread the peanuts on a rimmed cookie sheet or sheet-cake pan. Add the oil and toss until the nuts are coated.

2. Roast the peanuts in the upper third of the oven until they are crisp and lightly browned, about 1 hour. Salt them liberally and toss until they are uniformly coated. Drain them briefly on absorbent paper and serve warm or at room temperature.

Verte's Goobers and Greens

"Goober" and "goober pea" are just two of the dozens of folk names that have been given to peanuts. They are thought to derive from an African name for the legumes, and here they most definitely give away the African roots of this variation on that pot of greens common to all Southerners of African descent.

The recipe is from National Public Radio personality and culinary anthropologist Vertemae Grosvenor, whose memoir/cookbook *Vibration Cooking* has become a modern classic. Though Verte has lived all over the world, her mouth has never lost its Geechee lilt, nor its taste for the cooking of her native South Carolina Lowcountry. She says she was nearly grown before she found out that there were people in the world who did not eat rice every day. True to that tradition, rare is the day that she still does not eat rice. She even suggests adding shrimp to the greens and serving them over Carolina-Style Rice. (page 43).

SERVES 4

2 pounds fresh spinach; or spinach and beet greens, mixed (see note); or Swiss chard
½ cup roasted peanuts (see page 165; do not use dry-roasted; see note)
3 tablespoons extra virgin olive oil
1 small yellow onion, split, peeled, and thinly sliced
1 clove garlic, crushed, peeled, and minced
Salt and black pepper in a peppermill
Whole nutmeg in a grater

1. Pick over the greens and remove any wilted or discolored leaves. Strip away and discard any tough stems (if you are using beet greens or chard, remove all the stems; see notes). Wash them in several changes of water to remove all the grit. Drain, shake off the excess water, and coarsely chop the greens. Set aside.

2. Grind the peanuts through a meat grinder or in a blender or food processor. They should be the texture of coarse meal or raw grits, so don't grind them too fine, or you'll release the oils and end up with peanut butter.

3. Put 2 tablespoons olive oil and onion in a large saucepan or lidded skillet that will hold all the greens comfortably and turn on the fire to medium. Sauté until the onion is softened, about 3 minutes. Add the spinach (and greens) and sauté, stirring frequently, until they are wilted, about 5 minutes.

4. Sprinkle the garlic and peanuts over the greens and, if they appear to be too dry, a few spoonfuls of water. Cover, reduce the heat to medium low, and cook until the greens are tender, about 10 minutes. Check the pot about half way through to make sure that the moisture has not completely dried up and the greens are not sticking. If it has, sprinkle in a few more spoonfuls of water.

5. Uncover the pan, add the remaining tablespoon olive oil, a healthy pinch of salt, a few liberal grindings of pepper, and a generous grating of nutmeg to taste. Cook, uncovered and stirring frequently, until the flavors are blended and the excess moisture is evaporated, about 3 minutes more. Turn off the heat, taste and adjust the seasonings, and serve at once.

Note: *Beet greens are a delicious addition to this dish, but they are a pushy vegetable; they tend to take over. To combat this, be sure to remove all but the smallest stems. Chard stems look very much like celery, and make a wonderful vegetable on their own. They can be cooked in any way that asparagus is on pages 62 through 69, except for the soup.*

Don't use dry-roasted cocktail peanuts for this dish; they are coated with a combination of sugar and spices that would be out of place in this dish.

To turn this into a main course dish, substitute hot red pepper flakes to taste for the black pepper and add a pound of peeled, deveined shrimp at the beginning of step 5. Serve the shrimp and greens over Carolina-Style Rice (page 43).

PEANUT SAUCE

This sauce has African roots but has developed a distinctly Southern accent. It is the perfect mate for grilled chicken, fish, or meat kabobs and is good with roast poultry of almost any kind. It also makes a fine sauce for steamed or baked sweet potatoes, pumpkin or winter squash, or Carolina-Style Rice (page 43).

If you have access to a grocery or natural-food store that grinds peanut butter to order or sells an all-natural peanut butter with nothing added to it, you can substitute 1/2 cup of either of these for the peanuts. Just make sure that the peanut butter contains only peanuts.

³/₄ cup Roasted Peanuts (page 165)
¹/₂ cup water
2 tablespoons peanut oil
1 small onion, peeled and chopped fine
2–3 large cloves garlic, crushed, peeled, and minced
2 tablespoons tomato paste
2 cups Chicken Broth (page 23)
Salt, cayenne, and black pepper in a peppermill
2 tablespoons chopped parsley
¹/₂ teaspoon Worcestershire sauce
Juice of ¹/₂ lemon

1.   Grind peanuts to a paste, either with a mortar and pestle or in the food processor fitted with a stainless-steel blade. Gradually add the water until it is a smooth paste. Set it aside.

2.   Put the oil and onion in a saucepan that will comfortably hold all the ingredients and turn on the heat to medium high. Sauté, tossing and stirring frequently, until the onion is softened and beginning to brown, about 5 minutes. Add the garlic and continue sautéing until it is fragrant. Add the peanut and tomato pastes, stirring until the onion and garlic are incorporated. Gradually beat in the broth until it is incorporated and there are no lumps of peanut paste. Add a large pinch of salt, a small one of cayenne, and a few grindings of black pepper. Bring the liquid almost to a boil and lower the heat to a slow simmer. Simmer, stirring frequently, until the sauce is thick, about 15 to 30 minutes, depending on how thick you want the sauce to be. Stir in the parsley, Worcestershire sauce, and lemon juice, then taste and adjust the seasonings. Serve hot.

Note: *For a chunkier sauce, substitute ³/₄ cup (about 1 large) peeled, seeded, and chopped tomato for the tomato paste, and add a diced green bell pepper along with the onion in step 2. For a meatless sauce, use the chopped fresh tomato and diced bell pepper, and substitute Vegetable Broth (page 24) for the chicken broth.*

Peanut Ragout with Tomatoes and Country Ham ◄

This stew may seem exotic to those unaccustomed to thinking of peanuts as beans, but there's really nothing new about it. This is the way that most Southern cooks would cook any kind of beans. It's an excellent accompaniment for any pork or poultry dish that does not already have tomatoes in it, or when served over rice, it makes a fine vegetarian main dish.

SERVES 4 TO 6

1½ pounds (4 cups, shelled) green peanuts or other acceptable legumes
(see note, page 170)
2 cups Chicken Broth (page 23) or canned broth
1 medium yellow onion, peeled and chopped
2 tablespoons bacon drippings or extra virgin olive oil
2 large cloves garlic, peeled and minced
2 ounces (1 thick slice) julienned country ham or prosciutto
2 pounds ripe tomatoes, blanched, peeled, seeded, and chopped as
directed on page 117, or 1 28-ounce can Italian plum tomatoes,
seeded and chopped, with their juice
1 tablespoon chopped fresh thyme or 1 teaspoon dried thyme
1 tablespoon chopped parsley
1–2 bay leaves, depending on size
1 whole pod hot red pepper
Salt

1.   Wash the peanuts, drain them well, and shell them. Put them in a pot with 2 cups of water and the broth. Place over medium-high heat and bring the liquid to a boil. Skim the scum that rises, reduce the heat to a slow simmer, loosely cover the pot, and let the peanuts cook until they are nearly tender, about 1 hour.

2.   Put the onion and bacon drippings or olive oil in a sauté pan and place it over medium-high heat. Sauté, tossing frequently, until the onion is softened and beginning to

color, about 8 to 10 minutes. Add the garlic and ham, and continue sautéing until the garlic is fragrant, about a minute more. Turn off the heat.

3. Add the onion-and-garlic mixture to the peanuts, then add the tomatoes, thyme, parsley, bay leaves, and pepper pod. Raise the heat to medium high and let the liquid come back to a boil, then reduce the heat to low. Loosely cover the pot and simmer slowly until the peanuts are very tender, about an hour longer. Taste and correct the salt, and let the peanuts simmer for about 5 minutes more to allow the seasonings to blend. If the liquid isn't thick, raise the heat and quickly boil it down. Turn off the heat, remove and discard the pepper pod and bay leaves, and serve hot.

Note: *Any fresh beans, such as cranberry beans or field peas, work well in this recipe. Substitute 4 cups fresh beans or field peas, or 2 cups dried beans or peas. Soak the dried beans or peas for 6 hours or overnight in water to cover by at least 3 inches. Drain them and proceed with step 1. Cured peanuts and dried beans will need more time in the preliminary cooking in step 1, about 2 hours.*

As a matter of fact, cooking times can vary a lot even with green peanuts. A lot depends on their freshness, size, and maturity. The younger and fresher they are, the quicker they'll cook, so don't take the cooking times as gospel, and keep an eye on the pot.

For a meatless version, use all water or substitute Vegetable Broth (page 24) for the meat broth, omit the country ham, and add a small dash of soy sauce.

SUMMER SQUASH

The zucchini war. It strikes, in the South, in midsummer, late summer in the North. Overzealous gardeners, who cannot imagine that those tiny little seeds can possibly produce all that many squash, plant two hills too many. The plants flourish and mature and all at once start to produce—like nothing has ever produced before. Those gardeners go from being crazy for summer squash to just being crazed. They show up at your house, at church, at roadside stands, anywhere they think they have a prayer of unloading their surplus, with brown grocery sacks overloaded and splitting with glossy green things the size of baseball bats. The truly desperate will drop them on your doorstoop like foundlings, ring your bell, and run.

Poor things, they've compounded the problem by letting the zucchini get too big. A squash the size of a baseball bat is not a gardener's pride; it ought to be a gardener's embarrassment. All summer squash—yellow crooknecks or cymlings (those little flying-saucer–like squash, also known as pattypan) or zucchini—are best when still quite immature. In fact, the name *zucchini* means "little squash." There's not much you can do with an overgrown one.

In spite of the annual war, we Southerners love summer squash, whether they are those Italian newcomers, zucchini, or our own yellow crooknecks. We steam them whole, mash them up with butter and cream, braise them with onions, fry them, stuff them, bake them in casseroles, and even turn them into pickles. Here is a sampling of some of our best recipes.

Yellow Summer Squash Soup with Sage and Thyme

Served hot or cold, this soup is the very essence of summer—from its bright, sunny color to its light, fresh flavor. Its secret lies in the youth and freshness of the main ingredient. Any variety of yellow summer squash will do; just make sure that they are very young, small, and impeccably fresh, with clear, taut skins and bright green stems.

SERVES 4

1 pound yellow crookneck or yellow zucchini squash
1 medium leek
1 large yellow onion
2 tablespoons unsalted butter
1 cup Chicken Broth (page 23), or ¹/₂ canned broth mixed with ¹/₂ cup
*   water, or use all water*
1 Bouquet Garni (page 36), made with a sprig each of thyme, parsley,
*   and sage*
Salt and whole white peppercorns in a peppermill
2 cups half-and-half
¹/₄ cup heavy cream (optional)
4–5 fresh sage leaves, thinly sliced, or 1 tablespoon chopped fresh chives

1. Scrub the squash under cold running water, being careful to remove all the grit and sand that may be stuck to them. Trim off the blossom and stem ends, and slice the squash crosswise into ½-inch rounds. Set them aside. Split the leek lengthwise and wash it well under running water to remove the grit and sand from between the leaves. Remove the green part of the leek and set it aside. Thinly slice the white part of the leek. Split lengthwise, peel, and thinly slice the onion.

2.   Put the sliced leek, onion, and butter in a soup kettle that will hold all the ingredients comfortably, and turn on the fire to medium. Sauté until the onion is softened but not browned, about 5 minutes. Add the sliced squash and toss well.

3.   Pour the broth or water over the vegetables and raise the heat to medium high. Bring the liquid to a boil and add the bouquet garni, a pinch or so of salt (go easy on this if your broth is already salted; you can correct the seasonings later), and a liberal grinding of white pepper. Reduce the heat to low, cover, and simmer the soup until the vegetables are tender, about 20 minutes. Turn off the heat.

4.   With a slotted spoon, take up about 1 cup of the solids and set them aside. Remove and discard the bouquet garni. Puree the remainder of the soup through a food mill, or in batches in a food processor or blender. Return the puree to the kettle and stir in the half-and-half. Thinly slice the inner light green leaves of the leek. Roughly chop the reserved solids and add them with the leek to the soup. Bring it back to a simmer over medium heat and simmer until the leek is just tender, about 5 minutes. (Note: the soup can be made several days in advance up to this point. Pour the soup into a bowl and set it in a basin of ice water. Stir until the soup is cold, then cover and store it in the refrigerator.)

5.   To serve the soup hot, heat it gently over medium heat, stirring occasionally to prevent scorching. Taste and correct the seasonings. Ladle the soup into heated soup plates. Garnish with a drizzle of cream and a sprinkling of the fresh sage or chives.

6.   To serve the soup cold, taste and correct the seasonings after it is chilled. Garnish as you would the hot soup, or whip the cream until it forms soft peaks, put a dollop on each serving, and sprinkle with the chopped herbs and a grinding of white pepper.

Note: *To make a meatless version of this soup, use water instead of broth and add a small pinch of Curry Powder (page 31). Keep the curry accent subtle; the idea isn't to make it a curried soup, but to compensate for the depth of flavor of the chicken broth. Don't omit the half-and-half—the soup is lackluster without it.*

SUMMER SQUASH
WITH ONIONS

We tend to associate braising, with its caramelized surfaces and hefty flavors, with cold-weather cooking, but even in the hottest weather, a warm dish of braised summer squash makes an appealing foil for any cold meat. And the rich aroma goes a long way toward reviving appetites that have been wilted by the heat. It has long been a favorite in my house.

SERVES 4

1½ pounds very young yellow crooknecks, cymling (pattypan) squash,
    or zucchini
2 medium onions
2 tablespoons bacon drippings or unsalted butter
Salt and black pepper in a peppermill
1 tablespoon each chopped parsley and summer savory or chives

1. Scrub the squash under cold running water to remove any dirt and grit that may be clinging to them. Trim off the blossom and stem ends and slice them crosswise into ¼-inch rounds. Set them aside. Trim the root and stem ends from the onions, halve them, then peel and cut them into ½-inch dice.

2. Put the bacon drippings or butter and the onions into a lidded skillet that will comfortably hold all the ingredients and turn on the heat to medium. Sauté, uncovered, until the onions are translucent, about 5 minutes. Add the squash, toss until they are well mixed, and let them heat through. Add a healthy pinch or so of salt, a few liberal grindings of pepper, and stir them in. Reduce the heat to medium low and cover the pan. Cook, shaking the pan occasionally to prevent sticking, until the squash and onions are golden and tender, about 15 to 20 minutes.

3. Remove the lid and, if there is any liquid in the pan, raise the heat to medium high and quickly boil it away. Add the chopped herbs, gently stir them in, and turn off the heat. Taste and adjust the seasonings, transfer the squash to a warm serving bowl, and serve at once.

Note: For a vegetarian version, substitute peanut or olive oil for the fat and add a small pinch of Curry Powder (page 31) with the salt and pepper in step 2. The Curry Powder will lend the squash a dusky, meaty taste that it loses if you omit the bacon fat, yet will still be recognizably Southern in flavor and aroma.

The flavor of fresh herbs is important, but if you don't have summer savory in your garden but have a nice stand of basil, use that. If you haven't any basil, but your sage is thriving, use it. Likewise, if you lack sage, use thyme.

Baked Stuffed Summer Squash

Stuffed squash have traditionally been served as a side dish in the South. However, baked squash have a meaty flavor that allows them to hold their own as a main course, especially when reinforced, as they are here, with a bit of flavorful country ham. The neat, self-contained portions make it an appealing dish to serve at a luncheon or buffet.

SERVES 4

4 medium yellow crookneck squash
3 tablespoons unsalted butter
1/2 cup minced green onions, green and white parts, or yellow onion
2 ounces country ham, chopped fine (a 1/8-inch-thick slice)
3/4 cup soft bread crumbs
2 large eggs, well beaten
Cream or milk
Salt and pepper
1 tablespoon chopped fresh thyme or 1 teaspoon dried thyme

1.   Position a rack in the center of the oven and preheat it to 350 degrees F. Half-fill a large kettle that will hold all the squash comfortably with water. Bring it to a boil over high heat. Meanwhile, scrub the squash under cold running water. When the water is boiling, add the squash. Let the water come back to a boil and cook until the squash are nearly tender, about 10 minutes.

2. Lay the squash on a cutting board so that they will lie flat without rolling. Horizontally cut off ¼ inch of the side of the squash that is facing up, and set these slices aside. Using a melon baller or small spoon, carefully scoop out the center pulp of each squash, leaving about ¼ inch of the outer flesh intact, taking care not to puncture the shell. Set the squash aside. Chop the reserved slices and pulp, and put it in a mixing bowl.

3. Put 2 tablespoons of the butter and the onions in a shallow pan and turn on the heat to medium. Sauté, stirring constantly, until the onion is transparent and soft but not colored. Add the ham and sauté for a minute more. Turn off the heat. Add the onions, ham, bread crumbs, and beaten egg to the chopped pulp. Mix thoroughly, moistening it with a little cream or milk, if needed, keeping in mind that the filling should not be too wet. Add a healthy pinch of salt, a few grindings of pepper, the thyme, and mix well.

4. Lightly grease a shallow, flat pan (such as a cookie sheet) or a pottery casserole, and arrange the hollowed-out squash casings open side up so that they do not touch. Spoon the filling into each, carefully packing it in as you go to prevent air pockets, and mound it up on the top. Dot the tops with the remaining 1 tablespoon of butter and bake in the center of the oven until the filling is set and the tops are browned, about 30 minutes. Serve either hot or at room temperature.

Note: *For a meatless stuffed squash, omit the ham and use a full cup of bread crumbs. Add a small pinch of Curry Powder (page 31) to the filling mixture along with the salt and pepper in step 3, to compensate for the depth of flavor that the ham lends.*

Jo Bettoja's Georgia Pasta

Jo Bettoja is an extraordinary Italian author and cooking teacher, born and raised in a little town called Millen near Rome—only it's Rome, Georgia—not Italy. It was only after she married Angelo Bettoja that she found herself living *in* Rome, this time in Italy. Now when she comes back to Georgia, newspapers occasionally report, to her combined embarrassment and amusement, that "Contessa Bettoja" is in town, even though she is not really a contessa.

What happens when a fine Southern cook moves to Italy? She becomes a fine Italian cook, that's what happens, and two wonderful cuisines collide in her kitchen, getting happily muddled. There are many parallels between Italian and Southern cooking, and Jo has lived with them for nearly her entire career as a cook. Nothing illustrates the blend of traditions better than this dish, which is a cross between a Southern squash casserole and Italian *pasta al forno*. In Georgia she makes it with that most Southern of squash, yellow crooknecks, but in Rome, she says, she "makes do" with zucchini. It's powerfully good no matter which squash you use.

SERVES 4 TO 5
(4 ITALIANS, 5 SOUTHERNERS)

2 pounds young, small zucchini or yellow crookneck squash
Salt and black pepper in a peppermill
4 tablespoons unsalted butter
Handful fresh basil leaves (about ¼ cup, tightly packed)
⅔ pound sedanini or pennette (small penne) or other small, tubular
    imported Italian pasta
¼ pound Parmesan (preferably Parmigiano-Reggiano), freshly grated
1 large egg
2 tablespoons fresh dry bread crumbs

1.   Thoroughly wash the squash under cold running water, trim them, and cut them into chunks. In a kettle that will comfortably hold the squash, bring enough water to just cover them to a boil over high heat. Add a large pinch of salt and the squash, bring it back to a boil, and cook the squash until they are tender, about 5 minutes. Drain them well and

roughly mash them with a fork or potato masher. Add a liberal grinding of pepper and 2 tablespoons of the butter. Chop two-thirds of the basil and stir it into the squash. Set aside. (The squash can be prepared to this point a day ahead.)

2.   Position a rack in the upper third of the oven and preheat the oven to 350 degrees F. Bring 3 quarts of water to a boil and add a small handful of salt. Add the pasta and cook for half the time indicated on the package (about 4 to 5 minutes—the pasta should be under-done). Thoroughly drain the pasta and spread it on a large platter. Add to the pasta the remaining 2 tablespoons of butter and three-fourths of the Parmesan, mixing it in well, and spreading the pasta to arrest the cooking.

3.   Break the egg into a separate bowl and beat until it is smooth. Add it to the squash and mix well. Combine the squash and pasta mixtures together, and stir until they are thoroughly combined. Lightly butter a 2¹/₂-quart baking dish (preferably pottery) and pour in the pasta and squash.

4.   Chop the remaining basil and mix it with the bread crumbs. (This can be done in a food processor: put both basil and crumbs in the processor bowl fitted with a steel blade and pulse until the basil is finely chopped.) Mix the crumbs with the remaining Parmesan and sprinkle the mixture over the top of the pasta and squash. Bake in the upper third of the oven until the pasta is done and the top nicely browned, about 30 minutes. Serve hot.

Note: *Jo advises that the squash can be prepared ahead of time, but don't mix it with the pasta until you are ready to bake it. If you make the squash a day ahead and refrigerate it, let it come back to room temperature before adding it to the pasta. The pasta cannot be made ahead, but since it only partially cooks before it goes into the casserole, it doesn't take long to get it ready.*

FRIED SUMMER SQUASH

Dyed-in-the-wool Southerner that I am, this is my favorite way of doing any young summer squash—whether yellow crooknecks, pattypans (or cymlings), or zucchini. The secrets to success are two: the squash should be very fresh and still quite young (leave the more mature ones for the stewing pot), and the cornmeal should be fresh, clean-smelling, and really stone-ground.

SERVES 4

1¹/₂ pounds young summer squash
1 cup fine stone-ground cornmeal
Lard or vegetable oil, for frying
Salt and black pepper in a peppermill to taste

1.   Position a rack in the upper third of the oven and preheat the oven to 150 degrees F. Scrub the squash under cold running water to remove any grit that may be clinging to them, dry them, trim off the stem and blossom ends, and cut them into slices a little more than ¹/₈ inch but less than a ¹/₄-inch thick—crosswise in rings if the squash are long and thick, or lengthwise if small.

2.   Spread the meal on a dinner plate and have both squash and breading close by the cooking surface.

3.   Put enough lard or oil in a wide, cast-iron or other heavy-bottomed skillet to come up the sides by at least ¹/₂ inch. Turn on the fire to medium high. When the melted fat is hot but not smoking (around 375 degrees F), roll the squash slices in the meal until they are coated, and gently shake off the excess. Slip them into the hot fat as soon as they are coated, and keep adding more slices until the pan is full but not crowded.

4.   Fry the squash until the bottoms are golden brown, about 3 minutes, then carefully turn them and let the other side brown. As soon as they have evenly browned, take them up with a slotted spatula or spoon and lay them on a wire rack set over a cookie sheet to drain. Keep them in the warm oven while the remaining squash cook. Add more squash to the pan as soon as there is space, until all the slices are cooked.

5.   Season them lightly with salt and a few good grindings of pepper. Fold a cotton or linen napkin to fit and place it on a serving platter. Place the squash on the napkin in a single layer and serve hot. Never crowd or stack them or they will get soggy.

Note: *I find it best to drain all fried vegetables on a wire rack set on a cookie sheet rather than on the usual butcher paper or paper towels. The vegetables are full of moisture that seems to be naturally drawn to absorbent paper, making the bottom crusts limp and soggy.*

Mama's Fried Summer Squash in Parmesan Batter: My mother often fries summer squash in a Parmesan cheese breading. Substitute 1 cup finely grated Parmesan (preferably Parmigiano-Reggiano) for the cornmeal. Fry the slices in very little fat—use just enough to coat the pan. For a crispier texture, mix ¹/₂ cup Parmesan with ¹/₂ cup dry bread or cracker crumbs; dip the squash first in 1 beaten egg, then coat them with the crumb and cheese mixture, and deep-fry them as directed above.

MARYLAND
SQUASH CROQUETTES ⤴

This old Maryland recipe is sometimes called "mock crab" because it is supposed to imitate the flavor of those famous Chesapeake Bay blue crab. Well, I don't know that they really taste all that much like crab, but they taste pretty good, and the boiling spices, which were designed primarily as a seasoning for seafood, do give the squash a hint of the seacoast.

MAKES ABOUT 12 CROQUETTES,
OR 6 SERVINGS

1 pound zucchini or yellow crookneck squash
1 small yellow onion
1 large clove garlic
1½ cups fine cracker crumbs
1 tablespoon Homemade Mayonnaise (page 53)
2 teaspoons Seafood Boiling Spice (page 31) or Old Bay brand
  seasoning and ½ teaspoon salt
1 large egg
½ pound (2 sticks) unsalted butter or ¼ pound butter and ½ cup
  peanut oil, mixed
1 lemon, cut into 8 wedges
Parsley sprigs, for garnish
1 recipe Savannah Sweet Red Pepper Sauce (page 56) or Herb
  Mayonnaise (page 55)

1. Position a rack in the upper third of the oven and preheat the oven to 150 degrees F. Scrub the squash under cold running water to remove any grit that may be clinging to them. Cut off the stem and blossom ends and grate the squash through the large holes of a hand grater or food processor. Put the grated squash in a colander and let it stand in the sink for half an hour. Squeeze it to remove as much moisture as possible and transfer it to a mixing bowl.

2. Peel the onion and grate it to the same size as the squash. Crush, peel, and mince the garlic. Add both to the squash along with the cracker crumbs, mayonnaise, and spice mix. Break the egg into a separate bowl and beat lightly until the yolk and white are evenly mixed. Add it to the squash and mix it in well.

3. Put the butter or butter and oil into a 9- or 10-inch skillet and turn on the heat to medium. When the butter is melted and the foaming subsides, take up about 2 tablespoons of the squash mixture and slip them into the fat until the skillet is full but not crowded. Fry the croquettes until the bottoms are golden brown, about 3 minutes, carefully turn them, and continue cooking until uniformly browned and the center is set, about 3 minutes more.

4. Take them up onto absorbent paper, drain briefly, then transfer them to a cookie sheet and put them in the warm oven. Slip the remaining croquette batter into the pan and repeat until all the batter is cooked. Transfer the croquettes to a serving platter, garnish with lemon wedges and sprigs of parsley, and serve at once, passing the pepper sauce or mayonnaise separately.

Note: *Draining the grated squash well is a critical step, as they throw off a lot of liquid that would otherwise make the batter too soupy. Don't let the batter sit once it is made, and don't make the croquettes too large or you'll have trouble handling them and they will break up when you try to turn them.*

SWEET POTATOES IN SUMMER

There are many people who think that sweet potatoes are only for the fall and winter, who have never seen them without a thick covering of marshmallows, or brown sugar and pecans, or on a table that did not also have a turkey on it. In the South, sweet potatoes have never been relegated only to Thanksgiving dinner, but have long been a year-round staple. In the summer, we roast them on the grill or slice them and grill them directly over hot coals. We turn them into fries and salads—just like white potatoes—and serve them up in cooling Sweet Potato Vichysoisse (page 225). They'll even put in an appearance at dessert.

SWEET POTATO SALAD

Southern sweet potato salads are often so full of sugar, apples, raisins, and marshmallows that they seem more like dessert than salad. So people meet this salad with surprise, since it contains few ingredients besides potatoes, and none of them are sweet—green onions, red bell peppers, and a light vinaigrette. However, surprise usually turns into enthusiasm after the first bite.

This fits all my requirements for a great summer salad: it's nice to look at, simple to make, and, best of all, can be made on the morning before you plan to serve it, when the air is still fairly cool and you can deal with boiling potatoes. Its sweet-tangy flavor makes it a perfect accompaniment for grilled or barbecued meat of any sort.

Of course, the most appealing thing of all is that it also happens to be very, very good.

SERVES 6 TO 8

3 pounds sweet potatoes
2 red bell peppers
8 scallions or other green onions
Red wine vinegar
Salt and black pepper in a peppermill
Extra virgin olive oil
2 tablespoons chopped parsley

1. Scrub the sweet potatoes under cold running water. Put them in a large kettle that will just hold them. Add enough water to cover them by an inch and lift out the potatoes. Cover the kettle and place it over high heat. When the water is boiling briskly, add the sweet potatoes, cover, and let the liquid come back to a boil. Reduce the heat to medium, skew the lid on the kettle, and simmer until the potatoes are just tender and can be pierced through with a sharp knife. Drain and let them cool enough to handle.

2. Meanwhile, wash the bell peppers and scallions, and drain them well. Cut off the tops and bottoms of the peppers, remove the seed cores, and cut the peppers into small dice. Cut the onions crosswise into thin slices. When you can handle the potatoes, peel them and cut them into 1/2-inch dice.

3. Put the potatoes, bell peppers, and scallions in a large serving bowl. Sprinkle generously with wine vinegar, salt, and pepper to taste, and toss well. Let the salad stand for a minute or two, then taste and adjust the seasonings. Drizzle the salad well with olive oil—enough to lightly coat the potatoes—and toss again. Let cool completely. (The salad can be made ahead and refrigerated, but take it out of the refrigerator at least half an hour before serving it to let it lose some of the chill.) Just before serving, sprinkle the top of the salad with the chopped parsley.

GRILL-ROASTED SWEET POTATOES ◢

These potatoes are an ideal accompaniment to barbecued spareribs, chicken, or any other meat that cooks slowly on the grill. You just put them on the back of the grill while the meat is cooking and give them an occasional turn—and when the meat is ready, so are they.

SERVES 4

4 small sweet potatoes (about 8 ounces each)
Unsalted butter or peanut oil
Salt and black pepper in a peppermill

1.   Prepare a grill with coals—preferably of natural hardwood—and ignite them. While the coals are burning down, scrub the potatoes under cold running water. Pat them dry and rub lightly with butter or peanut oil. Put them on a plate and set aside.

2.   When the coals are ready, spread them so that there is a clear spot at the back of the grill without any coals. Put the potatoes over this bare spot, making sure there are no coals directly beneath them. Roast the potatoes, turning them frequently so that the skin browns evenly, until they are tender and yield easily when pressed with your finger, about 45 minutes. Serve hot, passing more butter, salt, and the peppermill separately.

SWEET POTATO ICE CREAM ◢

This is really just a frozen version of a sweet potato custard pie. The flavorings are the same—lemon peel, nutmeg, and bourbon—and they are kept subtle so that the flavor of the sweet potatoes is allowed to come through. The pecan topping is a nice finish, but you can omit it and splash a spoonful of bourbon over each serving if you don't like chewy things in your ice cream.

There are several important secrets to ensure success in making this ice cream. The potatoes must be mature: new sweet potatoes that have not properly cured are often stringy and tend to "seize up" when frozen. Also make sure the potatoes are absolutely smooth and free of lumps *before* adding the cream: if you try to beat them smooth after the cream is added, the cream is likely to break and turn to butter, leaving hard little granules of fat in your base mixture.

MAKES ABOUT ¹/₂ GALLON

1 pound (about 2 medium) sweet potatoes
1 cup sugar
3 cups half-and-half
1 cup heavy cream (minimum 36 percent milkfat)
1 tablespoon bourbon
Grated zest of 1 lemon
Nutmeg in a grater
1 cup chopped toasted pecans or pralines (optional)

1.   Position a rack in the center of the oven and preheat the oven to 400 degrees F. Scrub the sweet potatoes under cold running water, remove any root tendrils, and pat dry. Prick them in several places with a carving fork or paring knife, and place them on a baking sheet. Bake in the center of the oven until the potatoes are tender and easily pierced through with a carving fork, about 45 minutes. Let the potatoes cool enough to handle, peel them, and while they are still warm, force them through a potato ricer or coarse sieve. You should have at least 1 cup of puree. Stir the sugar into the puree until it is dissolved, and let the mixture cool completely.

2.   Gradually add the half-and-half and then the cream, stirring well after each addition until smooth. The mixture should be the consistency of a thick custard. Add the bourbon, lemon zest, and a few gratings of nutmeg to taste. Stir well until thoroughly blended, cover, and refrigerate until well chilled—2 hours or overnight.

3.   Prepare an ice-cream freezer according to the manufacturer's directions, and freeze the sweet potato mixture until it is thick and nearly set. Pack it into freezable containers or ice cream molds, cover, and let it solidify in the freezer, about 2 hours more. If you like, serve the ice cream sprinkled with the chopped pecans or pralines.

Note: Because of the rich, starchy qualities of the sweet potatoes, I've found that too much fat in the base mixture results in an unpleasant, waxy after-feel in the mouth, so don't be tempted to enrich the base with more cream: trust me, I've tried it. If you have more than a cup of puree from the potatoes, don't worry about it—a little more shouldn't make much difference. A pound will produce 1 cup of puree.

Summer Fruit

Southern summers may be muggy and hot, but they have always had their compensations—even before Coca-Cola came along and we all became imprisoned in our houses by air-conditioning. We iced our tea, we froze our cream, we juleped our bourbon, we moved the living room out onto the front porch and our parties out under the shade tree in the yard. And yes, we invented Coca-Cola.

The best and most satisfying compensation was always the plenitude of summer fruit that the hot climate made possible. A picnic without a sweet, crisp watermelon chilled in the nearest creek or spring is just not a Southern picnic; a church summer social that does not include peach ice cream is doomed to failure; a midday Sunday dinner without a bowl of sliced sweet cantaloupe is a dinner that is happening somewhere north of the Mason–Dixon line.

And a summer without a fresh fruit cobbler is a summer that is not worth living.

BLACKBERRIES

In late summer, blackberry brambles grow wild all over the pastures and thickets of the South. As children, we ate them in prodigal quantities because they were plentiful and free for the picking. We would go out early and come home late with gallons of luscious deep-purple berries, our fingers stained and our stomachs full of the berries that didn't make it into the bucket. Mama would be up late that night putting up countless jars of jam, because jam was a family favorite, but she always saved enough berries for a cobbler. It would come to the table, its golden crust glistening with butter and oozing thick purple juice, the most beautiful thing, for the moment, that we'd ever seen. And then, in short order, it was gone.

*B*LACKBERRY COBBLER

If you live in a place where the only fresh blackberries you ever see are sold in expensive little plastic packets, buy them anyway and make this; it's worth every penny.

FOR THE CRUST:
2 cups unbleached all-purpose flour
2 teaspoons baking powder, preferably single-acting
1/2 teaspoon salt
1/4 pound (1 stick) chilled unsalted butter, cut into bits
1 tablespoon chilled lard
2/3 cup buttermilk or 1/2 cup plain, all-natural yogurt mixed with
enough skimmed milk to make 2/3 cup total

FOR THE FILLING:
5 cups ripe blackberries, washed and drained
Sugar
2 tablespoons flour
2 tablespoons bourbon
2 tablespoons unsalted butter, cut into bits

1. Sift the flour, baking powder, and salt together into a mixing bowl that will comfortably hold all the crust ingredients. Add the butter and lard, and cut it in with a pastry blender, fork, or two knives until the flour has the consistency of coarse meal. Make a well in the center and add 1/2 cup of the liquid. Lightly but thoroughly mix it in. The dough should be fairly soft; if it is too crumbly or stiff, add the rest of the liquid by spoonfuls until you get the right consistency. Gather the dough into a ball and divide the ball into two parts—one slightly larger than the other.

2. Position a rack in the center of the oven and preheat the oven to 375 degrees F. Lightly flour a work surface and roll out the larger piece of dough to a thickness of about 1/8 inch. Line a deep dish, such as a 9-inch pottery casserole or soufflé dish, with this dough. Trim off the excess dough and set it aside.

3. To make the filling, sprinkle the bottom of the dough with a spoonful of sugar, and spread half the berries over it. Sprinkle them generously with sugar (how much will depend on how sweet the berries are), 1 tablespoon of flour, and 1 tablespoon of bourbon. Lay the strips of excess dough trimmed from the bottom crust over the berries.

4. Roll out the remaining dough to the same thickness as the bottom crust. If there are gaps in the layer of dough on top of the berries, cut enough dough from the edges of the remaining dough to fill them in. Sprinkle the strips of dough with sugar and put in the rest of the berries. Sprinkle the second layer with more sugar and the remaining tablespoons of flour and bourbon. Lay the top crust over the berries, seal the edges to the bottom crust by moistening them with a little water or milk. Crimp the edges decoratively and cut several gashes in the top crust. If you like, you can also cut decorative shapes from any scraps of dough that remain, brush the backs of the shapes with milk, and decorate the top crust with them. Place the cobbler on a rimmed cookie sheet (to keep the juices from dripping on the oven floor). Bake the cobbler in the center of the oven for 20 minutes.

5. After 20 minutes, the crust should be beginning to color. Rub it with 2 tablespoons of butter and dust it well with sugar. Return the cobbler to the center of the oven and bake until the top is golden and the filling is bubbling, about 40 more minutes more. Serve warm with vanilla ice cream, Sweet Potato Ice Cream (page 182), or a pitcher of very cold heavy cream, passed separately.

BLACKBERRY (OR RASPBERRY) BOURBON SAUCE

The first time you make this sauce, you're going to suspect that I have been lying down with too many of those bottles of bourbon I keep talking about. The method is the same as Cherries Kentuckian (next page), except that here the heat and flaming liquor must be applied behind the scenes in the kitchen because the berries disintegrate into a hopeless-looking mush. Don't give up: while they surrender their shape and texture altogether, they are transformed into a silky sauce that glides over ice cream like melted rubies.

This sauce is wonderful served over homemade peach or vanilla ice cream or, especially if you've made it with raspberries, over chocolate ice cream or your favorite chocolate mousse. Pooled underneath a slab of chocolate pound cake, it will make your company roll over and play dead.

MAKES 4 SERVINGS

¹/₂ pound fresh blackberries or raspberries
2 tablespoons unsalted butter
3–4 tablespoons sugar, to taste
¹/₄ cup warm bourbon

1.   Gently rinse the berries under cold running water and drain them well. Put the butter in a sauté pan that will comfortably hold the berries and turn on the heat to medium high.

2.   When the butter is melted and the foaming begins to subside, add the berries and sprinkle them with the sugar. Cook, shaking the pan constantly, until they are beginning to dissolve, about a minute (raspberries will do this right away; blackberries will take a little longer because of the center core).

3.   Add the bourbon and—leaning well away from the pan—ignite it. The flames will shoot straight up, so be very careful. Shake and stir the berries until the flame dies out.

4.   Strain the sauce to remove the seeds through a fine wire-mesh sieve set over a warm serving bowl, pressing well on the solids. Stir the sauce well and serve warm.

$\mathcal{C}$HERRIES KENTUCKIAN

This is not just cherries jubilee with a Kentucky twist. There are a couple of important differences. Instead of brandy or cognac, I use bourbon, Kentucky's national beverage. This is no mere substitution; bourbon lends a smoother, richer flavor. Also, instead of pouring the cherry sauce over the ice cream while it is still flaming, I let it cook until the alcohol has completely burned off. It may not be as showy, but the taste is mellower—and that's what really matters.

The original cherries jubilee was always done tableside by a waiter, but I put it together in the kitchen. You, of course, may do it in a sauté pan over a portable burner at the table if you want to show off.

SERVES 4

10 ounces (about 3 dozen) Bing or other dark cherries
2–3 tablespoons sugar (see step 1)
2 tablespoons unsalted butter
$^1/_3$ cup bourbon, warmed but not hot
1 pint French vanilla ice cream, preferably homemade

1.   Wash the cherries, split them with a paring knife, and give each one a twist to loosen the pits. Remove and discard the pits. Sprinkle the cherries with 2 to 3 tablespoons of sugar—depending on how sweet the fruit is—to suit your taste. Stir until the sugar is

nearly dissolved and set the cherries aside. Refrigerate 4 individual serving bowls for at least half an hour before you plan to serve the cherries and ice cream.

2. Put the butter in a sauté pan that will comfortably hold all the cherries and place it over medium-high heat. When the butter is melted and hot, add the cherries and any juice that has accumulated and sauté them until they are heated through, about 3 minutes.

3. Add the bourbon, stir, and—*leaning away from the pan*—ignite it, either by tipping the pan toward the flame if you have a gas stove, or by putting a long lighted match near the surface. Continue cooking, shaking the pan and stirring when the flame subsides enough, until the flame goes out and the juice is thick.

4. Quickly scoop the vanilla ice cream into chilled individual serving bowls. Pour the sauce over them and serve at once.

Peaches or Mangoes Kentuckian: Peaches and cherries are close kin to one another, and peaches are slap wonderful substituted in this recipe. So are mangoes. Allow 1 cup of peaches or mangoes (about 2 large ones), blanched, peeled, and pitted as directed in Georgia Peach Soup (page 197). Cut the peaches or mangoes into $1/2$-inch chunks. If you do this ahead of time, squeeze a little lemon juice over them to keep them from discoloring.

$\mathcal{F}$IGS AND COUNTRY HAM

Southern country ham and Italian prosciutto are very much alike. In the South, in season, country ham is sometimes served with fresh fruit, just as its Italian cousin is. Even out of season, a fruit conserve will be passed along with it. Here it is happily paired with succulent, sweet, perfectly ripe figs. I like to also pass warm Corn Sticks (page 40) with this.

The ingredients are few, but the strength of this dish lies entirely in the quality of those few ingredients: the figs must be perfectly ripe, the ham of the best quality—not too salty with just an undertone of sweet smokiness—and the butter fresh and creamy.

SERVES 4

4 large, ripe figs (or 8, if they are small)
2 lemons
16 paper-thin slices of raw (preferable) or cooked country ham
$1/4$ pound unsalted butter, softened
Black pepper in a peppermill

1. Cut the figs lengthwise into quarters and lemons into 8 wedges.

2. Fold the ham slices double and arrange them 4 per plate on salad plates, folded side out and centers overlapping. Arrange the figs and lemons in an alternating pinwheel pattern on top of the ham.

3. Whip the butter until fluffy and light, and put a large dollop in the center of each plate. Serve at once, passing the peppermill or a shaker of freshly ground pepper separately.

MANGOES

This tropical fruit, while it is not native to Florida, has long been a fixture in Florida gardens and kitchens. Floridians look forward to their mangoes ripening the way Georgians and Carolinians look forward to the season's first peaches. In Florida the mango trees are so plentiful and prolific that it seems that every other corner has a child selling the family's surplus from a little red wagon.

Aside from chutney, that Far Eastern condiment that Southerners have adopted and made their own, most Southern cooks prepare mangoes as they would peaches. The fruit can be substituted in any of the peach recipes on pages 197–201.

MANGO OR PEACH CUSTARD TART (KUCHEN)

After finishing graduate school, I worked through my architectural internship in West Palm Beach, Florida. There, I met up with tree-ripened mangoes and a brilliant teacher, painter, and interior designer named Wayne Jung. Both remain among my best memories of Florida, and here, they are combined in Wayne's favorite dessert.

A variation on that Southern classic custard pie, Wayne's kuchen is typical of the eclectic cookery of the Gold Coast, the southeastern arc of the Florida peninsula, where Southern and Caribbean flavors are blended and accented with the borrowed foodways of the region's diverse population. Here, the accent is German and Norwegian.

1 cup unbleached all-purpose flour
1 tablespoon sugar
Salt
$\frac{1}{4}$ pound (1 stick) unsalted butter, softened
1 tablespoon cider vinegar
4 large eggs
1 cup light cream
1 cup sugar
1 heaping cup mangoes or peaches, peeled, pitted, and cut into cubes, or
    other fresh fruit (see note)

1. Position a rack in the center of the oven and preheat the oven to 400 degrees F. Combine the flour, sugar, and a small pinch of salt in a mixing bowl. Work in the butter until the mixture resembles cookie dough (you can do this with a pastry blender or simply use your fingers). Work in the vinegar, then press the dough evenly over the bottom and up the sides of an 8-inch square casserole or 9-inch round pie plate. Bake in the center of the oven until the crust is beginning to color, about 10 minutes. Remove it from the oven and reduce the temperature to 375 degrees F.

2. Add water to the bottom of a double boiler. Bring the water to a simmer over medium heat. Break the eggs into a mixing bowl and beat until they are smooth. Whisk in the cream until smooth, and then stir in the sugar and a tiny pinch of salt. Transfer the custard mixture to the top half of the double boiler and place it over the simmering water. Cook, stirring constantly, until the custard is thick enough to coat the back of the spoon. Remove it from the heat.

3. Spread the fruit over the crust and pour the custard over them. Bake in the center of the oven until the custard is set and the crust lightly browned, about 40 minutes. Serve warm or at room temperature.

Note: Aside from mangoes and peaches, raspberries are my favorite fruit to use for this recipe, but you can also use fresh blackberries, blueberries, or sliced strawberries.

    If you enjoy gilding lilies, you can, as many Germans do, pass a pitcher of cold heavy cream along with the kuchen, but Wayne would ask you what in the world you thought you were doing.

St. John's Golden Mango (or Peach) Chutney

Every November the Episcopal churchwomen of St. John's Church, Savannah, hold a pre-holiday bazaar to raise money for various charities and for maintenance of the historic Green-Meldrim house, built in 1851–1853, which is the church's parish house. One of the star attractions of these events is the sale of homemade baked goods, frozen foods, and preserves—especially the preserves.

The canning team, "Jane's Canners," spends the dog days of August over steaming kettles, making countless batches of chutneys, relishes, jellies, and pickles. Most of their effort goes into the chutneys, because it doesn't matter how much, or even what kind, they make, they're always a sellout.

This gorgeous chutney is the best of the lot, as golden in color as its name implies and of equally golden flavor. The ideal fruit to use for it is green mangoes, but underripe peaches or pears also work well.

MAKES 7 TO 7 1/2 PINTS

8–10 green mangoes (12 cups when diced) or about 2 dozen
 underripe peaches
3/4 cup chopped candied ginger
6 small red hot chile peppers, split, seeded, and chopped
4 large cloves garlic, peeled and minced
3 cups golden raisins
1 large onion, split, peeled, and chopped
2 tablespoons whole mustard seeds
1 tablespoon salt
3 cups cider vinegar
7 cups sugar

1. Peel the mangoes, cut the flesh from the seed, and then cut it into small dice until you have 12 cups (the exact number of mangoes you need will vary, depending on size). Mix in the ginger, hot peppers, garlic, raisins, onion, mustard seeds, and salt. Set aside.

2. Put the vinegar and sugar in a stainless or enamel-lined kettle that will comfortably hold all the ingredients, and stir until the sugar is dissolved. Place the kettle over medium-high heat, bring it to a boil, and let it boil for 5 minutes.

3. Add the mango mixture, stir it well, and bring it back to the boiling point. Reduce the heat to a steady simmer, and simmer until the fruit is just tender and the chutney is thick, about an hour. Don't overcook it or the mangoes will go mushy on you. Pack the chutney in sterilized jars, leaving ¼ inch of headroom in the jar. Discard any leftover juice. Seal with sterilized new lids and process the jars in a boiling water bath (see pages 9–11 for detailed canning instructions) for 10 minutes.

MELONS

An enduring cliché of Southern culture is the image of a thick wedge of watermelon, its bright red, green-edged grin punctuated with impossibly regular rows of black seeds. From hand-painted produce stand signs to elaborate porcelain dinnerware, it's an image that never seems to go away. This is due, in part, to the fact that we Southerners really do love melons of all kinds. The vines thrive in our hot, humid summers, providing plenty of cooling fruit to refresh spirits that have wilted in the very heat that made the melon vines thrive.

Southern recipes for melons are few, because no one needs a recipe for the best way to prepare and eat them: chill them in the creek, cut them into wedges, and dig in. However, occasionally melons do get dressed up for the table.

CANTALOUPE One of my most vivid memories of my grandmother's summer table is a pink Depression-glass bowl filled with orange wedges of chilled cantaloupe. It was a better table decoration than any flower you can name: it wasn't just pretty, we could eat it.

Choosing a ripe cantaloupe can be mysterious business for the uninitiated. Ripe ones are tan with blushes of yellow. Hard, green melons aren't ripe and were probably picked too green to have much flavor. The most important signal is aroma: the stem end should have a distinct melon fragrance. If it doesn't smell like ripe cantaloupe, it won't taste like it either. Press the stem scar gently with your thumb; it should yield slightly but not be mushy.

CANTALOUPE WITH COUNTRY HAM AND REDEYE GRAVY

An old favorite for breakfast (and sometimes supper) on many farms in the South is cantaloupe doused with milk or redeye gravy, and maybe served with ham or bacon, depending on what else there is on the table. Most people who weren't raised on it meet the idea with a wrinkle of the nose, yet they don't seem to have a problem pairing melon and prosciutto—which is exactly the same taste combination. Go figure.

Here, the contrast of the cool melon against the warm ham and gravy gives still another dimension to the salty-sweet flavor combination. It would be appropriate served for breakfast, brunch, or even as a first course at dinner.

SERVES 4

1 small ripe cantaloupe or honeydew melon
4 thin slices of raw country ham (about 8 ounces)
¼ cup flour, spread on a dinner plate
½ cup freshly brewed coffee or tea
½ cup water
Salt and black pepper in a peppermill
Sprigs of mint (optional), for garnish

1. Cut the melon in half lengthwise, scoop out the seeds, cut it into 8 even wedges, then peel each wedge. Arrange the melon, 2 wedges per serving, on individual plates and set them aside.

2. Trim some of the fat from the ham and put it into a skillet that will comfortably hold the ham in a single layer without crowding. Turn on the heat to medium and cook until the fat is rendered and the crackling is brown and crisp. Meanwhile, cut the ham into medallions about 2 inches across, slashing the membranes around the edges of the pieces to keep them from curling up when the ham is cooked. Lay the medallions on a flat work surface and lightly pound them with a mallet or the edge of a saucer.

3. When the fat is rendered, remove the browned cracklings. Roll the ham medallions in the flour, shake off the excess, and slip them into the pan. Cook for a minute, turn, and cook until they are just heated through and beginning to brown, about a minute longer. Take the ham up and divide it among the plates with the cantaloupe.

4. Raise the heat under the skillet to medium high. Pour the coffee or tea into the skillet and deglaze it, stirring and scraping to loosen any bits of cooking residue that may be stuck to the pan. Add the water and let it come to a boil. Cook rapidly until the gravy is reduced and lightly thickened, about 4 minutes. Turn off the heat. Taste the gravy and season with salt, if necessary, and a liberal grinding of black pepper. Pour the gravy directly over the melon and ham, garnish with the optional mint, and serve at once.

WATERMELONS   If there is anything more satisfying or cooling on a hot summer day than a thick wedge of chilled watermelon, I've never found it. It's a fixture at virtually any outdoor event in the South from late June well into September. The genteel eat it with a knife and a fork, but children happily bury their faces in it, and I'm not sure they don't have the best idea.

Occasionally, a host will cut a plug out of the melon and pump it full of rum, but don't count me as a fan; I think the harsh taste of alcohol does not do the clean, sweet flavor of this melon any favors.

A WATERMELON FRUIT BASKET

A classic at dressy summer receptions, the basket itself can be as simple or as elaborate as your inclinations and carving skills allow. Don't feel bound by the fruits that are given here, either, but do taste them in combination with the melon to make sure they don't fight with one another before you dump them in.

The handle of the basket is only decorative; don't try to pick the melon up with it or it will break, especially after it is filled with fruit.

SERVES 10 TO 12

1 large watermelon, about 18 pounds
1 large cantaloupe
1 large honeydew
1 pint (2 cups, or 12 ounces) blueberries
$^1/_2$ cup chopped fresh mint leaves
5–6 sprigs of mint, for garnish

1.   Wash the outside of the watermelon and pat it dry. With a long, sharp knife, make 2 parallel cuts halfway through the center of the melon on one side. This will create the "handle" of the basket. Now make a horizontal cut from each end of the melon to the center cuts. Lift off the 2 top pieces and set them aside for another use. Cut the red inner flesh from the handle part, being careful not to cut through the rind. If you like, you can decorate the basket by fluting the edges, by carving designs into the rind, anything that gets you excited.

2.   Using a melon baller, scoop out the red part of the melon, leaving at least $1/2$ inch of rind around the edges. Remove the seeds from the balls and put them in a separate bowl as you go. Strain the juice that remains in the melon basket through a sieve to catch the seeds, and pour it over the melon balls. Set aside.

3.   Split the other 2 melons lengthwise, scoop out and discard the seeds, and cut out the flesh with the melon baller. Put them in the bowl with the watermelon balls.

4.   Wash the blueberries and drain them well. Combine them with the melon balls and reserved juice. Add the chopped mint leaves and toss gently to mix. Pour the fruit back into the basket and chill until you are ready to serve it. (The basket can be made several hours or even a day ahead. Cover it well with plastic wrap.)

5.   When ready to serve, garnish the basket with the mint sprigs, set it on a tray (in case the basket springs a leak or tips over), and serve, providing a slotted spoon for dipping out the fruit.

Note: Some people add rum to the fruit. I don't care for it myself, but if it appeals to you, allow $1/2$ cup rum and mix it in when you add the mint leaves.

$\mathcal{W}$ATERMELON SALAD

Here, watermelon gives up its usual place at the table as a fruit and goes to work in a role that its cousin, the cucumber, usually occupies. The melon is a lovely foil for the salty feta, spicy onion, and tart vinegar. It makes a refreshing and unusual salad for any summer brunch, luncheon, or dinner.

SERVES 6

$^1/_2$ *small watermelon, about 5 pounds*
1 medium Vidalia or other sweet onion
$^1/_4$ *cup red wine vinegar*
Salt and black pepper in a peppermill
$^1/_2$ *cup extra virgin olive oil*
2 tablespoons chopped fresh mint
4 ounces feta cheese, crumbled
6 whole sprigs mint, for garnish

1. Cut the inner flesh from the melon and cut it into bite-sized pieces, removing and discarding the seeds as you go. Set aside. Peel and slice the onion into thin rings. Set aside.
2. Put the vinegar in a bowl and add a large pinch of salt, a few liberal grindings of pepper, and whisk until the salt is dissolved. Slowly whisk in the oil a few drops at a time. Stir in the chopped mint, taste and correct the seasonings, and set aside.
3. Combine the melon, onion, and feta in a bowl, pour the dressing over them, and toss gently until they are coated and evenly mixed. Garnish with the sprigs of mint or divide the salad among individual salad plates and garnish each serving. Serve at once.

PEACHES

The only place that I could go through a summer without eating a single peach is Bonaventure Cemetery—because I'd have to be dead as a doornail. Peaches are the very essence of a Southern summer, lending their spicy, floral perfume and tart, yet mellow flavor to countless buttery cobblers, soothing ice creams, potent, bourbon-laced conserves, and spicy chutneys. But the best way to eat them is still the simplest—right out of your hand.

Ironically, peaches—at least the variety that we know and cultivate—are not native to the South or even to North America. They are one of the many imports that European settlers introduced to Colonial America. They are thought to have originated in China, where they have been cultivated for at least ten thousand years. Their introduction to Europe is usually credited to the Persians, as suggested by their botanical name, *Prunus persica*. As that name also suggests, peaches are a part of the large botanical family of plums and are closely related not only to plums, but to apricots and cherries.

Perhaps even more ironic is the fact that Georgia, though officially known as the "Peach State," does not (and probably never has) led the country in peach production. We have long been outdistanced by California and South Carolina, but we Georgians don't care and continue to plaster pictures of peaches on everything from lottery tickets to license plates, and give the name "Peach State" to everything from fairs to our public-radio system.

GEORGIA PEACH SOUP

Fruit soups are not intended to be sweet. They are served, not as a dessert, but as a first course in much the same way as a fruit salad. This particular fruit soup is popular in Georgia hotel dining rooms and in restaurants that cater to visitors.

SERVES 8

> 6 medium, ripe yellow peaches (about 2 pounds)
> 1 lemon, cut in half
> 2 tablespoons unsalted butter
> 1/4 cup chopped shallot or yellow onion
> 2 cups Chicken Broth (page 23) or 1 cup canned broth mixed with 1
>   cup water
> 2 1/2 cups heavy cream (minimum 36 percent milkfat)
> Nutmeg in a grater
> 1 tablespoon bourbon
> 1 tablespoon chopped fresh mint

1. Put the peaches in a heatproof bowl or stockpot. Bring a large teakettle of water to a boil and pour it over the peaches. Let them stand in the hot water for 30 seconds and then drain the water off. Rinse the peaches in cold water. Peel them (the peels should now slip right off), cut them in half, and remove the pits, then cut them into thin wedges. Squeeze the lemon juice over them, then toss to coat them well. Set them aside.

2.   Put the butter and shallot or onion in a pan that will hold all the ingredients and place it over medium-high heat. Sauté, tossing frequently, until the onion is softened and transparent but not in the least colored, about 4 minutes. Add all but 1 cup of the peaches and stir until they are warmed. Add the broth and let it come to a boil. Reduce the heat to low and simmer until the peaches are tender, about 10 minutes. Turn off the heat.

3.   Puree the soup in a blender or food processor, and return it to the kettle. Cut the remaining peaches into small chunks and add them to the puree. Stir in 2 cups of the cream and season to taste with a few generous gratings of nutmeg. Stir until smooth. The soup can be made several days in advance up to this point. Let it cool uncovered, and then cover and refrigerate it until needed. If the soup is too thick (a result of the acid in the fruit reacting with the cream), thin it with a little milk but don't add more cream or broth. Serve cold or gently reheat it if desired.

4.   Just before serving, stir in the bourbon. Whip the remaining 1/2 cup cream until it forms soft peaks and use it to garnish each serving, adding a sprinkling of mint and freshly grated nutmeg over the top.

GEORGIA PEACH ICE CREAM

Rich, luscious, and tasting intensely of fresh peach, this ice cream is the essential ingredient of any church ice-cream social in the summer. It also makes the perfect ending to a summer barbecue, and it is the most graceful way I know to beat the heat of a Savannah summer.

MAKES ABOUT 1/2 GALLON,
OR 6 TO 8 SERVINGS

4–6 ripe, juicy peaches
2 teaspoons lemon juice
1/2 pound (1 cup) sugar
1 quart heavy cream (minimum 36 percent milkfat)
Salt
1 tablespoon bourbon or 2 teaspoons vanilla extract
1 recipe Blackberry (or Raspberry) Bourbon Sauce (page 186,
*   optional), or Amaretto, or a dozen amaretti cookies*

1.   Peel the peaches over a large bowl to catch their juices. Halve them, remove the pits, and chop them roughly, almost pureeing some of the peaches and roughly chopping the rest to give added texture to the ice cream. Sprinkle them with the lemon juice and ¼ cup of the sugar. Let them macerate for at least half an hour.

2.   Dissolve the remaining ¾ cup sugar in the cream, stirring carefully to make sure that no granules remain. Add a tiny pinch of salt and pour the cream over the prepared peaches. Stir well and thoroughly chill the cream in the refrigerator (about 2 hours, or you can make the cream a day ahead and let it chill overnight).

3.   Prepare an ice-cream freezer with ice and rock salt according to the manufacturer's directions. Pour the cream into the freezing cylinder and freeze, following the manufacturer's directions. The cream should be still creamy, not frozen hard .

4.   Pack the ice cream into a mold or deep container and put it in the freezer to completely solidify. When it has hardened, dip the mold in a basin of hot water (or wrap it with a towel that has been heated in the clothes dryer for a few minutes). Invert the mold over a serving plate and lift off the mold. If it won't come off, dip the mold again or rewarm the towel and wrap it for a minute or two more.

   If you like, serve the ice cream with the Blackberry (or Raspberry) Bourbon Sauce (page 186), or drizzle a tablespoon of Amaretto liqueur, or crumble up a couple of amaretti cookies over each serving.

PEACH AND BLUEBERRY COMPOTE

This recipe may not be old, but it's Southern to the bone. I developed it while in graduate school nearly—well, it's none of your business how long ago—taking advantage of three wonderful (and, most important to a tuition-poor student, free) local products: peaches, blueberries, and sourwood honey.

   Peaches and blueberries have a great affinity for one another, and, when well doused with a good sourwood honey, they take on a subtle, spicy flavor that is hard to describe, but not at all hard to eat. The only problem you'll have is making enough.

SERVES 6

6 medium, very ripe peaches, preferably freestones
1 tablespoon freshly squeezed lemon juice
2 cups (1 pint container, or 8 ounces) blueberries
1/2 cup (or to taste) honey, preferably sourwood (see note)

1. Wash the peaches and rub them well to remove all the fuzz. You don't actually need to peel them, but many object to the peels, so you can do so if you must. Halve them and remove the pits, then cut them lengthwise into thick wedges. Put them in a stainless or glass bowl that will hold all the ingredients, sprinkle with lemon juice to prevent them from discoloring, toss well, and set aside.

2. Rinse the blueberries well and pick through them to remove any stems and bad fruit. Add them to the peaches. Add the honey to taste, and toss until the fruit is well coated. Cover and set in the refrigerator to macerate for at least an hour. Serve cold—alone or with Cold Cream Sauce (page 60) or vanilla ice cream.

Note: *Sourwood honey is a specialty of the mountain regions of the South, particularly the Carolinas, Georgia, and Tennessee. Its distinctive flavor comes from bees having gathered pollen from the blossoms of sourwood trees. It is available mostly from local vendors and occasionally from specialty groceries. So, while the flavor of this honey is preferable, you can substitute any good honey.*

JESSICA HARRIS'S
PEACH FRITTERS

Fellow culinary historian and Southern food lover Dr. Jessica Harris is not actually a Southerner by birth. While she was born and raised in New York, her family roots go back to Virginia and, like most African Americans, her culinary roots are solidly grounded in the South. As she puts it, "We lived in New York, but we ate in the South."

Dr. Harris explains that African American cooking developed from centuries of improvisation, which continues even today. Her peach fritters are a prime example. When she came South to do a cooking demonstration at Macon's Georgia on My Plate festival, she wanted to use Georgia products. Her solution?—her grandmother's banana fritters, but using Georgia peaches instead of bananas.

The recipe is also exemplary of the "fritter factor" of the African diaspora. While deep-fat frying cannot, by any stretch of the imagination, be called African, fritters turn up wherever there are African cooks in the Americas—from Brazil to Nova Scotia.

SERVES 4 TO 6

4 ripe, but firm, freestone peaches (about 1 pound)
1/2 lemon
Peanut oil, for frying

FOR THE FRITTER BATTER:
2 large eggs, lightly beaten
1/2 cup cold milk
3 tablespoons light brown sugar
1 cup flour
Pinch baking soda
2–3 tablespoons confectioners' sugar

1. Peel the peaches, halve them, and cut them into thin wedges (don't make them too thick or they won't cook evenly). Put the wedges in a bowl and squeeze the lemon juice over them. Toss to distribute the juice evenly and set the peaches aside.

2. Put enough peanut oil in a deep skillet or deep fryer to come halfway up the sides (if you are using a skillet, it should be deep enough to hold an inch of fat and still be only half-full). Turn on the heat to medium high and heat the oil until it is around 375 degrees F. (A small spoonful of batter should sizzle happily, but not start browning right away.)

3. While the oil is heating, put the eggs, milk, and sugar in a large mixing bowl that will comfortably hold all the batter ingredients and give you room to slosh around. Lightly beat them until they are well mixed, then gradually beat in the flour until the batter is smooth. Finally, beat in the soda.

4. When the oil is hot, put the peach wedges in the batter a few at a time, lift them out with a fork or slotted spoon, and slip them into the oil. Fry until they are golden brown, about 3 minutes, turning them halfway through the cooking. Drain them on absorbent paper and transfer them to a serving dish. Put the confectioners' sugar in a wire sieve, dust it over the fritters, and serve hot.

Autumn

Sweet Potatoes, Nuts, and Crisp Mountain Apples

The line between summer and autumn in the South is never distinct; the autumnal equinox frequently comes and goes without a flicker on the heat index or a single leaf changing color and detaching itself. It stays warm and green right into October and sometimes into November. Our only clues that change is on the way are subtle ones: the trees begin to look heavy and tired; the light, though less direct, is brighter; the days begin to get shorter while, conversely, evening shadows get longer.

Even the local produce stands are slow to change; in most places, they are still sporting voluptuous, deep purple eggplants, glossy zucchini, bright peppers, and the reddest of tomatoes well into October. In fact, it isn't unusual to find fresh tomatoes right up to Thanksgiving. At home, we've sometimes had fresh tomatoes (picked from the freezing vines and stored in a cool room) at Christmas. It's often just sheer exhaustion, instead of the weather, that makes the plants stop bearing fruit.

Because of all this, autumn almost always takes us by surprise. One day, we realize with a start that summer is over. The lingering bright colors of its produce are gone, having given way to softer hues. Crisp, purple-topped turnips appear, bright orange pumpkins and winter squashes, dusky cabbages, collards, kale, and broccoli. Okra and tomatoes gradually dwindle and vanish, peaches and blueberries lose their place to apples and persimmons. And as the vegetables and fruits begin to whisper of cooler days to come, slowly, subtly, as if preparing us for the cold weather ahead, our palate begins to shift.

The cooking methods begin to change, too. Braising, roasting, gentle stewing, and slow baking, used less in the summer kitchen, dominate, replacing quicker, cooler methods. Dishes become richer, spicier, denser, and more complex. Even the produce that lingers from summer gets more complex treatment.

Autumn is the time of year when I am happiest in the kitchen. The abundance of produce can make summer cooking less monotonous, and the bright flavors certainly make cooking simpler, but the limited range of autumn produce makes that season's cooking more of a challenge. The summer kitchen is a bit like Carnival in Rio, an explosion of brilliant fruits and vegetables vibrating with intensity. The autumn palate is gentler, more like a subdued country fair, less excitable, perhaps, but with a sense of comfort that exuberant summer produce can't touch.

APPLES

In the Appalachian mountains that stretch across western Virginia and the Carolinas, northern Georgia and Alabama, and eastern Tennessee and Kentucky, the cool nights, abundant moisture, and warm, sunny days of August and early September lead to two of the greatest miracles of autumn: a brilliant red, orange, yellow, and rust display of turning leaves and the mellowest, sweetest apples in the world. As the first blush of color touches the tips of the dogwoods and sweet gums, apple stands begin to sprout along the scenic roadsides like mushrooms after a hard rain.

There are many varieties of apples sold, each coming to market at different times as they ripen. First are the familiar red and gold Delicious apples, then the Romes, Yorks, McIntoshes, and Winesaps. My own favorites are the Arkansas Blacks (so called because of their deep wine color), which are so hard that you can almost play baseball with them and still keep them over the winter. Unlike many varieties, they are both superb cooking and eating apples.

Naturally, some of the roadside vendors are scoundrels, selling Washington State apples and commercial cider to unsuspecting tourists, but plenty of good apples and real cider are there for the wily apple lover who knows where—and how—to look. Luckily for me, though I can't always go foraging on my own, I can count on having a good selection without leaving Savannah. Every October, like clockwork, a box of the season's best arrives on my doorstep, thanks to Betty and Carlisle Hoadley up in Walhalla, who were my surrogate parents while I was in graduate school. By the time it arrives, my mind has already started cooking with them.

$\mathcal{F}$RIED APPLES ✒

Fried apples used to be a common breakfast dish, and an indispensable accompaniment for that luxurious hog-killing–time breakfast of fresh pork tenderloins. They still make a fine showing for breakfast or brunch but can serve as a side dish for any pork, game, or poultry that does not already have a sweet sauce. Needless to say, they also make a good dessert.

In most of the traditional recipes, apple rings or wedges were fried in bacon drippings without any kind of breading, but this is how my grandmother used to do them.

In choosing apples for frying, look for tart, firm fruit such as my favored Arkansas Blacks, Winesaps, or Granny Smiths. There is a very brief period in the beginning of apple season when Red and Gold Delicious apples will work, but they must be very firm. If they don't have a crisp snap when you bite into them raw, they'll only turn to mush when cooked. Leave them for making applesauce.

SERVES 4

Lard, bacon drippings, clarified butter, or vegetable oil for frying
4 small, tart apples, or 2 if large
1/2 cup all-purpose flour
Confectioners' sugar in a shaker
Powdered cinnamon in a shaker
1 recipe Bourbon Custard Sauce (page 59), optional

1. Preheat the oven to 150 degrees F. Put enough lard, drippings, butter, or oil in a skillet to completely coat the bottom by about 1/4 inch.

2. Peel the apples, cutting out the stem and blossom ends of the fruit, and slice them crosswise into 1/4-inch rounds. Turn on the heat beneath the skillet to medium high. Spread the flour on a dinner plate and have it ready by the pan. When the fat is very hot, but not smoking (about 375 degrees F), roll the apple slices in the flour one at a time, shake off the excess, and slip them into the hot fat until the pan is full but not crowded. Fry until the bottoms are nicely browned, about 3 minutes, then turn them and fry until evenly brown, about 3 minutes more.

3. Drain the apples briefly on absorbent paper, then transfer them to a baking sheet lined with a rack and put them in the warm oven while you fry the rest of the apples.

4.   Dust the apples with confectioners' sugar and a sprinkling of cinnamon. If the apples are to be an accompaniment for meat, you can omit the sugar dusting. If you are serving the apples for dessert, film the bottoms of 4 dessert plates with the bourbon custard sauce, tipping and turning the plates until they are evenly coated. Arrange the fried apples on the plates and drizzle a little more custard sauce over them. Serve at once.

*A*PPLES AND HONEY
MUSHROOMS

Bill Neal was a gifted North Carolina chef who fathered the renaissance of traditional Southern cooking in restaurants. His Chapel Hill restaurant, Crook's Corner, set a standard of excellence for a new generation of Southern chefs. When he published *Bill Neal's Southern Cooking* in 1986, it became a classic and set a standard for Southern cookbook authors as well. This was a cook who could write circles around the best. Unfortunately, his untimely death in 1991 robbed the South of one of its greatest champions.

Bill Neal's cooking was always Southern to the bone, even when he used a seemingly unorthodox ingredient or technique, because it was so firmly rooted in Southern traditions and because he was never preoccupied with being clever or innovative (which was why his cooking usually seemed that way). This recipe illustrates that point. It takes advantage of two standard North Carolina ingredients—apples and local wild mushrooms—and pairs them in a way that seems fresh, new, and wholly unorthodox but is actually an adaptation of an old mountain recipe.

SERVES 4

*6 tablespoons bacon drippings, pan drippings from roast pork or poultry,
    or unsalted butter*
1½ cups (about 2 medium) thinly sliced yellow onions
4 large, green (underripe) cooking apples (Granny Smiths are fine)
1 large clove garlic, peeled and minced
¼ cup sugar
*1 cup (about 6 ounces) thinly sliced honey mushrooms or other wild
    mushrooms (see note)*
Salt

1.   Put 3 tablespoons of the fat in a lidded skillet or sauté pan that will comfortably hold all the ingredients. Turn on the heat to medium low. When the fat is melted, add the sliced onions and sauté until it is tender, shaking the pan from time to time.

2.   While the onions cook, peel, core, and thinly slice the apples. When the onions are tender, add the apples to the pan and toss until they are well mixed. Add the garlic and sprinkle the sugar evenly over the mixture. Shake the pan to distribute the garlic and sugar, cover it, and steam until the apples are tender. Give the pan a vigorous shake from time to time to prevent sticking.

3.   When the apples are tender, put the remaining 3 tablespoons of fat in a separate sauté pan and turn on the heat to high. When it is hot, add the mushrooms and sauté them quickly, shaking and tossing to prevent them from burning, until they are golden. Turn off the heat.

4.   Add the mushrooms to the apple-and-onion mixture, toss to mix, and raise the heat to medium high. Sauté, shaking the pan frequently, until the excess moisture is evaporated. Turn off the heat. Taste and adjust the seasoning with a pinch or two of salt (the amount of salt will depend on what kind of fat is used). Serve warm with roasted pork or poultry, or with sautéed pork chops.

Note: *Honey mushrooms* (Armillariella mellea), *so called because of their yellow-brown color, are indigenous to the eastern portion of the country. But unless you know what you are looking for, don't go foraging for them, since they resemble certain poisonous varieties. Common field mushrooms, morels, or* Boletus edulis *(porcini or cepes) can be substituted for honey mushrooms. Commercial champignons are a poor substitute, but cremini mushrooms (sometimes labeled "Italian Golden") and commercially cultivated "wild" mushrooms, such as shiitakes or morels, work well in this recipe.*

You can also substitute 1 ounce of dried porcini or cepes. Soak them in a cup of hot water for half an hour, lift them gently out of the soaking water, dipping them in it to rinse off any sand that may be stuck to them. Filter the soaking water through a paper towel or coffee filter. Put the reconstituted mushrooms, their filtered liquid, and 3 tablespoons of the fat in a sauté pan over high heat. Cook, stirring frequently to prevent scorching, until the liquid is evaporated and absorbed into the mushrooms (this concentrates their flavor), then proceed as directed in step 4.

BAKED APPLES WITH BOURBON AND PECANS ≪

There is nothing more old-fashioned and homey than baked apples—and also nothing better to warm up autumn's first cold night. No matter how sophisticated your company may be, they will meet this dish with murmurs of delight.

SERVES 4

4 medium, firm apples (such as Arkansas Blacks or McIntoshes)
1/2 cup raw pecans, roughly chopped
1/4 cup brown sugar
1/4 cup bourbon
2 tablespoons unsalted butter, plus more, for greasing
1 recipe Bourbon Custard Sauce (page 59)

1. Position a rack in the center of the oven and preheat the oven to 350 degrees F. Wash the apples and pat them dry. Cut out the stem ends with a paring knife and scoop out the cores with a melon baller, leaving the blossom ends intact. Lightly butter a 9-inch square baking dish or pie plate, and put in the apples, stem side up.

2. In a separate bowl, combine the pecans and sugar until they are evenly mixed. Pack this into the core cavities of the apples, mounding it up on top. Spoon the bourbon into the centers of the apples and top each one with 1/2 tablespoon of the butter.

3. Bake the apples in the center of the oven, basting occasionally with pan juices, until they are tender, about 45 minutes to an hour. Let the apples stand for a few minutes to dissipate some of the intense heat. Serve warm or at room temperature with a pitcher of bourbon custard sauce passed separately.

APPLE AND ONION BISQUE ≪

Though this is not an old, traditional soup, its flavors are very much so. The savory combination of apples, onions, and sage has long been enjoyed in the South.

All onions, not just Vidalias and their sweet cousins, have a great deal of natural sweetness that is often overshadowed by their peppery bite. Because of this, they may seem unlikely companions for apples, but in fact they make a perfect foil for each other. The sweet-savory flavor that results is difficult to describe but is understood when tasted.

SERVES 6

2 medium yellow onions
2 tablespoons unsalted butter
2 medium tart, firm apples, such as Granny Smiths
3 cups rich chicken broth
1 teaspoon dried sage
White peppercorns in a peppermill
1 pint half-and-half
Salt
6 fresh sage leaves (optional)
6 tablespoons heavy cream

1. Have all the rest of the ingredients handy so the apples will not have a chance to turn brown once they are peeled. Peel the onions and slice them crosswise into thin rings. Put the onions and butter in a kettle that will comfortably hold all the ingredients and place it over medium heat. Sauté until the onions have wilted and are a pale gold, but don't let them scorch, about 10 minutes.

2. Meanwhile, wash, peel, and core the apples, and cut them into thin slices or chunks (whichever is easiest for you). When the onions are colored and softened, add the apples and continue cooking until the apples also begin to color. Add the broth and raise the heat to medium high. Bring the soup to a boil, then reduce the heat to a simmer, add the dried sage and a liberal grinding of white pepper. Don't add salt yet. Loosely cover and simmer until the onions and apples are tender, about 20 minutes.

3. Puree the soup in batches in a blender or food processor. Put it back in the kettle and stir in the half-and-half. Taste and correct the seasonings.

4. If you are using them, slice the fresh sage leaves crosswise. Ladle out the soup into individual soup plates, pour a tablespoon of heavy cream into the center of each, garnish with the sliced sage leaves, and serve at once.

Note: To make a meatless version, add the sliced white part of a leek and substitute Vegetable Broth (page 24) for the chicken broth. For strict vegetarians, sauté the apple and onion in peanut oil and substitute the vegetable broth for both the chicken broth and the half-and-half. Omit the cream and garnish the soup with chopped apple and sliced green onions.

Apple, Pecan, and Clemson Blue Cheese Salad

For decades, the agriculture department of South Carolina's Clemson University has produced an admirable blue cheese, which was originally aged in nearby abandoned Confederate railway tunnels. It used to be hard to come by, as supply always fell far short of demand, but when we could get it, Mama would enliven our winter salads by mixing tart apples, a handful of pecans, and a crumbling of this creamy, sharp cheese with the late fall lettuce from the garden. It became a traditional fall salad in our family.

Though Clemson blue cheese is now marketed nationally, and is available through a few mail-order catalogs, its availability is sometimes still spotty. Gorgonzola, Roquefort, or Danish blue all make acceptable substitutes.

SERVES 4

4 scallions or other green onions
1 small head romaine or large head Boston lettuce
1 tart, firm apple, such as Granny Smith or Arkansas Black
4 ounces Clemson or other blue cheese (see headnote), crumbled
¹/₂ cup whole Toasted Pecans (page 219)
2 tablespoons chopped parsley, or 1 tablespoon parsley and 1
*   tablespoon fresh sage or winter savory, chopped*
Extra virgin olive oil
Salt and black pepper in a peppermill
Cider vinegar

1. Wash the green onions and trim the roots and discolored leaves. Thinly slice the onions and set aside. Wash the lettuce, dry it, and break it into bite-sized pieces. Peel, core, and cut the apple into small dice.

2. Combine the onions, lettuce, apple, crumbled cheese, pecans, and chopped herbs in a salad bowl, and toss to mix. Add a pinch of salt and generously sprinkle the salad with olive oil. Toss the salad until the greens are glossy and taste it to see if more oil and salt are needed—it should taste distinctly of the oil, but not be overpowering or greasy. Lightly sprinkle on a little cider vinegar, toss until it is mixed in, and taste to see if it is tart enough to suit you. Don't overdo the vinegar. Sprinkle on a few liberal grindings of pepper and toss until mixed. Divide the salad between individual salad plates or bowls and serve at once.

BRUSSELS SPROUTS

Brussels sprouts *(Brassica oleracea gemmifera)* are of course a relative of cabbage. But unlike their larger cousins, which form heads at the top of their stalks quite close to the ground, sprouts form in clusters on the sides of a tall, slender plant. Legend has it that they have been grown in Belgium since time immemorial, even though they aren't mentioned in botanical records until the nineteenth century. Sprouts are relatively new in Southern kitchens but have become very popular here as a staple green vegetable throughout the cold months of autumn and winter.

This is one of the vegetables with which I prefer steaming above any other cooking method. Even when I sauté sprouts, they get a brief steambath first. A quick blanching in boiling water, while it may be suitable and even preferable for other vegetables, seems to take something away from Brussels sprouts. One of the simplest and tastiest ways of preparing sprouts is to steam them until they are just tender—even large ones are done in under 10 minutes if they are split in half before being cooked. Sauce them lightly with a little unsalted butter or, for a really sumptuous dinner, serve them with Hollandaise Sauce (page 52), Sauce Creole (page 124), or any of the drawn butter sauces on pages 51–52.

ℬRUSSELS SPROUTS
WITH PECANS

Brussels sprouts paired with chestnuts are a timeless classic. Here, the idea develops a Southern accent by combining the sprouts with that most Southern of nuts—pecans—which makes for an equally felicitous marriage.

SERVES 4

2¹/₂ dozen small Brussels sprouts (about 1 pound)
Salt
5 tablespoons unsalted butter
¹/₂ cup pecans

1.   Fill a basin with cold water. Trim the sprouts at the cut, rinse them well, and drop them into the basin of water. Let them soak for at least 30 minutes.
2.   Put an inch of water in a large pot (or the bottom of a double-boiler–type steamer), fit it with a vegetable steamer basket, cover the pot, and turn on the heat to high. Bring the

water to a rolling boil. Drain the sprouts and put them in the steamer basket. Sprinkle them with a liberal pinch or so of salt, cover the pot, and reduce the heat to medium. Steam until the sprouts are tender but still bright green, about 12 to 15 minutes.

3. Turn off the heat, remove the Brussels sprouts, and refresh them under cold running water to arrest the cooking. Drain well and set them aside.

4. Put the butter in a skillet that will hold all the sprouts in one layer and turn on the heat to medium high. When the butter is melted, add the pecans and sauté, tossing frequently, until the pecans begin to color, about 3 to 4 minutes. Add the Brussels sprouts and continue sautéing, tossing constantly, until the sprouts are heated through and well coated with the butter. Turn off the heat. Taste for salt and adjust it accordingly. Pour the sprouts into a warm serving dish and serve at once.

Note: *There is no substitute for the butter in this dish, since no other fat will react with the pecans and give the sprouts a lovely glaze.*

You can precook the sprouts several hours ahead up through step 3, but don't try to finish the dish completely and reheat it later, as the pecans will lose their crispness and get flabby. When the sprouts have steamed, drop them into a bath of ice water to arrest the cooking, drain them well, and keep them covered until you are ready to finish them up.

MUSHROOMS

Developments in the domestic cultivation of mushrooms over the last few decades have changed the face of American restaurant menus and created one of the most delicious of oxymorons in our modern culinary lexicography—the "cultivated wild" mushroom. Well, naturally any mushroom that is cultivated is no longer wild in any sense of the word. Indeed, the most commonplace, shiitake, had been cultivated in Japan for so long that it was as domesticated as button mushrooms when it was introduced to America. Yet "wild" does give a menu description a bit of cachet and daring.

Actually, mushroom agriculture in the West is a relatively recent development. Most of the fresh mushrooms available to early American markets were truly wild, though the most common—ordinary field mushrooms *(Agaricus campestris)*—are closely related to the cultivated variety. Field mushrooms are easily identified and are the least likely to be confused with poisonous fungi.

Except for Japanese enoki and shiitake, most cultivated mushrooms in America are still of the Agaricus family, but oyster mushrooms, chanterelles, and a few others have also been successfully cultivated.

Mushrooms are available in most supermarkets, but take the trouble to look for them in natural-food or specialty groceries that sell mushrooms in bulk; these vendors often buy from local growers, so the mushrooms are naturally fresher. Avoid any that have moist, dark spots. If you must buy plastic-wrapped mushrooms, remove the plastic as soon as you get them home and, if you don't plan to cook them right away, cover the package with a dry paper towel and refrigerate it promptly. In any case, use the mushrooms as soon as possible.

Here are some notes on the most readily available mushrooms:

COMMON WHITE MUSHROOMS OR CHAMPIGNONS: The pearly white color of these mushrooms is owed in part to their cultivation in caves, cellars, or special "mushroom houses." They are closely related to common field mushrooms. The caps should be firm, creamy white, and dry.

CREMINI OR CRIMINI: also marketed as "Italian golden" or "brown" mushrooms. Because their flavor is more distinctive than that of white mushrooms, they are preferable when you can find them. Try to buy them in bulk and look for tight, firm, dry caps.

PORTOBELLO OR PORTABELLA: Resembling overgrown cremini mushrooms in color and flavor, portobellos are never sold in their button stage, and their broad caps range from 4 to 6 inches across. They are often sold as "griller mushrooms," but don't confuse them with the creamy-white griller mushrooms, which are really just large champignons.

OYSTER MUSHROOMS: A tree-growing fungus, cultivated oyster mushrooms are usually a soft grayish brown. They are the most delicate of the many cultivated varieties, which also means they are the most perishable. Unless they are very fresh, their texture will be mushy and their flavor practically nonexistent. If they're wilted and damp-looking, don't waste your money.

SHIITAKE: Native to Asia, shiitake (also called Chinese and Black Forest mushrooms) are so called in Japan because they are found in the wild growing on *shii* trees. Possibly the most common "wild" mushroom used in restaurant kitchens, they are widely cultivated.

MORELS: Until very recently, these mushrooms defied all efforts to cultivate them. Consequently those that were available in the market were all gathered in the wild during the spring, their natural growing season, and were wildly expensive. Larry Lonick, founder and president of Mr. Mushroom, a mushroom farm and packing company in the Carolina Lowcountry, has been successfully cultivating morels year round, and dried morels are becoming more widely available. Fresh morels must be cooked before you can eat them.

TRUE WILD MUSHROOMS: All along the eastern seaboard there are a number of highly prized indigenous mushrooms—the *Boletus edulis*, called porcini in Italian and cepes in French, chanterelles, morels, chicken mushrooms, common field mushrooms, and puffballs. But don't go foraging for them unless you are thoroughly familiar with both the edible and poisonous types and know exactly what you are looking at. Take an experienced gatherer with you or stick to cultivated mushrooms.

GRILLED MUSHROOMS WITH BOURBON HERB BUTTER

Grilling large mushrooms concentrates and enhances the earthy flavor of the wild ones and gives cultivated varieties such as portobellos a depth of flavor that they don't possess on their own. Here, they get an additional lift by bathing them with a sage and bourbon-scented herb butter.

The herb butter is also fine for other grilled vegetables that are compatible with sage—such as sweet potatoes or squash—and has a particular affinity for grilled pork (especially tenderloin), lamb, chicken, and virtually any game bird.

SERVES 4

¹/₄ pound unsalted butter, softened
1 tablespoon chopped fresh sage (do not use dried sage)
1 tablespoon chopped fresh parsley
1 medium shallot, peeled and finely minced
1 tablespoon bourbon
Salt and whole white peppercorns in a peppermill
4 large portobello, shiitake, or porcini mushrooms (about 2 pounds)

1. Knead together the butter, herbs, shallot, and bourbon. Season to taste with a healthy pinch of salt and a few liberal grindings of white pepper, and knead until the seasonings are well blended. Roll the butter into a log. This is easiest done by rinsing your hands with cold water, then gently rolling the butter on a flat surface covered with wax paper. (If the butter has gotten too soft, let it sit in the refrigerator until it is firm enough to handle.) Fold the wax paper around the butter and refrigerate it until firm.

2. Prepare a charcoal grill with coals (preferably hardwood) and light it. When the coals have burned down, carefully wipe the mushrooms with a dry cloth or paper towel to remove any dirt that may be clinging to them, and trim the stems so that the mushrooms will lie flat when turned stem-side down. (If you are using shiitakes, cut the stems off altogether and discard them.)

3. When the coals are ready, spread them and position the grill rack about 3 inches above the heat. Put on the mushrooms, stems down, and grill until they are hot and beginning to color around the edges of the gills, about 5 minutes. Meanwhile, cut the herb butter into tablespoon-sized slices. Rub the tops of the caps with a piece of the herb butter and turn them over. Put a tablespoon-sized slice of the herb butter into the center of each mushroom and continue grilling until the mushrooms are just cooked through and the caps are beginning to color, about 3 to 5 minutes more. Smear a serving platter with 2 tablespoons of the herb butter. Put the mushrooms on the platter, stems up. Sprinkle them lightly with a little salt, dot with a little more of the herb butter, and serve at once, passing more salt and pepper separately.

Note: *The whole point of the herb butter is the flavor of fresh herbs, so don't use dried sage for this recipe. If fresh sage is unavailable, substitute another fresh herb that is compatible with mushrooms, such as thyme, savory, or basil. And while we're on the don'ts, don't be tempted to add more bourbon to the butter. Too much whiskey will impart a raw, harsh alcohol aftertaste.*

WILD MUSHROOMS
IN CREAM

When the mushrooms are impeccably fresh, there is nothing to equal this sumptuous dish, and no other way of doing them is more useful. Over toast points or puff pastry, they make the most elegant first course imaginable. When ladled over broiled fish or roasted poultry or an omelet, they turn a plain main course into a gastronomical event. They are also exceptional on egg pastas, such as fettuccine, or short, sturdy factory pasta like rotelle or rigati.

And they are absolutely stellar all by themselves.

SERVES 4

1 pound small shiitake, cremini, or other mushrooms
4 tablespoons unsalted butter
Salt and whole white peppercorns in a peppermill
1 cup heavy cream (minimum 36 percent milkfat)

1. Gently brush the dirt from the mushrooms and trim the stems (cut off all the stems from shiitakes; they're too tough to eat). Cut the larger mushrooms into halves or quarters, but leave the rest whole.

2. Put the butter in a large sauté pan that will hold all the mushrooms and turn on the heat to medium high. Add the mushrooms and sauté, tossing them frequently, until they are beginning to color. Add a healthy pinch of salt and a grinding or two of white pepper, and pour in the cream. Toss until the mushrooms are coated and cook, again tossing frequently, until the cream is beginning to thicken (it becomes even thicker after coming off the heat, so don't let it get too thick). Turn off the heat, pour into a warm serving dish, and serve hot.

$\mathcal{C}$REAM OF MUSHROOM SOUP

One of my first insane acts as a cook occurred while I was in graduate school in Genoa: I decided to cook a five-course dinner for my fellow students, our cook, Ilda, and the rest of the school staff—some thirty-odd people. Somehow (and how, I don't know) it all came together and the meal was a success. This soup led the way, and Ilda asked for the recipe, even though it was she who had made it a success by coaching me to use dried mushrooms.

The original was thickened with flour, but over the years the pasty quality that flour thickening often lends to food began to bother me, and I learned to use purees and real cream instead.

SERVES 6

1 ounce dried porcini mushrooms
1 cup boiling water
12 ounces (³/₄ pound) cremini (brown or golden) mushrooms
¹/₄ cup minced shallot or yellow onion
3 tablespoons unsalted butter
2 cups Chicken Broth (page 23)
Salt and whole white peppercorns in a peppermill
2 cups heavy cream (minimum 36 percent milkfat)
3 tablespoons chopped fresh chives or parsley

1. Put the dried mushrooms in a heat-proof bowl and cover them with the boiling water. Let them soak for 30 minutes. Meanwhile, wipe the dirt from the fresh mushrooms and cut off the stems. Thinly slice the caps and roughly chop the stems. Set them aside separately.

2. Put the shallot or onion and butter in a 3-quart soup kettle, and turn on the heat to medium. Sauté until the shallot is softened, about 8 to 10 minutes.

3. Meanwhile, lift the dried mushrooms out of their soaking water, dipping them several times to remove any sand that may be stuck to them. Strain the soaking water through a paper towel or coffee filter, and set it aside. Roughly chop the dried mushrooms and add them to the kettle along with the chopped mushroom stems. Stir until the stems wilt, about 4 minutes, then add the reserved soaking water, chicken broth, a large pinch of salt, a few grindings of white pepper, and bring to a boil. Reduce the heat to low and simmer until the vegetables are tender, about 20 minutes. Turn off the heat.

4. Puree the mixture in a blender or in batches in the food processor. Return it to the kettle, add the cream, and turn on the heat to medium. Bring the soup back to a simmer, add the sliced mushroom caps, and simmer until they are tender and the cream is lightly thickened, about 10 minutes more. Taste and correct the seasonings, and ladle the soup into a heated tureen or soup plates. Garnish with the chopped chives or parsley and serve at once.

Note: *For a meatless soup, substitute Vegetable Broth (page 24) for the chicken broth. However, there is no substitute for the cream. The character of the soup depends on the silkiness of mushrooms and cream in combination. If you must avoid dairy products, you can make a respectable clear soup using all broth. Just omit the puree step and garnish the soup with the chives, parsley, and a few croutons (page 43) toasted in oil instead of butter.*

Mushrooms Stuffed with Country Ham ⤺

Stuffed mushrooms are so popular at Savannah parties that I've always wished that I could be more enthusiastic about them. Yet the first bite usually leaves me feeling vaguely disappointed. The mushrooms seldom have any real flavor and the filling, inevitably, has too much. The problem is that the cook is using the wrong mushroom and a filling that fights with it. All the same, I didn't think there was anything wrong with the basic idea, so I went to work looking for a stuffing that was flavorful on its own without dominating the mushrooms. And here it is, enlivened with a touch of garlic and a splash of bourbon.

SERVES 4

¹/₂ ounce dried porcini mushrooms
¹/₂ cup boiling water
4 large portobello or shiitake, or 1 dozen small shiitake or large cremini
*   mushrooms (see note)*
5 tablespoons unsalted butter
2 large cloves garlic, crushed, peeled, and minced
¹/₄ cup (about 1 ounce) minced country ham or prosciutto
2 tablespoons chopped parsley
¹/₂ cup dry bread crumbs
Salt and black pepper in a peppermill
3 tablespoons bourbon

1.   Put the dried mushrooms in a heatproof bowl and pour the boiling water over them. Set them aside to soak for at least 30 minutes.

2.   Position a rack in the upper third of the oven and preheat the oven to 375 degrees F. Brush away any dirt or moss that may be clinging to the mushrooms with a clean, dry cloth or mushroom brush. Remove the stems from the caps and chop the stems fine (if you are using shiitake and the stems are tough, discard them and chop a couple of extra caps for the stuffing—see note). Set both stems and caps aside.

3.   Lift the reconstituted dried mushrooms out of their soaking water, dipping them to remove any sand that may be clinging to them, and put them in a sauté pan that will hold all the chopped stems comfortably. Strain their soaking liquid through a coffee filter or paper towel and add it to the pan. Turn on the heat to medium high, bring the liquid to a

boil, and cook, stirring frequently, until all the liquid is absorbed and evaporated. Turn off the heat. Remove the mushrooms from the pan, chop them fine, and set them aside.

4. Add 3 tablespoons of the butter and stir until it is melted. Add garlic and sauté, tossing frequently, until the garlic is fragrant and golden. Add the chopped stems and sauté until they are wilted and their moisture is mostly evaporated. Add the ham and parsley, stir well, and turn off the heat.

5. Add the crumbs to the stem mixture, toss until well mixed, and season well with a pinch of salt (go easy on this if the ham is especially salty) and a few grindings of black pepper. Toss to blend the seasonings.

6. Lightly butter a baking dish that will hold all the mushrooms and put the caps into it, stem side up. Sprinkle them lightly with a little salt, and divide the stuffing mixture among them, mounding it up in the center. Sprinkle the bourbon over the mushrooms, dot them with the remaining 2 tablespoons of butter, and bake until the filling is lightly browned on top and the mushroom caps are tender, about 20 minutes (shiitake often take less time; start checking them after 10 minutes). Serve at once; stuffed mushrooms don't reheat very well.

Note: *If you are using shiitake, check the stems in the market to see if they are tough, as they often are, especially on the larger, more mature mushrooms. If they are tough, buy one or two extra large mushrooms or half a dozen small ones to substitute for the chopped stems in the stuffing mixture.*

Don't use white champignon mushrooms for this recipe, even the ones sold as "stuffers"—their flavor is too mild and dull to stand up to the stuffing.

If you want to serve the mushrooms as a cocktail party pickup food, the recipe doubles beautifully. However, if you double it, only increase the butter by half.

PECANS

Pecans *(Carya olivaeformis)* are native nuts, indigenous to the South. They are actually a variety of hickory (the Latin name means olive-shaped hickory). They were well known to many Native Americans, who relished them and even used their extracted oil as a seasoning. This fondness was passed on to the early European settlers, and wild pecans were used in the South as an inexpensive substitute for walnuts and imported almonds. During this century, pecans have been widely cultivated as a commercial crop in the Deep South.

Shady pecan groves dot Georgia, Alabama, Mississippi, and Louisiana. In these areas, where the nuts are cheap and plentiful, were born some of the South's most famous confections—pecan pie, Creole pralines, and butter pecan ice cream, to name a few. Unfortunately, the trees cannot survive a really severe winter, so their growing area is limited, and outside it pecans can be an expensive luxury.

Not so in my family. I grew up in borrowed houses. My father was (and is) a minister, and those were the days when churches still provided a residence for their pastor. We were lucky—those pastoriums were all wonderful old houses with lots of character and, best of all, a humongous pecan tree in the backyard (one of them had six!). So for our family, pecans weren't a luxury—they were free. Then my father retired and bought his first house. The place has many assets. It is peacefully secluded on an old farm road; from the back porch and kitchen there is a spectacular view of the Blue Ridge Mountains; the garden spot is ideal. But for the first time in my living memory there is no pecan tree in the yard.

We still don't know what Daddy was thinking.

$\mathcal{T}$OASTED PECANS

When it came to entertaining at our house, toasted pecans were pretty much taken for granted. We ate and served them in prodigal quantities, and I was grown before I knew that many people considered them a luxury. I've never tired of them. To this day, they're my favorite snack food, and the one sure given when company comes to my house.

A pound of toasted nuts will serve 4 to 6 people through about two rounds of drinks. If you are serving other things along with them, allow 1 pound of nuts for 8 people. The quantity in this recipe is only a pound, but you can actually toast up to 4 pounds at one time. Choose a large, deep-rimmed pan that will hold the nuts in no more than two layers. A 9 × 14-inch sheet-cake pan is perfect for up to 2 pounds of nuts. For larger quantities, a large roasting pan or two pans side by side will do.

MAKES 1 POUND

> *1 pound whole pecan halves (or other nuts; see note)*
> *2 tablespoons unsalted butter (no substitutes)*
> *Salt*

1.   Position a rack in the center of the oven, and preheat the oven to 275 degrees F. Spread the pecans on a wide, deep-rimmed pan. Roast them in the center of the oven, stirring occasionally until they begin to color, about 45 minutes to an hour. The nuts will continue to darken and crisp as they cool, so don't let them get too dark.

2.   Cut the butter in bits, and add it to the pecans. Stir until it has just melted and the nuts are evenly coated. Return them to the oven and toast for about 10 minutes more.

3.   Salt the pecans to taste while they are still hot and toss them until they are uniformly coated. Usually, the pecans are allowed to cool completely before serving, but in the winter, I serve them still toasty-warm from the oven. To store them (assuming you have very strange company and actually have leftovers), make sure the pecans are completely cool and place them in a tightly sealed container, such as a glass jar, a plastic storage bowl, or a tin box.

Note: *You can follow this recipe to toast almost any nut—almonds, cashews, filberts, and walnuts all work well. The cooking time is the same for all of them.*

Curried Pecans: Curry spices are a popular seasoning for toasted pecans in the South, especially during the holiday season. Allow 1 tablespoon of Curry Powder (page 31) for a pound of pecans. Add it with the butter in step 2, before the final toasting, which will help the curry flavor develop. Serve warm.

PECAN PIE

Most versions of this famous Southern pastry are corn-syrup–based custards. I like them fine, but corn syrup is intensely sweet, and there is something cloying about those syrup-based pies. For years I have looked for a pecan pie without that drawback, but which still had the satisfying balance of flavors that had made it a classic. Unfortunately, I met with little success.

Then, on what was probably the saddest day of my life, I discovered such a pie. We had just laid my sweet grandmother to rest beside my grandfather and watched as the dirt was piled onto the end of an era. The family retired to the homeplace over in Hartwell, beautifully refurbished by Ma Ma's cousin Dorothy Marrett, a soothing place to heal our wounds, surrounded by lovely memories, and by Aunt Fanny Lou's fragrant old rose bushes. And there, in the midst of it all, was the best pecan pie I had ever tasted, courtesy of my cousin Tillie Bannister.

As is typical of the best cooks when they are confronted wi\
Tillie was mildly surprised and even a little embarrassed by my ent\
was just a plain old thing, nothing fancy, which was of course why it\
anced. Luckily, Tillie was not so embarrassed that she wouldn't share t\

MAKES TWO 9-INCH PIES

1 recipe Basic Pastry (page 47)
¹/₄ pound (1 stick or ¹/₂ cup) unsalted butter
6 eggs
3 cups (tightly packed) brown sugar
¹/₂ teaspoon salt
2 cups pecans, roughly chopped

1. Roll out the pastry to a thickness of about ¹/₈ inch and line two 9-inch pie plates with it. Prick it well, flute or decorate the edges, and chill the pastry for 30 minutes to allow it to relax.

2. Position a rack in the center of the oven and preheat the oven to 425 degrees F. Put the butter in a saucepan and melt it over low heat. Turn off the heat and let it cool. Meanwhile, break the eggs into a mixing bowl and beat them until smooth. Add the sugar and stir until it is dissolved. Stir in the butter and salt, and mix until smooth (don't beat the mixture). Stir in the pecans and then pour the filling into the prepared pastry.

3. Put the pies on the center rack of the oven. Bake for 10 minutes and immediately reduce the heat to 325 degrees. Bake until the custard is set and the top of the pies is nicely browned, about 45 minutes.

𝒲ILTED SALAD

When the weather finally begins to cool across the Deep South, the late crop of lettuce, which withered in the blistering summer heat, revives and flourishes again. But since cooler weather has also stimulated heartier appetites, autumn is the season when one of our best-loved dishes of greens—a wilted salad—is especially popular.

Wilted salads are traditionally made by pouring sizzling red-eye gravy over the greens, or by wilting the greens in a pan with rendered fat and vinegar. Here is a modern version in which the traditional idea remains intact, but the wilting hot fat is a fruity extra virgin olive oil. The taste is very different, but still satisfyingly familiar.

Choose tender, leafy salad greens—bibb, Boston, or red-tipped leaf lettuces. Romaine [is] ather too sturdy for this salad, and iceberg lettuce is too watery and loses what little fla- [vor] it had when heated.

SERVES 4

½ pound leaf lettuce (see headnote)
4 green onions
¼ cup fresh herb leaves, such as basil, oregano, tarragon, or mint (torn
into small pieces if large)
⅓ cup extra virgin olive oil
⅓ cup red wine or cider vinegar
Salt and black pepper in a peppermill
1 recipe Corn Sticks (page 40)

1. Wash the lettuce carefully and thoroughly dry it. Put it in a heat-proof or wooden salad bowl. Trim the roots and yellowed leaves from the green onions and thinly slice them. Add them along with the herbs to the greens, and toss to mix. Set aside.

2. Put the oil and vinegar in a pan, and bring them to a boil. Season with a liberal pinch of salt, a few grindings of black pepper, and turn off the heat.

3. Pour the hot dressing over the salad and toss rapidly until the greens are well coated and beginning to wilt. Taste and correct the seasonings, toss again to mix, and serve at once with hot corn sticks.

SWEET POTATOES VS. POTATOES VS. YAMS

Now, here's a real mess—a history of confused interrelations that is more convoluted than that of any first family of Virginia. First, we have sweet potatoes, *Ipomoea batatas*—the root of a tropical vine in the morning-glory family. Apparently native to Central America, it spread to South America, the Caribbean, and probably Asia. This vegetable was "discovered" by the Spanish and introduced to continental Europe early in the sixteenth century. Eventually, the name *batatas* was corrupted to "potatoes"—they were sometimes even referred to as "Spanish potatoes"—and were certainly the first tuber to be called a "potato."

Fine, that's simple enough. But then the Spanish ran across South American *pappus (Solanum tuberosum)*, a tuber in the nightshade family that is not even remotely related to *Ipomoea batatas*. They introduced this vegetable to Europe sometime later in the sixteenth century, at which point the words *pappus* and *batatas* somehow got hopelessly mashed together and both vegetables came to be known as "potatoes."

Enter the African slave trade and the plot thickens. Africans and those Europeans who were trading with Africa knew another edible tuber—yams, of the family *Dioscoreaceae*, which is probably native to tropical Asia—but never mind. Now, yams and sweet potatoes are not remotely related to one another, but both the early *batatas* (not as orange nor as sweet as modern hybrids) and yams had a not dissimilar color and texture. Africans began calling sweet potatoes "yams" and, unfortunately, the name stuck. By the late 1930s it was so commonplace that a hybrid deep orange sweet potato introduced in Louisiana was officially called a "yam." Add to that Margaret Mitchell's constant references to "yams" in her novel *Gone with the Wind*, which for some reason is constantly being referenced as history, throw in the sweet potato's reputation for "procuring bodily lust," stir in the fact that real yams were introduced to the Caribbean in the seventeenth century—and are still sold in West Indian markets—and you have a story so steamy, confused, and convoluted that it would make even a romance novelist's head spin.

In any case, the sweet potatoes that nearly everyone expects on the Thanksgiving table, the ones that we Southerners continue—stubbornly—to call yams, are all hybrids of those ancient *batatas*. Sweet potatoes are not nearly as starchy as true yams, and their flavor is much sweeter. Their skin is very smooth and their color, a deep hue of the inner flesh, ranges from yellow to deep orange (almost red), and they weigh from 8 to 10 ounces each. Real yams have a rough skin, a mildly sweet, starchy pale-yellow to white flesh, and can weigh up to 5 pounds. In other words, the two vegetables are not at all alike.

In Florida, *boniatos*, a variety of sweet potato that is close to the older types, is being grown. Available in Latino markets and specialty groceries in many parts of the country, *boniatos* can be used in any of these recipes, as can any variety of Southern orange sweet potatoes, even the ones called "yams." Avoid real yams—and I'll try to avoid the Southern habit of calling sweet potatoes by that name—aren't you glad?

Sweet Potato and Leek Soup ✒

The simple substitution of sweet potatoes turns this reliable old workhorse of the French kitchen into something at once both refreshingly new and yet comfortingly familiar. While I am reluctant to call a recipe "Southern" just because it contains a "Southern" ingredient, this one does have a distinct drawl.

SERVES 6

2 pounds sweet potatoes
3 large leeks
1 medium yellow onion, peeled and chopped
2 tablespoons unsalted butter
2 cups Chicken Broth (page 23) or 1 cup canned chicken broth mixed
 with 1 cup water
1 Bouquet Garni (page 36), made with 1 sprig each parsley, sage, and
 thyme, and 1 bay leaf
Salt and whole white peppercorns in a peppermill
1 cup light cream or half-and-half
1 tablespoon chopped fresh sage or parsley

1. Scrub the potatoes well, peel them with a vegetable peeler, and cut them into small dice. Split the leeks and wash them under cold running water until all dirt and grit have been removed. Trim off the roots and any tough or discolored leaves. Separate the green tops from the white parts of the leeks and set aside. Slice the white parts thinly.
2. Put the sliced leeks, onion, and butter in a kettle that will comfortably hold all the ingredients, and place it over medium heat. Sauté until the vegetables are softened but not browned, about 5 minutes. Add the potatoes and toss until they are warm. Add the broth, the bouquet garni, a healthy pinch of salt, and a liberal grinding of pepper. Raise the heat to medium high and bring the soup to a boil, then reduce the heat to low and simmer until the potatoes are tender, about 12 minutes. Turn off the heat.
3. Take up and set aside 1 cup of the potatoes. Puree the rest of the soup through a food mill or in batches in a blender or food processor. Return the soup to the kettle, add the cream or half-and-half, and bring the soup back to a simmer over medium heat.

4.   Meanwhile, thinly slice the reserved leek greens. When the soup is simmering once more, add them along with the reserved potatoes and simmer until the leek greens are tender but still bright green. Taste the soup and adjust the salt, then season with a few liberal grindings of pepper. Pour the soup into a heated tureen or divide it among heated soup plates, and serve at once with chopped sage or parsley sprinkled over the top of each serving.

Note: *For a meatless version, substitute Vegetable Broth (page 24) for the chicken broth and increase it to 3 cups. If you want to avoid dairy products, use peanut or olive oil for sautéing the leeks and onion, and omit the cream. The flavor will be very different, but it is still pretty doggone good.*

Sweet Potato Vichyssoise: My friend Dean Owens makes this into a superb summer soup by pureeing the entire soup. He chills and serves it exactly like vichyssoise, topped with a dollop of heavy cream, a sprinkling of white pepper, and some chopped fresh chives.

OVEN-ROASTED
SWEET POTATOES

Originally, sweet potatoes were roasted in the hot ash of the kitchen hearth. This gave them a smoky, earthy flavor that cannot be imitated in a modern oven. When I've got the grill fired up, I'll roast the sweet potatoes on the back of the grill (see page 182 for the method), which comes close to giving them that ash-roasted flavor. However, when roasted in a cast-iron Dutch oven or an unglazed clay baking dish, as directed here, they can still taste awfully good.

SERVES 4

4 medium sweet potatoes (about 2 pounds)
Unsalted butter, softened
Salt and black pepper in a peppermill

1. Position a rack in the center of the oven and preheat it to 400 degrees F. Scrub the potatoes well under cold running water, removing any root tendrils that may still be attached, and pat them dry.

2. Prick them in several places with a fork and lightly grease them with butter. Put the potatoes in a cast-iron Dutch oven or Romertopf that will hold them in one layer (it's okay if they touch slightly, but don't crowd them). Put on the lid and place them on the center rack of the oven. Roast them, turning them occasionally so that the bottoms don't get too brown, until they yield easily when pressed with your finger, about 1 hour.

3. To serve the potatoes, slit them lengthwise with a sharp knife, wrap a kitchen towel around a potato, and gently press until it splits and "puckers." Repeat with the remaining potatoes and serve at once with butter, salt, and black pepper passed separately, or filled with peppers and onions (see next recipe).

OVEN-ROASTED SWEET POTATOES WITH PEPPERS AND ONIONS

The most sublime topping of all for an oven-roasted sweet potato is an unapologetically large lump of butter. But in the fall, when the last of the bell peppers are sweet and ripe, novelist Dori Sanders keeps alive an old tradition by making this savory filling, which she recorded in her lovely book *Dori Sanders' Country Cooking.*

Ms. Sanders modernized her version by using olive oil, but wrote: "If you want to make it like the old-timers did, substitute rendered pork fat for the olive oil." Well, Miss Dori, I do, and I did: the smell of onions and peppers simmering in bacon drippings is one of the world's great gastronomical sensations. However, if you want, you can omit the bacon and use 2 tablespoons of extra virgin olive oil instead.

SERVES 4

4 medium Oven-Roasted Sweet Potatoes (page 225)
4 slices bacon
1 medium yellow onion, thinly sliced
1 medium ripe (red or yellow) bell pepper, seeded as directed on page
    116, and thinly sliced

Salt and black pepper in a peppermill
6 tablespoons homemade Crème Fraîche (page 18) or sour cream
2 tablespoons chopped fresh chives or scallion tops

1.   While the potatoes are roasting, put the bacon in a medium skillet, preferably of cast iron, and turn on the heat to medium. Fry the bacon, turning it occasionally, until it is browned and crisp, about 8 to 10 minutes. Turn off the heat.

2.   Remove the bacon, drain it well on absorbent paper, then crumble and set it aside. Drain off all but 2 tablespoons of the fat, and add the onion and bell pepper to the skillet. Turn up the heat to medium and sauté, tossing frequently, until the vegetables are tender, about 8 to 10 minutes. Turn off the heat. Season with a pinch or so of salt and a liberal grinding of black pepper.

3.   Meanwhile, mix the crème fraîche or sour cream with the chopped chive or green onion tops and set it aside. When the potatoes are tender, remove them from the oven, slit each one lengthwise, and wrap a kitchen towel around it, pressing gently until it splits and "puckers." Gently reheat the onion-and-pepper mixture over medium heat and spoon them into the potatoes. Serve at once, with the cream-chive mixture and crumbled bacon passed separately.

Bubber's Stuffed Sweet Potatoes

This is my kind of sweet potato dish. It isn't so sweet that it hurts your teeth, and the fine flavor of the potatoes isn't smothered with a lot of spices. The nutmeg and sherry enhance rather than mask the flavor, and the cheese lends a welcome savory contrast to the natural sweetness.

I'd better explain the name. To say Southerners are a bit "family proud" would be the understatement of the century. We are so much so that there's a long-standing tradition of naming the firstborn son after his proud daddy. Naturally, proud Daddy was named for *his* proud daddy, who had been in turn named for *his*—and so on. The result is half a dozen men in the same family with *exactly* the same name, the only difference being a number at the end. To distinguish them from one another, each ends up being tagged with a boy-hood nickname that he never outgrows. That's why the South is populated with grown men called "Sonny," "Bud," "Red," "Skip," "Rip," and the now infamous "Bubba." "Bubber," in this case, is Adam Howard of McClellanville (a fishing village near Charleston) who has single-handedly added a whole paragraph to the dictionary definition of eccentric. Adam is also a slap-wonderful cook, as this recipe clearly demonstrates.

SERVES 4

4 Oven-Roasted Sweet Potatoes (page 225)
Salt and whole white peppercorns in a peppermill
1 blade of mace, crushed, or ¹/₄ teaspoon ground mace, or whole nutmeg
  in a grater
³/₄ cup grated sharp Cheddar
¹/₄ cup heavy cream (minimum 36 percent milkfat)
3 tablespoons melted unsalted butter
1 tablespoon dry sherry (such as Amontillado)
Sweet paprika

1.   After you take the potatoes from the oven, preheat the broiler. Allow the potatoes to cool enough to handle comfortably, but don't let them get cold. Cut a slice from the top of each potato, and with a spoon or melon baller, scoop out the insides, leaving a shell about ¹/₄ inch thick. Set the shells aside.

2.   Mash the scooped-out pulp smooth and season it with a healthy pinch of salt, a liberal grinding of white pepper, and the mace or a liberal grinding of nutmeg. Beat into it ¹/₂ cup of the cheese, the cream, butter, and sherry. Taste and adjust the seasonings to suit, and continue beating until the potatoes are fluffy. Spoon the whipped potatoes back into the shells, mounding them up on top. Sprinkle the tops with the remaining cheese and paprika.

3.   Place the shells on a shallow pan or cookie sheet and broil until the tops are lightly browned, about 5 minutes.

Note: *You can also make the potatoes completely ahead and reheat them in the oven. Position a rack in the center of the oven and preheat the oven to 400 degrees F. Put the potatoes on a shallow baking dish or cookie sheet, and bake them in the center of the oven until they are heated through and the tops are lightly browned, about 20 minutes.*

If you can't find whole-blade mace, you can use the ground variety, but it won't have nearly as much flavor. I would encourage you to use freshly grated nutmeg instead. The two spices are actually parts of the same fruit, and their flavor is similar. In my opinion, freshly grated nutmeg always has a finer flavor than powdered mace.

$\mathcal{M}$A MA'S SWEET POTATO CUSTARD PIES

When my first book, *Classical Southern Cooking*, came out, I had tried to be very careful about staying within the known traditions of antebellum Southern kitchens, and was braced for the inevitable "That's not the way *my* grandmother did it" with a ready answer: "Well, it's not the way *my* grandmother did it, either." What I wasn't prepared for was a complaint from Ma Ma herself. My sweet potato pies, she informed me, both while I was stirring them up for Christmas dinner and while we were eating them, were nothing like hers. They were perfectly good, she said, but then promptly launched into a long list of what was the matter with them. Well, she was right: I had gotten so caught up with historical accuracy that my grandmother's recipe—the one I truly loved—had completely disappeared. I knew then that I'd have to do something about it. But sadly, I never got to cook with her again. Still, she is always nearby whenever I make this pie.

Get ready for a religious experience.

MAKES TWO 9-INCH PIES

1 recipe Basic Pastry (page 47)
3 pounds (5 to 6 medium) Oven-Roasted Sweet Potatoes (page 225)
1 cup sugar
2 ounces (4 tablespoons or ½ stick) unsalted butter
4 large eggs
Salt
Whole nutmeg in a grater (optional)
1 tablespoon bourbon or ½ teaspoon vanilla extract (optional)
Lightly sweetened whipped cream

1.   Position a rack in the center of the oven and preheat the oven to 375 degrees F. Line two 9-inch pie plates with the pastry and prick them all over with a fork. Chill them in the refrigerator while you make the filling.

2.   Peel the sweet potatoes while they are still hot (they are easier to peel) and puree them through a ricer or sieve into a large mixing bowl, or cut them in chunks, put them in the bowl, and mash them well with a fork.

3.   Add the sugar and butter, and stir until they are dissolved into the potatoes. In a separate bowl, lightly beat the eggs until the yolks and whites are well mixed, then stir them

into the potatoes. If you like, add a generous grating of nutmeg and the bourbon or vanilla, and mix well.

4.   Pour the filling into the prepared pastry and place the pies in the center of the oven so they are not touching each other. Bake them until they are set and the pastry is nicely browned, about 40 minutes.

5.   Serve the pies at room temperature or cold with a healthy dollop of lightly sweetened whipped cream.

Note: I do like to flavor the pie with my own homemade bourbon vanilla extract or a bit of plain bourbon (I don't use commercial vanilla extract), but good Baptist that she was, Ma Ma never used whiskey and cast a rather disapproving eye my way when I added it.

Myrtice's Crunchy Sweet Potato Soufflé

Don't put me in the same room with marshmallows and sweet potatoes. If I never saw another one of those syrupy so-called soufflés with rows of brown mush on top, it would not be a moment too soon. All that sweet goop just covers up the lovely flavor of the potatoes.

Well, my prejudice aside, sweet potato soufflé is a Southern standard on Thanksgiving and Christmas tables. Not to include one in a book on Southern vegetables would be like leaving fried chicken out of a book on Southern poultry. Happily, Myrtice Lewis, my friend and fellow parishioner at St. John's Church, makes a stellar sweet potato soufflé topped with pecans and coconut, without a single marshmallow in sight.

Myrtice is heir to a long tradition of fine cooks by way of her mother, Nianza Freeman James. With wonderful food always around, Myrtice didn't spend much time in the kitchen as a girl, and claims that she was grown before she prepared her first complete meal. That may be so, but today she's one of the best home cooks I know.

SERVES 6

2 pounds sweet potatoes
1¹/₂ cups sugar
¹/₄ teaspoon salt

3 large eggs, slightly beaten
¹/₄ pound (1 stick) unsalted butter
6 ounces evaporated milk
1 teaspoon vanilla extract
1 teaspoon freshly grated nutmeg
¹/₂ teaspoon cinnamon

FOR THE PECAN CRUNCH TOPPING:
¹/₄ pound (1 stick) unsalted butter
1 cup brown sugar
1 cup chopped pecans
1 cup grated unsweetened coconut

1. Position a rack in the center of the oven and preheat the oven to 350 degrees F. Wash the sweet potatoes and put them in a deep pot. Completely cover them with water and then lift out the potatoes. Cover the pot and place it over high heat. Bring the water to a boil and carefully add the potatoes. Cover and let the liquid return to a full boil. Reduce the heat to medium and simmer until the potatoes are tender, about 20 to 30 minutes, depending on the size and age of the potatoes. Drain them well, let them cool enough to handle, and peel them. Put them into a mixing bowl and mash them to a pulp.

2. Add the sugar, salt, eggs, butter, evaporated milk, vanilla, and spices to the potatoes, and stir until well mixed. Lightly grease a 2-quart glass or pottery baking dish and fill it with the potato mixture, smoothing the top with a spatula or wooden spoon. Set it aside.

3. To make the topping, melt the butter in a saucepan that will comfortably hold all the ingredients over low heat. Turn off the heat and mix in the brown sugar, pecans, and coconut until all the ingredients are moistened with the butter. Spread or sprinkle this mixture evenly over the potatoes.

4. Bake until the topping is nicely browned and the filling is set, about 35 to 40 minutes.

BAKED PEARS IN WHITE WINE

Some of the best fruit desserts in Lettice Bryan's wonderful book *The Kentucky Housewife* (1839) were hidden as afterthoughts in a chapter on fruit sauces intended for meat. This is one of them.

Look for small pears: the ones that Mrs. Bryan used would have been much smaller than the behemoth hybrid fruit that is available to most of us these days. The pears make a showier presentation when cooked whole and presented standing upright. If you can find only the larger pears, don't despair: you can still use them in the recipe, but they'll need to be split. Refer to the note at the end of the recipe for cooking larger fruit.

SERVES 4

4 small Bosc or firm Bartlett pears (about 1¹/₂ pounds, see note)
1 cup dry white wine or vermouth
1 lemon
Sugar
Whole nutmeg in a grater
¹/₂ cup heavy cream (minimum 36 percent milkfat) or Bourbon
    Custard Sauce (page 59)

1. Position a rack in the center of the oven and preheat the oven to 350 degrees F. Wash and peel the pears. Cut out the cores by cutting from the bottom of the fruit with the aid of a paring knife and a small melon baller.

2. Lightly butter a deep, lidded baking dish that will just hold the pears upright with the lid on. Put the pears in the dish and pour the wine over them. Cover and bake the pears in the center of the oven until tender, about 1 hour, basting them occasionally with the wine.

3. Meanwhile, cut the zest from the lemon with a vegetable peeler and cut it into fine julienne. When the pears are tender, take them up onto a serving platter or individual serving dishes. Halve the lemon and squeeze a few drops of lemon juice over each pear.

4. If the casserole in which the pears cooked isn't flameproof, transfer the wine mixture to a saucepan. Sweeten it with a tablespoon or so of sugar and place it over medium-high heat. Bring it to a boil and reduce it to a thick, syrupy glaze. Freshen it with a squeeze or two of lemon juice and pour it over the pears. Sprinkle the pears with the lemon zest, a grating or so of nutmeg, to taste, and serve warm, with a pitcher of the heavy cream or custard passed separately.

Note: *If the pears are large ones (weighing more than 6 ounces), you will need only 2 for this recipe. Split them lengthwise after peeling them and bake them lying cut side down in one layer. If you don't have a baking dish with a lid that is large enough, use an open casserole and cover the pears with a sheet of buttered parchment paper or foil.*

PERSIMMONS

Persimmons are native to our continent and were once plentiful in the wild, a free and delectable late autumn treat after the frost had nipped most of the other, less hardy fruits. In fact, a frosty nip helps this fruit ripen fully and render it edible. Nothing can equal the meltingly sweet flavor of a ripe persimmon, but when not perfectly ripe, its pulp is so astringent that it will turn your mouth inside out.

Today, as rural areas give way to urban development, wild persimmons are becoming rarer. Both domestic (developed from imported hybrids) and large Japanese persimmons are available in the markets from autumn through late spring. These commercial fruits do not have the distinctive flavor of wild fruit, in part because they do not ripen on the tree. Consequently, they are often hard and a little green, especially the large Japanese variety. Pastry chef Karen Barker says that this can be remedied by freezing the fruit overnight. This is supposed to simulate the frost that helps break down the persimmons in the wild. Let them thaw completely before using. They will collapse and look shriveled and wrinkly, but that's the way they're supposed to be.

PERSIMMON PUDDING
MAGNOLIA GRILL

A favorite way of using persimmons in the South used to be the brewing of persimmon beer. That art, however, like the wild fruit, is fast disappearing. Old-time persimmon pudding is still popular in our region, even in upscale restaurants like the celebrated Magnolia Grill in Durham, North Carolina. Known for the innovative yet traditional elegance of its menu, this old-fashioned pudding is one of the restaurant's seasonal favorites. The recipe is from Karen Barker, who with her husband, Ben, is coproprietor of the Grill and the restaurant's pastry chef. Karen is originally from Brooklyn, yet both her pastries and her tongue have long since developed a distinctly Southern accent.

When selecting persimmons for this recipe, Karen advises: "Be sure the persimmons are perfectly ripe (i.e., ugly, mushy, and shriveled) or else they will provide you with one of the world's worst taste sensations." A mild understatement. If you are using the large commercial Japanese persimmons found in supermarkets, see above for Karen's tips on using this fruit.

1¼ cups flour
¾ teaspoon baking soda
¾ teaspoon baking powder, preferably single-acting
½ teaspoon powdered ginger
½ teaspoon powdered cinnamon
⅛ teaspoon freshly grated nutmeg
⅛ teaspoon powdered cloves
⅓ teaspoon salt
3½ ounces (7 tablespoons) butter
¾ cup plus 1½ tablespoons sugar
3 large eggs
1½ cups plus 1 tablespoon half-and-half
1½ cups strained persimmon puree (see note)
2 tablespoons apricot jam
1 Recipe Bourbon Custard Sauce (page 59) or vanilla ice cream

1. Position a rack in the center of the oven and preheat the oven to 350 degrees F. Prepare a teakettle full of water and put it on to boil. Butter a 10-inch round, 1-inch deep cake pan, line the bottom with parchment or wax paper, and butter the paper. Set aside.

2. Sift together the flour, soda, baking powder, ginger, cinnamon, nutmeg, cloves, and salt and set aside. In a separate mixing bowl, cream the butter and sugar until fluffy. One at a time, break the eggs into a separate bowl and incorporate them into the butter and sugar mixture, beating well after each addition.

3. Alternating, gradually add the sifted dry ingredients and the half-and-half. When both are incorporated, stir in the persimmon puree and the apricot jam. Pour the batter into the prepared cake pan and put the pan in a larger sheet-cake pan.

4. Place the pans on the center rack of the oven and carefully pour the water into the larger pan until it comes halfway up the sides of the smaller pan. Bake the pudding until golden brown and firm, but still moist, about 1 hour and 10 minutes. The center should be moist but not wet and runny. Serve the pudding warm, with Bourbon Custard Sauce or with your favorite vanilla ice cream.

Note: To puree persimmons, stem them and cut them in half lengthwise. Remove the seeds and scrape the flesh away from the skins. Discard the skins and place the whole fruit in the food processor. Process until smooth. If you don't have a processor, you can puree them with a food mill or force them through a wire strainer.

WINTER

BEANS, GREENS, AND SWEET FLORIDA CITRUS

A Southern winter is perhaps the most difficult season of all to pin down with any accuracy. A Southern summer is hot and humid—and just how hot and humid is only a matter of degrees. Winter, on the other hand, can be just about anything, depending on where you are—from brisk snow-skiing temperatures to balmy sunbathing weather. Among the factors that play into this are the vast differences in our geography. From the blustery, snowy crests of the Great Smoky Mountains to the palm-edged beaches of Key West and delta bayous of Louisiana, the South has just about every imaginable terrain except desert. It isn't so much a single region as it is a collection of many regions. Each meets the winter months in its own way, and even within a given region, there are wild fluctuations in weather patterns and temperatures. Perhaps it isn't surprising, then, that winter cooking is the most varied in our repertory.

Still, cold is relative, and even areas with the mildest of winters experience at least a few weeks of chilling weather. Midwinter visitors to Savannah are unpleasantly shocked to find that we can have weeks of subfreezing weather, and they scramble to locate long trousers and an extra sweater.

At any rate, even if the dip in temperature is only a drop from bikini to sweater weather, something on the table that warms both the insides and the imagination can be a welcome thing indeed, and all Southern kitchens respond accordingly.

Before rapid air freight made possible the mass distribution of produce from other parts of the globe, the winter selection of vegetables was limited to hefty winter squashes and root vegetables, the sturdier greens of the cabbage family, dried beans, fruits, and vegetables, and our ever-present hominy. Yet, traditionally at least, winter vegetable cookery is one of our most varied and imaginative—in part because of the limited variety, and in part because the season is punctuated by exuberant religious festivals where feasting (and therefore elaborate cooking) figure prominently.

Whether it is Thanksgiving, Chanukah, Christmas, the relatively new festival of Kwanza, or only a ritual celebration of the crowning of the year, from late November until the beginning of Lent, Southerners are busy cooking and eating as at no other time. Regardless of the cook's tradition, the object is a celebration, and this time of limited culinary resources is when we do some of our most imaginative cooking.

DRIED BEANS AND PEAS

Dried beans and peas have long been an important winter staple food for much of the world, since they are cheap and easy both to grow and store. In the South, certain varieties are so common in a given region—red beans in New Orleans and cowpeas in the Carolina Lowcountry, for example—that they have become an identifying element of the region's cuisine. But regardless of the variety, most of the ways of preparing them have hints of African cookery about them. It's interesting and probably instructive that the most "Southern" of all peas—cowpeas and black-eyes—are native to Africa.

On the other hand, not all our beans are African imports. Most of them are native to this country, members of the extensive kidney-bean family, which includes such well-known varieties as black beans, navy beans, Great Northerns, pintos, and those famous Creole red beans. Aside from these familiar types of beans, there are dozens more, some of which are slipping sadly into obscurity, while others are being planted again. At Seabrook Village Museum, an early free-black community south of Savannah, there has been a valiant effort not only to preserve the homes and one-room school of this Lowcountry farming community, but also one of its crops—the seminole pea. Only a few years ago, this little red pea faced almost certain extinction, and even though seminoles are once again being cultivated, their future is still by no means secure.

PRESOAKING AND PARBOILING DRIED BEANS AND PEAS

Dried beans are usually soaked and parboiled before they are used in a given recipe. There are some cooks who don't soak them, on the theory that there is a loss of flavor and nutrients, but this isn't a problem if you cook them in their soaking liquid. Conversely, there are many cooks who do soak the beans but don't use the soaking liquid, maintaining that it causes more gas. Well, in that department, I can't tell the difference, so I opt for the route with more flavor.

SERVES 8

1 pound dried beans or peas

1.   Pick over the beans and remove any stones and beans that are defective. Place them in a colander and rinse them under cold running water. Transfer the washed beans to a glass or stainless bowl that will comfortably hold 3 times their volume. Add enough cold, preferably soft water (see note) to cover them by 2 inches. Allow them to soak for at least 6 hours or overnight.

2.   Transfer the beans with their soaking water to a stainless kettle and add enough additional soft water to cover them by 2 inches. Or you can pour off the soaking water, rinse the beans, and put them in the kettle with enough fresh soft water to cover them by 2 inches. Place the kettle over medium heat and bring the liquid to a boil, carefully skimming off the scum as it rises to the top. Reduce the heat to medium low and simmer the beans until they are tender, about 1 hour. The beans are now ready to use in any of the following recipes.

Note: *Dried beans cook best in soft water that hasn't been salted; both salt and the minerals in hard water inhibit the beans' ability to soften. If your tap water is especially hard, use distilled water or add a pinch of soda to the cooking liquid, though many cooks object to adding soda.*

Stewed Dried Black-Eyed Peas

This basic recipe can be used for finishing any dried beans or peas that have been prepared by the previous recipe. Salt pork is essential for a traditional flavor, but you can omit it and substitute 2 tablespoons of butter or olive oil for the rendered fat—though the flavor will not be remotely the same, it'll still be very good.

SERVES 6

¼ pound lean salt pork
1 medium yellow onion, peeled and chopped
1 pound dried black-eyed peas, soaked and cooked as directed on page
  237, with their cooking liquid
1 whole pod fresh or dried cayenne pepper
Salt
1 tablespoon chopped parsley or fresh mint

1. Cut the salt pork into thin slices and rinse it thoroughly under cold running water. Pat it dry and put it into a pot that will comfortably hold the peas. Turn on the fire to medium and cook the pork until it is crisp. Remove it from the pan and pour off all but 2 tablespoons of the rendered fat. Add the onion and sauté until it is translucent and softened but not browned.

2. Return the pork to the pan. Add the peas with their cooking liquid and the pod of cayenne. Bring the peas to a boil and reduce the heat to a slow simmer. Simmer until the peas are very tender and the liquid is somewhat reduced and lightly thickened, about 45 minutes to an hour.

3. Taste and add a pinch or so of salt, if needed, and let the peas simmer for a couple of minutes more. Remove and discard the pod of cayenne, and pour the peas into a warm serving dish. Sprinkle them with the chopped parsley or mint and serve at once.

Note: *If you are cooking the peas without meat, a dash (and only a dash) of Thai fish sauce or soy sauce can be added to give the peas the subtle depth of flavor that the pork lends to them. Strict vegetarians who do not eat fish can add a dash of soy sauce.*

ℬLACK-EYED PEA FRITTERS ⪻

Wherever an African cook has touched the cuisines of the Americas, there are pea fritters. In South America and the Caribbean, the fritters are known by various derivations of the African name *akkra*—*akaras*, *aklas*, and *acarajes*, and even *calas*. In the South, they are usually called "fritters" or "croquettes," and in New Orleans, *calas* are rice fritters. Classic African *akkras* are made from a paste of raw dried peas that have been soaked, skinned, and ground up but not precooked. Southern pea fritters deviate in that they are made from leftover cooked peas. The paste tends to fall apart in the hot fat, so they must be bound together with egg and covered with crumbs.

Black-eyed peas are most frequently used for these fritters, but any leftover beans will do; in Creole New Orleans, they are made with red beans. Regardless of what kinds of beans or peas were used, traditional recipes called for the skins to be removed before the peas were mashed up. Peeling cooked peas is a royal pain, and you know me—lazy to the bone—so I've never bothered. If you use the food processor, it purees the skins so well that you don't even know they are there.

SERVES 6

2 cups stewed dried black-eyed peas (previous page), drained
1 small yellow onion, minced fine
1 teaspoon Pepper Vinegar (page 27) or cider vinegar mixed with a
　　　dash of hot sauce or pinch of cayenne
Salt
1 large egg
1 cup dry bread crumbs
Lard or peanut oil (for frying, see step 4)

1. Puree the beans in a food processor fitted with a steel blade. Transfer them to the mixing bowl. If you don't have a processor, you can puree the beans in small batches in a blender, or just put them into the mixing bowl and mash them to a smooth pulp with a fork. Add the minced onion, vinegar, and a healthy pinch or so of salt. Mix well. Taste and adjust the seasonings.

2. Break the egg into a separate bowl and beat it until it is well mixed. Add it to the pea mixture and thoroughly work it in. Let the mixture stand for a few minutes. The peas will absorb some of the liquid of the egg, and the mixture will get a little stiffer.

3.   Spread the crumbs on a dinner plate. Drop a rounded tablespoon of the pea puree onto the crumbs, then roll it until all sides are lightly coated and the lump forms a 1-inch ball. Repeat with the remaining puree until all the croquettes are formed. They can be prepared several hours ahead up to this point. Set them aside on a platter or cookie sheet.

4.   Preheat the oven to 150 degrees F. Put enough oil or lard in a deep skillet or deep-fat fryer to come halfway up the side of the pan. Turn on the heat to medium high, and when the oil is hot but not quite smoking (375 degrees F), put in enough of the croquettes to fill the pan without crowding. Cook until they are uniformly browned, about 4 or 5 minutes, turning them halfway through if they are not completely covered by the fat. Handle them as little as possible; they tend to break up. Lift them out with a slotted spoon, drain them briefly on absorbent paper, and keep them in the warm oven while the rest of the croquettes cook. Repeat until all the croquettes are fried and serve them at once with more pepper vinegar passed separately.

Note: *An important aspect of frying is getting the fat hot enough. This is particularly true with pea fritters. The egg and breading are critical; otherwise, these little critters disintegrate into the fat, especially if it isn't hot enough. If a few fall apart anyway, don't panic. Just lift out the browned bits, drain them well, and have cook's treat.*

You can use any cooked, leftover beans for these fritters, and dress them up with a tablespoon of chopped fresh herbs (or a teaspoon of dried herbs). Thyme and sage are good with any variety; mint is especially lovely with black-eyed peas. You could also substitute 4 green onions, finely minced, for the yellow onion or add a minced clove of garlic.

LIMA BEAN SOUP

Lima beans, a legume native to America, are indispensable in Southern vegetable soup but are not often turned into a soup on their own. Too bad; their creamy yellow flesh and delicate, distinctive flavor make an especially fine soup that'll persuade even the most hardened winter-hater that cold weather does have its benefits and that life, even in January, may be worth living after all.

1 pound dried large lima beans, washed, soaked, and parboiled as
directed on page 237
1 quart Chicken Broth (page 23)
2 medium yellow onions, peeled and chopped
2 sprigs parsley, plus 2 tablespoons chopped parsley
Salt and whole white peppercorns in a peppermill
1 cup heavy cream (minimum 36 percent milkfat) or 1/2 cup finely
julienned, uncooked, dry-cured (country) ham (optional)

1. Put the parboiled beans, their cooking liquid, and the broth in a kettle that will hold all the ingredients and bring it slowly to a boil over medium heat.

2. Add the onions, whole parsley sprigs, a healthy pinch or so of salt to taste, and a liberal grinding of white pepper. Let the soup come to a boil, then reduce the heat, and simmer until the beans and onions are very tender, about 1 to 1 1/2 hours.

3. Puree half the beans through a food mill or sieve, or in a blender or food processor. Stir the puree back into the soup, thinning it a little with water if it is too thick, and bring the soup back to a simmer. Remove and discard the parsley sprigs. Stir in the optional cream or ham, let it just heat through, and serve at once, sprinkling each serving with the chopped parsley.

PEAS (OR BEANS) AND RICE

If I had to choose a single dish that summarized the African influence on Southern tables, it would be peas and rice. Whether it is our lowly hoppin' John, served on New Year's Day for luck (or any day when our luck has not been so good), South Florida's Cuban black beans, or Creole red beans (both of which are cooked without rice but always served over it), the soul-satisfying combination of peas and rice is directly descended from West African cooking. As slaves from that region were brought to the Caribbean and rice-growing regions of South Carolina and Georgia, they made a distinct and lasting impression on the cooking of these areas. Many elements of Southern cooking are a part of this legacy, but the rice and peas combination is perhaps the most enduring of all.

$\mathcal{M}$y Hoppin' John

Every Lowcountry cook has his own version of this classic African dish of peas and rice, ranging from the starkly simple to the painfully elaborate. When I am teaching it as a historical recipe, I feel bound to stay within traditions, but here's how I make it for myself.

Hoppin' John differs from other pea and rice dishes in that the rice and peas cook together. It's really a pilau—a dish in which rice cooks in a rich, aromatic broth—in this case, the flavorful cooking liquid from the peas.

Folk etymologists and pop historians like to tell cute stories about the origins of the name "hoppin' John," and they can keep right on telling them for all I care. I adhere to culinary historian and author Jessica Harris's theory that it's an Anglicized corruption of an old West African name.

SERVES 4 TO 6

2 cups dried cowpeas, black-eyed peas, or crowder peas
¹/₂ pound lean salt-cured pork or one country ham hock
1 large onion, peeled and finely chopped
2 ribs celery, strung and diced
2 large garlic cloves, peeled and minced
1 whole pod red pepper, preferably cayenne
1 Bouquet Garni (page 36), made with a healthy sprig each fresh
    parsley, mint, thyme, a leafy celery top, and 2 bay leaves (see note)
Black pepper in a peppermill
Salt
1 cup raw rice, washed and rinsed as directed on page 44
10–12 fresh mint leaves

1. Sort the peas to remove any stones and blemished peas, wash and drain them, and put them in a nonreactive bowl that will hold more than twice their volume. Add enough cold (preferably soft) water to cover them by 2 inches and soak the peas for 6 hours or overnight.

2. Put the peas into a large pot with their soaking liquid and enough water to completely cover them by at least an inch. Do not add salt. Place the pot over medium heat and bring the peas slowly to a boil; carefully skim off the scum as it rises. Reduce the heat to a slow simmer, cover the pot, and simmer for half an hour.

3. Put the salt pork or ham hock in an iron skillet, and turn on the heat to medium high. Cook the pork, turning it frequently, until 2 tablespoons of fat are rendered from it. Remove the pork and add the onion and celery. Sauté until they are softened, about 5 minutes, and add the garlic. Sauté until the garlic is fragrant but not colored. Transfer the vegetables to the peas along with the pork, whole pepper pod, bouquet garni, and a grinding or so of black pepper. Raise the heat to medium high and let the peas come back to a boil. Reduce the heat to a simmer, cover the pot, and cook until the peas are tender, about 1 hour.

4. Taste the peas and correct for salt. If the pork is very salty, they may not need any. But keep in mind that the broth must be highly seasoned in order to flavor the rice. Take up 2 cups of the broth into a separate pot and bring it to a boil over medium heat. Add the rice, bring it back to a boil, and reduce the heat to a slow simmer. Cover loosely and simmer for 12 minutes. Fluff the rice with a fork, cover it tightly, and let it sit for a minute to build steam inside the pot. Then turn off the heat and move the pot to a warm spot to let it steam for another 12 to 15 minutes.

5. When the rice is ready, remove and discard the pepper pod and bouquet garni and drain the remaining broth from the peas, but don't discard it. Fluff the rice with a fork and gently mix in the peas, tossing them with the fork rather than stirring. If the hoppin' John is too dry, add a little of the reserved broth.

6. If you like, you can remove the lean meat from the salt pork or ham hock, chop it, and stir it into the hoppin' John. Just before serving, cut the mint leaves into fine slivers and sprinkle them over the hoppin' John. Don't do this ahead, or the residual heat will make them turn brown.

Note: *You can omit the meat altogether and sauté the onion and garlic in 2 tablespoons olive oil or peanut oil, or in vegetable oil mixed with 1 teaspoon sesame oil for a touch of Africa. You must use a certain amount of fat in the dish to have an authentic pilau.*

If you don't have fresh thyme or oregano, substitute ½ teaspoon each of the dried herbs. If fresh mint isn't available, add ½ teaspoon of crumbled dried mint in step 3 and garnish the finished hoppin' John with 1 tablespoon of chopped parsley.

CREOLE RED BEANS AND RICE

Here come the letters from New Orleans saying that my red beans are all wrong—even though I have faithfully followed traditional recipes. Every New Orleanian, Creole and otherwise, has his/her own version of this, the Big Easy's staple Monday fare—and few of them agree with one another, so it's for sure they won't agree with somebody from Georgia. But here goes nothing.

SERVES 4 TO 6

1 pound red beans (see note)
1 tablespoon olive oil
1/2 pound andouille sausage (see note), sliced 1/4 inch thick, or diced
    country ham
1 large yellow onion, split, peeled, and chopped
1 medium green bell pepper, stemmed, seeded, and chopped
1 large carrot, peeled and diced
1 rib celery, strung and diced
2 cloves garlic, peeled and minced
1 Bouquet Garni (page 36) made from 1 bay leaf, 1 large fresh sprig
    each parsley, thyme, and sage or oregano
1 whole pod fresh hot pepper (omit if using andouille sausage)
1/2 cup red wine
Black pepper in a peppermill and salt
2 cups Carolina-Style Rice (page 43)

1. Wash, soak overnight, and parboil the beans as directed on page 237, until they are nearly tender, about 30 to 45 minutes. While the beans simmer, keep a teakettle of simmering water handy. There should always be enough liquid to cover the beans completely. If the liquid gets low, supplement it with the simmering water.

2. Meanwhile, put the olive oil and sausage or ham in a large skillet or sauté pan and place it over medium-high heat. Sauté until lightly browned on all sides and remove it from the pan. Pour off all but 2 tablespoons of fat (if there's less than 2 tablespoons, supplement it with more olive oil). Add the onion, bell pepper, carrot, and celery. Return the

pan to the heat and sauté until the vegetables are softened but not browned, about 5 minutes. Add the garlic and sauté until fragrant, about a minute more.

3. Transfer the vegetables and sausage or ham to the bean pot. Add the bouquet garni, pod of hot pepper (left whole, if using it), wine, and a grinding or so of black pepper. Raise the heat and bring the liquid back to a boil, then reduce the heat to low and simmer until the beans are very tender and thick, about 1½ to 2 hours. Taste and correct for salt, remove and discard the hot pepper and bouquet garni, and serve the beans over cooked rice.

Note: *You can make authentic-tasting Creole red beans and rice* au maigre *by omitting the meat. Increase the amount of olive oil to 2 tablespoons, or use 1 tablespoon each of oil and unsalted butter.*

The red beans are frequently garnished with thinly sliced scallions or green onions. Allow 1 scallion for every 2 servings.

Creole red beans are not remotely the same as red kidney beans. True Creole red beans are smaller, milder in flavor, and more of a ruddy red-brown than the deep red of the kidney beans. You can find them in specialty groceries and some natural-food stores. If you can't find true red beans, substitute kidney beans. Dried beans are preferable, but you can still make reasonably good red beans using the canned variety, provided that they do not have any added spices or other flavorings.

Andouille is a spicy smoked pork sausage that is a specialty of Louisiana cookery. It can sometimes be found in specialty groceries or can be mail-ordered from catalogs, such as Williams-Sonoma. Commercial kielbasa can also be substituted for it, though I prefer to use country ham when I don't have the right sausage for this dish.

BLACK-EYED PEA SALAD

Black-eyed pea salads and salsas are two popular and refreshingly new ways of serving an old Southern favorite. This version, which can be served as either salad or salsa, comes from one of Savannah's premiere chefs, Walter Dasher.

Walter apprenticed with Chef Gerry Klaskala in the kitchen of Savannah's 45 South. When Gerry left the restaurant to open the celebrated Buckhead Diner in Atlanta, Walter was invited to fill his mentor's shoes, which he did beautifully for eight years. He now presides over the kitchen of the Chatham Club, and his cooking classes, taught jointly with his wife, Alice, are very popular. Once you taste this salad, you'll know why.

SERVES 6

2 cups (12 ounces) dried black-eyed peas
3 ham hocks
$1/2$ medium red bell pepper, diced
$1/2$ medium yellow bell pepper, diced
1 shallot, chopped
$1/4$ small Vidalia or other sweet onion, chopped
1 tablespoon chives, chopped
1 recipe Balsamic-Ginger Vinaigrette (recipe follows)
8 to 10 fresh basil leaves

1. Soak the beans overnight as directed on page 237. Drain them and set them aside. Put the ham hocks in a 4-quart pot. Add 2 quarts water and bring the liquid to a boil over medium heat, reduce the heat to a simmer, cover, and cook for 1 hour.

2. Add the peas to the pot and raise the heat to bring the liquid back to the boiling point. Reduce the heat once more to low and simmer until the peas are tender, about 1 to $1\frac{1}{2}$ hours. The peas should remain covered with water, so keep a teakettle of simmering water handy in case more water needs to be added to the pot.

3. Drain the peas, discarding the ham hocks. Allow the peas to cool, then mix them with the red and yellow peppers, shallot, onion, and chives. Pour the dressing over the salad and toss until well mixed. The salad can be made a day or two ahead of time. Chill it until you are ready to serve it.

4. Just before serving, cut the basil into chiffonade (fine shreds) and strew it over the top of the salad. Serve cold.

Note: Walter especially favors this salad/salsa as an accompaniment to duck or quail. It's also wonderful with almost any grilled meat or poultry, or serve it as a salsa with a basket of tortilla chips on the side for dipping.

BALSAMIC-GINGER VINAIGRETTE

This dressing is great not only in the Black-Eyed Pea Salad (previous page), but it also makes a fine marinade for any poultry you plan on grilling.

MAKES ABOUT 1 CUP

1/8 cup (2 tablespoons) balsamic vinegar
1/8 cup (2 tablespoons) red wine vinegar
1/2 tablespoon finely minced fresh ginger root
2 tablespoons Dijon mustard
1 teaspoon sugar
Salt
3/4 cup extra virgin olive oil
Black pepper in a peppermill

Combine the two vinegars, ginger, mustard, and sugar in a glass or stainless mixing bowl. Add a small pinch of salt (to help the oil emulsify). Whisk until smooth. Gradually whisk in the olive oil, a few drops at a time, until it is all incorporated and emulsified. Season to taste with more salt, if needed, and a few liberal grindings of black pepper.

CABBAGE

Cabbage was once a winter staple, not only in the South, but everywhere it was grown. Packed in straw and stored in a cool, dark cellar, the tight heads kept through the winter, providing a reliable source of vitamins when other green vegetables weren't available. Another common method of preserving cabbage was to make sauerkraut—shredded cabbage pickled in salt. It was a tedious job, and Mother used to share the work with our neighbor from across the field. They shredded the cabbage with an old wood mandoline and layered it with salt in a heavy stoneware crock. They weighted it and covered it tightly with a clean cotton cloth, since the cabbage had to be kept completely submerged in brine and away from light and air—a tall order with curious little fingers like mine around.

The uninitiated may think it odd that this "German" dish was so popular in the South, but there were after all pockets of German settlers, and salt-pickling cabbage was a means of preservation that had been used by almost all Europeans, including the English, for millennia. Regardless of how it is kept, cabbage is still a winter favorite in the South.

In choosing a cabbage for the following recipes, look for heads with plenty of crisp, healthy-looking, dark green leaves still attached to the head. If the outer leaves have been stripped away from the cabbage, it is usually because the leaves have wilted, so cabbage heads that are stripped down to the tight, white inner leaves are usually not fresh.

$\mathcal{S}$TEWED CABBAGE

People who profess to hate stewed cabbage marvel at Nita Dixon's version of this commonplace dish. The secrets to its success are several. First, she never puts salt pork or bacon in the pot, explaining that there are other ways to make things taste good than always to put meat in them. Second, she says you must be careful not to overcook it; the cabbage should still be quite green and, though tender, have a pleasing firmness to the bite. Most important of all, the cabbage must be as fresh as possible. Says Nita, "Baby, if you want them vegetables to taste good, they better be *fresh*." Choose a cabbage with plenty of healthy, dark green leaves.

SERVES 4 TO 6

1 small, fresh green cabbage (about 2 pounds)
1 medium green bell pepper
1 medium yellow onion
2 tablespoons fat left over from frying chicken, or unsalted butter
1 clove garlic, crushed and peeled
Salt, sugar, and ground cayenne
2 tablespoons unsalted butter

1. Strip off any discolored, or withered leaves from the cabbage, but don't discard any of the healthy-looking, dark green leaves. Remove the dark green leaves, wash them thor-

oughly, roll them together, and cut them into thin strips. Set aside. Quarter the cabbage and cut out the core from each quarter. Sliver each quarter lengthwise into the thinnest possible strips. Set aside separately from the dark green leaves.

2. Stem, core, and seed the pepper and cut it into the thinnest strips you can manage. Cut off the root and stem ends of the onion, split it lengthwise, peel, and slice it into thin strips.

3. Choose a kettle that will comfortably hold all the cabbage. Put the 2 tablespoons of fat or butter into the kettle with the dark green cabbage leaves, bell pepper, and onion. Turn on the heat to medium and sauté until the vegetables are wilted. Add the garlic, give it a stir, and add just enough water to barely cover the cabbage. Cover and steam until crisp-tender, but still a little under done, about 5 minutes. Add the remaining cabbage, a couple of healthy pinches of salt, a large pinch of sugar, and a pinch of cayenne, and cover the kettle. Cook until the cabbage is tender but firm to the bite, about 15 minutes more. It should still be bright green and not army-fatigue brown. Stir in the butter, taste and adjust the seasonings, and serve hot.

Note: *As to seasonings, Nita cautions that you have to let your mouth guide you here. Keep tasting and play with them; some bell peppers can have a bitter edge and you'll want to use a little less. Some will be very mild and you may want to add more. She has given you free rein with the cayenne, but use discretion. Don't add so much that you can't taste anything else.*

MARY RANDOLPH'S CABBAGE PUDDING (STUFFED CABBAGE)

Here's an early nineteenth-century recipe, from a time when no household, rich or poor, ever wasted anything. This sturdy but lovely dish was one of many that provided a tasty and economical way of giving new life to leftovers. In more well-to-do households, it would have been considered a side dish and shared the table with other meat, but it makes a delightful winter supper on its own.

Variations on this dish survive in modern Southern cookbooks, though usually they follow the more common method of stuffing and rolling individual leaves. Stuffing the whole cabbage is a bit more troublesome, but it does make a spectacular presentation.

SERVES 4

1 large, whole cabbage (about 3 pounds)

1 medium onion, peeled

¹/₂ pound cooked meat or poultry, or ³/₄ pound ground beef or bulk
*   sausage*

2 tablespoons dry bread crumbs

1 tablespoon chopped fresh parsley

1 tablespoon chopped fresh herbs, such as thyme or marjoram, or 1
*   teaspoon crumbled dried herbs*

Grated zest of 1 lemon

Salt and black pepper in a peppermill

1 large egg

1 quart Meat Broth (page 21), optional (see step 9)

2 tablespoons unsalted butter, softened

1. Fill a large kettle that will easily hold the cabbage half-full of water and bring it to a boil over high heat. Meanwhile, strip off the outer green leaves of the cabbage, saving 2 or 3 if they are unblemished, and discarding any that are wilted or scarred. Wash everything well under cold running water.

2. When the water is boiling briskly, slip in the cabbage (and any reserved outer leaves) and let it come back to a boil. Cook until the outer leaves of the head begin to wilt and can be pulled back easily, about 15 minutes. Lift the cabbage out of the water and drain it well.

3. Without detaching them from the stem, carefully pull back 2 or 3 rows of leaves. Make a cross-shaped incision in the center of the cabbage, being careful not to cut through the bottom stem or to puncture any of the outer leaves. Pull back a few layers of the cut leaves, like the petals of a flower, and cut out the heart of the cabbage, leaving all the outer leaves attached to the stem.

4. Chop the heart and the onion fine, and put them in a large mixing bowl that will comfortably hold the next 7 ingredients.

5. If you are using fresh ground beef or sausage meat, put it into a skillet and brown it over medium-high heat, stirring until it just loses its raw, red color. Drain off the excess fat and add the meat to the mixing bowl. Otherwise, chop the leftover meat or poultry fine and add it to the cabbage. Add the crumbs, parsley, herbs, and grated lemon zest. Season with a liberal pinch of salt and a few grindings of black pepper. Toss until all is thoroughly mixed.

6.   Break the egg in a separate bowl and beat it until it is light. Add the egg to the stuffing mixture and mix it in.

7.   Spread a 14-inch square of cheesecloth on a work surface and place the cabbage shell in its center. Lay open the leaves and fill the center with the stuffing mixture, packing it gently so as not to break the outer leaves. Now carefully fold the leaves back over the stuffing as much like their original position as possible. If there is any leftover stuffing, work it into the layers of leaves.

8.   Wrap the reserved outer leaves around the cabbage, then pick up the corners of the cheesecloth and pull them up around the whole. Tie it securely with twine, making it as tight as possible, then wrap several lengths of twine around the cabbage and knot it well.

9.   If you are using broth, drain off the blanching liquid from the kettle and add the broth (or you may simply poach the cabbage in the blanching water; add a small handful of salt to it). Over a medium-high fire, bring the liquid to a boil and add the stuffed cabbage, gently lowering it into the liquid. Let it return to a boil, skim it well, and lower the heat to the slowest simmer you can manage, and let it simmer for 1 hour.

10.   Lift the cabbage out of the kettle, drain it, and lay it on a warm platter. Cut the twine, unwrap the cheesecloth, and carefully slip both twine and cloth out from under the cabbage. Spread the softened butter over the cabbage and serve at once.

$\mathcal{B}$RAISED CABBAGE
AND ONIONS ⤝

This is my favorite way of cooking cabbage. The old recipes invariably called this "fried cabbage," and at the end of cooking the liquid does indeed boil away and the cabbage and onions do "fry," lightly caramelizing and taking on a lovely golden color and marvelously concentrated sweetness.

Braised cabbage is a fine accompaniment for any roasted meat or poultry, but it is wonderful on its own, with cornbread and a dash or so of Pepper Vinegar (page 27).

SERVES 4

2 cups (tightly packed) shredded fresh cabbage (about ¹/₂ an average
head of cabbage)
2 cups thinly sliced yellow onion (about 2 medium)
2 tablespoons lard (preferred) or unsalted butter
¹/₄ cup Meat Broth (page 21) or water
1 tablespoon chopped parsley
Salt and black pepper in a peppermill

1. Put the cabbage, onion, fat, and broth or water into a large, heavy skillet fitted with a lid and cover it tightly. Turn on the heat to low. Cook slowly, stirring from time to time, until the vegetables are very tender, about 45 minutes to 1 hour. If the pan gets too dry, add a few spoonfuls of water—don't add more broth—but no more than is absolutely necessary to keep the vegetables moist.

2. When the vegetables are very tender, remove the lid and raise the heat to medium high. Cook, stirring constantly, until all the moisture in the skillet is evaporated and the cabbage and onions are both colored a rich gold. Be careful; they should brown but not scorch. Turn off the heat, stir in the parsley, and season to taste with salt and and a few liberal grindings of pepper. Serve warm.

Note: *Lard is an important element of this dish—both for flavor and color; no other fat allows the cabbage to brown as nicely. If you prefer not to use lard, however, butter will make an acceptable dish. If you wish to avoid animal fat altogether, the only plausible substitution for the lard would be olive or peanut oil.*

COLESLAW

The essential accompaniment for any fish fry or barbecue in the South, and *the* salad for any covered dish supper, is coleslaw. We love it as a side dish for fried fish and chicken, and often treat it like a condiment, slathering it thickly over barbecue sandwiches, hot dogs, and even hamburgers.

There are more Southern recipes for coleslaw than there are Southerners, but all of them fall into two basic categories. One is almost like a cabbage pickle, based on a thin, sweet-sour vinegar and oil dressing that is heated to the boiling point and poured hot over shredded cabbage; the other is creamy, dressed with mayonnaise or boiled dressing. This version is of the creamy persuasion.

SERVES 6 TO 8

1 medium green cabbage (about 2 pounds)
1 small yellow onion
1 medium carrot
1 recipe Boiled Dressing (recipe follows)
1 teaspoon celery seeds
1 teaspoon dry mustard
Salt and black pepper in a peppermill

1. Strip off the tough outer leaves of the cabbage, quarter it, and cut out the core. Discard the core or, if it's not bitter, set it aside and munch on it yourself while you make the slaw—it's delicious. Shred the cabbage, either by hand with a small paring knife (preferable) or with a food processor.

2. Put the cabbage in a large mixing or serving bowl. Peel the onion and grate it into the cabbage. Peel the carrot and shred it through the large holes of the grater or in the food processor. Add it to the cabbage and onion.

3. In a separate bowl, combine the boiled dressing, celery seeds, dry mustard, a large pinch of salt, and a few liberal grindings of black pepper. Mix well and pour the dressing over the slaw. Stir until the cabbage is uniformly coated. If the salad isn't creamy enough, stir in a little more boiled dressing. Let the salad stand for half an hour to allow the flavors to meld, and serve cold.

BOILED DRESSING

Since olive oil was always imported and expensive, Southerners long ago adopted this cream-and-egg–based dressing for salads. Though nowadays the dressing is considered a bit old-fashioned and olive oil is no longer so scarce, we still use it. Aside from coleslaw, it makes a good dressing for chicken or potato salads, especially if you are cooking for someone who for health reasons cannot eat uncooked eggs.

The name, of course, is an oxymoron: it doesn't really boil and can't—or it will curdle.

1 tablespoon sugar
1 teaspoon dry mustard
2 tablespoons all-purpose flour
Salt
¹/₂ cup water
¹/₄ cup vinegar
2 large egg yolks
1 tablespoon unsalted butter
¹/₄ cup heavy cream

1. Prepare the bottom half of a double boiler with water and bring the water to a simmer over medium heat. Mix together the sugar, dry mustard, flour, and a small pinch of salt in the top boiler. In a separate bowl, combine the water, vinegar, and egg yolks, and beat with a whisk until smooth. Slowly whisk this into the dry ingredients.

2. Place the top boiler over the simmering water, and cook, whisking constantly, until the dressing is thick, about 5 minutes. Don't stop whisking or take your attention away from it, because it thickens suddenly. As soon as the dressing is thick, immediately take the top boiler off the heat and beat in the butter and cream. Stir until cool and chill before using.

COLLARD GREENS

Collards are a variety of kale, a member of the extensive cabbage family (their name is thought to be a corruption of colewort, an old name for kale). They are native to Europe and not, as is often supposed, Africa. Yet collards have long been part of the diet of all Southerners, most especially those of African descent, maybe because collards bear a resemblance to a green that had been a staple of the cookery of their African homeland.

Once cut, collard greens won't keep well, but the plants are hearty enough to survive a mild frost and last well into the winter. Even in the colder regions of the South, they are almost always available through New Year's Day—at which time they are eaten for good luck. In the Deep South, collards often survive the entire winter, providing fresh greens when little else may be available.

Good collards are widely available in the South—at greengrocers, farmers' markets, and even supermarkets. Outside the South, they can often be found at West Indian markets or greengrocers that cater to African American or Portuguese communities. Collards are usually sold in whole plants (or heads) like a cabbage. A single plant weighs 1 to 2 pounds, depending on size, and will produce 3 to 5 servings. If you have trouble finding collards, move to a civilized part of the country—or, failing that, substitute either of their cousins, the curly or flat-leafed kale.

TWO CLASSIC WILTED WINTER GREENS

Slow stewing is the most traditional way of preparing collards and other winter greens in the South, but it isn't the only one. Slow cooking produces a distinctive (and strong) smell that many find objectionable. However, even Southerners who hate the smell will have their greens, and for them, braising (or wilting) is the traditional method of choice. The cooking time is considerably shortened and circumvents the permeating odor of a slow simmer. Out of the hundreds of variations, since practically every Southern cook has one, here are two from solidly traditional cooks who begin with the same idea and take it in two different directions. Both are served with Cornbread (page 40) and Pepper Vinegar (page 27), and in the Florida Keys, they pass a bottle of Old Sour (page 287). Either of these recipes makes an excellent accompaniment for pork, veal, chicken, or rice dishes.

BONNIE DAWSON'S WILTED WINTER GREENS

Bonnie Dawson is a traditional Southern cook in the best sense of both adjectives, as comfortable and accomplished on an open hearth as she is in a modern kitchen. Her pound cakes are still the standard by which I measure my own.

Bonnie developed this recipe for the hearth-cooking classes she occasionally teaches at the conservatory on Oatland Island, and it is at its best when cooked over fragrant hardwood coals but even tastes wonderful when the best fire you can manage is electric, so long as you use a well-seasoned iron skillet or Dutch oven.

2 pounds collards (1 large or 2 small plants) or kale
¼ pound thin-sliced bacon, cut into 1-inch pieces
1 medium yellow onion, peeled and sliced ¼ inch thick
Salt and black pepper in a peppermill
Pepper Vinegar (page 27) and/or Old Sour (page 287)

1. Fill a sink with water and add the collard leaves, shaking them around as you add them. Make sure they are completely free of dirt and grit; you may have to change the water several times.

2. Strip the greens from the stems, cut them into 1-inch wide strips, and set them aside. Put the bacon in a deep lidded skillet (preferably cast iron) or Dutch oven. Turn on the heat to medium high and cook, uncovered, until most of the fat has been rendered from the meat, about 5 minutes. Add the onion and sauté until softened, about 3 minutes. Add a large handful of greens with the water that is still clinging to them and stir until they are wilted. Keep adding the greens by the handful until they are all in the pan. Add a healthy pinch of salt and some pepper, cover tightly, and cook until the greens are nearly tender, about 8 to 10 minutes.

3. Remove the lid and continue cooking, stirring frequently, until the liquid is evaporated and the greens and onion are dry and tender, about 5 minutes more. Turn off the heat and serve at once with pepper vinegar or Old Sour.

JOHN TAYLOR'S WILTED GREENS

Cookbook author and culinary historian John Martin Taylor is best known for his work in reviving true Carolina Lowcountry cooking. His cookbook, *Hoppin' John's Lowcountry Cooking,* set a new standard for regional American cookbooks. But when I met John, I discovered that we shared a passion for a cuisine other than that of our native South—specifically, the herb-scented cooking of Genoa and the Ligurian coast known as the Italian Riviera.

Consequently, while John's kitchen is solidly Southern, it always has a hint of the Riviera about it. Says he: "My cooking will be forever influenced by my years in Italy, but nothing so marks it as my use of olive oil. I love the way it tastes and smells—and the way it looks on food, too." Here, he uses olive oil the way Bonnie Dawson uses bacon grease in the previous recipe.

This is a deceptively simple dish; its ingredients are few and its method virtually artless. Like most simple dishes, its strength lies in the quality of its ingredients. John advises: "You don't have to spend a fortune on a premium extra virgin oil for dishes like this one where the taste of the greens is paramount, but the better the oil, the better it'll taste." More important than good oil are good greens, as fresh as possible, preferably obtained from a local grower.

SERVES 6 TO 8

3 pounds collards (3 small plants or 2 large ones)
1/4 cup (4 tablespoons) olive oil
2 teaspoons salt
Pepper Vinegar (page 27) or Old Sour (page 287), optional

1.   Fill a sink with water and add the collard leaves, shaking them around as you add them. Make sure they are completely free of dirt and grit; you may have to change the water several times. When the greens are cleaned, remove them one leaf at a time from the water to a work surface near the stove.

2.   Trim the stalk from the leaf and discard it along with any wilted or discolored leaves. Repeat with several leaves, then stack them on top of each other and cut the leaves into 1-inch strips. Continue until you have trimmed all the collards.

3.   In a large stockpot or Dutch oven, heat about half the olive oil over high heat until it is just at the point of smoking. Pick up a large handful of the trimmed collards and add it to the pot, with the water that is clinging to the greens. Stir vigorously with a large wooden spoon until all the collards are wilted, then add another handful of wet collards, stirring until they wilt as well.

4.   Continue adding the collards until all of them are wilted, then add the salt and the remaining olive oil, and stir the pot well one last time. Immediately reduce the heat to low, cover, and braise for 15 minutes. Taste the greens, and if they need to cook a little more, replace the cover and continue cooking over low heat until they are done to your liking. Serve hot and pass pepper vinegar and/or Old Sour separately if you like.

CRESS, WATERCRESS, AND CREASIE GREENS

In the moist bottomland around the countless streams and rivers that ribbon the South, watercress grows in wild abundance. Most of us are familiar with the common hothouse variety, but many do not realize that it is just one of many varieties of cress, including the common land cress, sometimes called "creasie greens" and "peppergrass" in the South, which was even cultivated in many early gardens. It was used both as a salad green and as a cooked vegetable, especially among African American families, to whom greens of all kinds were very important, not only as part of their diet but as a tonic for the ailing.

Edna Lewis, the celebrated Southern chef, cookbook author, and national treasure, recalls that whenever one of her many brothers and sisters was ill, her mother would send the healthy children out into the snow-blanketed fields around their home in Freetown, Virginia, to gather the ground-hugging land cress that flourished beneath the snow.

Though Mrs. Lewis still prefers wild cress above the hothouse variety, she cautions against gathering cress from commercially farmed fields, maintained roadsides, or even your own lawn, where chemical plant control has often been used. Unless you are sure, it is safer to stick to the cultivated variety.

STEAMED WATERCRESS

In *The Taste of Country Cooking*, Mrs. Lewis suggests wilting cultivated cress in olive oil, like John Taylor's Wilted Greens (page 256). Here, the greens simmer luxuriously in ham broth, a very traditional way of cooking them, especially when they are the wild variety.

SERVES 4

2 cups water
¼ pound smoked pork or country ham
4 bunches watercress (about 1½ to 2 pounds)
Salt
Pepper Vinegar (page 27)

1.   Put the water and pork or ham in a lidded kettle that will comfortably hold all the cress at one time. Bring it to a boil, uncovered, over medium-high heat, then reduce the

heat to a slow simmer, cover, and cook until the pork or ham is falling apart tender, about 1 hour.

2. Wash the cress thoroughly (if it is wild cress, wash it in several changes of water, since it is usually very gritty). Drain it well, trim off any roots or tough stems, and add the cress to the pot. The liquid won't cover it at first, but as the cress wilts, it will throw off more liquid and also lose volume. Steam until the cress is completely tender, about 45 minutes for wild greens; cultivated cress will take less time. Taste and adjust the salt, if it needs any more, and simmer a minute or two more.

3. You can drain the cress or serve it with its pot liquor. Pass pepper vinegar with the greens.

GRITS AND GREENS

Nationally known author and television cooking teacher Nathalie Dupree is perhaps best known and loved by her viewers for what one critic calls her "endearing klutziness." This stems partly from the fact that she is hopelessly nearsighted, and partly from the fact that she wants her students to see that she's no more perfect than they.

Consequently, when I asked her for a recipe for this book, my first thought was to use the squash casserole that she had invented by mistakenly grabbing a bag of coconut out of the freezer instead of bread crumbs; it was classic clutzy Nathalie. But after poring over her two classics, *New Southern Cooking* and *Southern Memories*, we settled on this one because you don't get more innovative, yet more solidly Southern, than cooking grits and greens in the same pot.

SERVES 8

> 3 cups whole milk
> 1 cup heavy cream (minimum 36 percent milkfat)
> 1 cup quick grits (not instant)
> 6 tablespoons (3 ounces or ³/₄ stick) unsalted butter
> 1 pound greens (turnip, spinach, poke sallet, or chard), deveined and
>   stemmed
> 1¹/₂ cups freshly grated Parmesan (preferably Parmigiano-Reggiano)
> Salt and black pepper in a peppermill

1. Combine the milk and cream in a saucepan (preferably nonstick) that will hold all the grits. Turn on the heat to medium and bring the liquid almost to a boil. Stirring constantly, pour in the grits in a thin, steady stream. Bring back to a simmer and cook, stirring frequently, until the grits are thick and tender, about 5 to 10 minutes. Remove from the heat, stir in 2 tablespoons of the butter, and set aside in a warm place (a basin of hot water is ideal).

2. Wash the greens in a basin of cold water, changing the water if necessary, until all the sand and soil are removed from them. Lift them out of the water into a colander. Drain briefly but not thoroughly—there should still be plenty of water clinging to the leaves. Put the wet greens into a large, lidded frying pan that will hold all the greens at once. Cover and cook over medium-high heat until the greens are wilted, about 5 minutes. Immediately drain and refresh the greens in cold water. Drain well and gently squeeze the greens to remove all the water.

3. Put the remaining 4 tablespoons of butter in the frying pan in which the greens have cooked. Turn on the heat to medium. When the butter is melted, add the greens and sauté until they are heated through, about 2 minutes. Turn off the heat.

4. Stir the greens and Parmesan into the grits until the cheese is melted. Add a healthy pinch or so of salt and a few liberal grindings of pepper, both to taste. Pour the grits and greens into a warm serving dish and serve at once.

Note: *This dish can be made ahead and reheated over low heat or in a microwave oven, but wait until after reheating it to add the Parmesan. Nathalie sometimes garnishes the dish with poke shoots, the tender stalks of new poke plants that are no bigger than asparagus. If you have such wonders, blanch them in salted boiling water for about 5 minutes.*

JERUSALEM ARTICHOKES

When I first started teaching Southern cooking, I went around waving this little root vegetable like a Confederate flag. It became my symbol and example for the traditional Southern cooking that I had come to champion: a native American vegetable, once very popular on Southern tables, all but forgotten (except as an ingredient for pickles and relishes) in recent times. Even now, as it is beginning to be rediscovered, it is being treated mostly as an Italian vegetable.

Jerusalem artichokes are, of course, neither artichokes nor from Jerusalem. They are the tuber of a native American sunflower *(Helianthus tuberosus)*, one of several sunflower varieties that were cultivated by Native Americans for food. The charming and picturesque name, which goes almost all the way back to the vegetable's introduction to Europe, most likely derives in part from a corruption of an Italian name—*girasoli*. Though the usual explanation for why it was called an artichoke is that its flavor vaguely resembles that of artichokes, it may have a more curious derivation. According to some historians, the unopened flower buds, which look a bit like an artichoke, were once eaten by Native Americans in much the same way that we eat artichokes hearts today.

Nowadays, American growers are marketing these tubers as "sunchokes." Old crank that I am, I prefer the older, more picturesque name, but "sunchoke" is probably what you will have to ask for. This root is harvested after the plant blooms out. That happens at different times of the year throughout the country. In the South, Jerusalem artichokes begin to come into season in early autumn. In colder regions, they show up around Christmas and are available until spring. California sunchokes, a hybrid variety, are available almost year round, though they are sometimes hard to come by in late summer and early fall.

In spite of the vegetables' native origins, most of the old recipes for Jerusalem artichokes have a European lineage, which is betrayed by ingredients unknown to pre-Columbian America—butter, cream, bread crumbs, citrus juice, wine vinegar, and the like.

$\mathcal{B}$OILED JERUSALEM ARTICHOKES ⬩

This is the basic recipe for preparing Jerusalem artichokes. Once they are cooked, they can be scalloped, sauced with cream, breaded and fried, dressed as salad, or served just as they are—with perhaps a bit of melted butter. In selecting artichokes for boiling, remember that they should all be roughly the same size so that they cook evenly.

Though you can peel the artichokes after they are boiled or when they are to be cooked in other ways, never peel them before boiling them: the skins not only keep the flavor in, they also prevent the flesh from turning dark and getting soggy.

2 pounds Jerusalem artichokes as much the same size as possible
Salt

1. Scrub the artichokes under cold running water and pat them dry. Don't let them stand in water or they'll start to turn black. Put them in a kettle that will comfortably hold them with enough water to cover them by an inch. Lift out the artichokes, cover the kettle, and bring the liquid to a boil over high heat.

2. When the water is boiling, add a small handful of salt and the artichokes. Bring the liquid back to a boil, then loosely cover the kettle and reduce the heat to medium. Simmer until the artichokes are just tender, 12 to 20 minutes (the exact timing will depend on size). Don't overcook them or they'll get dark and soggy. Drain them quickly and, if you like, peel them. Serve hot, tossed with butter, a liberal pinch of salt, and a few grindings of black pepper to taste, or use them in one of the following recipes.

Scalloped
Jerusalem Artichokes

This sumptuous side dish is a fine companion for just about any meat, poultry, or fish that does not contain cream. It's also substantial enough to stand on its own as a main course.

The cream must have a fat content of at least 36 percent or it may never thicken properly. If you are unable to get cream that is rich enough, sprinkle each layer of artichokes with a tablespoon of soft bread crumbs. This will thicken the cream without giving it that disagreeable pasty quality that flour sometimes imparts.

SERVES 4 TO 6

2 pounds Boiled Jerusalem Artichokes (page 261)
Salt and black pepper in a peppermill
1 cup heavy cream (minimum 36 percent milkfat)
2 tablespoons unsalted butter
³/₄ cup dry bread crumbs

1.   Position a rack in the upper third of the oven and preheat the oven to 400 degrees F. While the artichokes are still warm, peel them if you like (the skins should slip right off) and cut them into ¼-inch slices. (It isn't necessary to peel them; I seldom do because I like the skins.)

2.   Lightly grease a 9-inch square (or equivalent oval or round) casserole with butter. Put in the Jerusalem artichoke slices in overlapping rows in no more than two layers, lightly seasoning the layers with a pinch or so of salt and a few grindings of black pepper. When all the artichokes are in the dish, pour the cream evenly over them.

3.   Put the butter in a skillet and place it over medium heat. When it is melted, turn off the heat, add the crumbs and toss until the butter is evenly absorbed. Sprinkle the crumbs over the casserole and bake in the upper third of the oven until the cream is thick and the crumbs are nicely browned, about half an hour.

JERUSALEM ARTICHOKE SALAD

While Jerusalem artichokes can be sliced paper thin and used raw in salads, old Southern cooks used to make salads with boiled artichokes, much like potato salad. It makes an interesting twist on that old picnic and dinner-on-the-grounds standard.

You can prepare the entire salad ahead of time, but don't cook the artichokes ahead of putting the salad together or they'll turn dark. Besides, they should still be a little warm when they are dressed so that they absorb some of the dressing.

SERVES 4

2 large hard-cooked eggs
½ teaspoon dry mustard
¼ cup red wine vinegar
2 tablespoons olive oil
Salt and black pepper in a peppermill
2 pounds Boiled Jerusalem Artichokes (page 261)
2 green onions
1 tablespoon capers, rinsed and drained
2 tablespoons minced parsley
4–6 fresh lettuce leaves, washed and drained

1.   Slice the eggs crosswise into rings and separate the yolks from the rings of egg white. Set the whites aside. Put the yolks in the bottom of a salad bowl with the mustard and mash them smooth with a fork. Gradually add the vinegar, stirring with the fork, until it forms a smooth paste. Add the oil, a drop at a time, beating until it is emulsified. The dressing can also be made in a blender or food processor (see note).

2.   While the artichokes are still warm, slice them into rounds about 1/4 inch thick. Don't peel them unless you dislike the skins. Add them to the dressing and toss until they are well coated. Add a healthy pinch of salt and a liberal grinding of pepper, and toss well.

3.   Wash the green onions and pull off any yellowed or discolored leaves. Trim off the roots and slice them thinly. Add the onions, the capers, and 1 tablespoon of the parsley to the salad. Toss again to mix them in, taste and correct the seasonings, and give it a final toss. Let the artichokes cool completely before serving.

4.   When you are ready to serve the salad, arrange the lettuce on a serving platter and turn the salad out onto it. Sprinkle with the remaining parsley, lay the reserved rings of egg white decoratively around the edges, and serve at room temperature.

Note: *To make the dressing in a blender or food processor, put all the ingredients except the oil in the bowl of the machine and blend. With the machine running, gradually add the oil through the feed tube (or hole in the blender lid) in a very thin stream and blend until it is emulsified.*

If you want to make this salad without eggs, put the dressing ingredients in a jar, put on a tight lid, and shake the jar until the dressing is well mixed.

MARYLAND JERUSALEM ARTICHOKE SOUP

This luscious, velvety soup is a perfect vehicle for the subtle but distinctive flavor of Jerusalem artichokes. The other ingredients are kept to a minimum and deliberately understated so that the flavor of the artichokes predominates. The recipe may look plain, and it is, but the resulting flavor is anything but simple.

Don't be tempted to enrich the soup by substituting cream for the half-and-half. The cooked and pureed artichokes have a creamy richness that neither needs—nor benefits from—added fat. Bet you thought you'd never hear me say that.

1 lemon

2 pounds Jerusalem artichokes

1 medium yellow onion, peeled and minced

2 tablespoons unsalted butter

2 cups Chicken Broth (page 23) or 1 cup canned broth mixed with 1
    cup water

1 Bouquet Garni (page 36), made with a healthy sprig each thyme and
    parsley, 1 leafy celery rib, and 1 bay leaf

1½ cups half-and-half

Salt and whole white peppercorns in a peppermill

1 tablespoon minced parsley

1. Have ready a basin of cold water that will comfortably hold all the artichokes. Cut the lemon in half. Set aside one of the halves. Squeeze the juice from the other half into the water and drop in the spent peel. Scrub the artichokes under cold running water and, one at a time, peel them with a vegetable peeler and cut them into ¼-inch slices. Put each one in the basin of acidulated water as soon as it is sliced (this keeps it from discoloring).

2. Put the onion and butter in a kettle that will comfortably hold all the ingredients and place it over medium-high heat. Sauté, tossing and stirring frequently, until the onion is softened but not colored, about 3 to 5 minutes. Add the broth and bouquet garni, and bring the soup to a boil, then reduce the heat to medium low, cover the kettle, and simmer for half an hour.

3. Drain the artichokes and add them to the soup, raise the heat to medium high, and bring the soup back to a boil, then reduce it once more to low, cover, and simmer until the artichokes are quite soft, about 25 minutes. Remove and discard the bouquet garni. Take up a cup of the artichokes, cut them into small cubes, and set aside.

4. Puree the soup in batches through a food mill or in a blender or food processor. Return the soup to the kettle, add the half-and-half and reserved cubed artichokes. Season with a healthy pinch or so of salt and a liberal grinding of white pepper. (The soup can be made several hours or a day ahead up to this point.)

5. To serve the soup, reheat it gently over medium heat, stirring frequently to prevent it from sticking and scorching. Take it from the heat and squeeze in the juice from the remaining lemon half. Stir, taste, and adjust the seasonings, and pour the soup into a heated tureen or divide it among warmed soup plates. Sprinkle each serving with the minced parsley.

Note: *This soup needs the substance of meat broth to give it the necessary body. If you are cooking without meat, however, you can substitute Vegetable Broth (page 24).*

POTATOES

Potatoes are so central to the average American diet that we forget that they have not always been so commonplace. They are not even native to our continent, but to South America. Just how this South American member of the nightshade family ended up in the North is a matter of some colorful debate. Historians disagree almost violently on the point. The most common theory is that they were introduced to North America by way of Europe. The fact that they are often called "Irish" potatoes by many Southerners, even today, is suggestive and has led a few pop historians to jump to the conclusion that they were imported to our continent by way of Ireland. That scenario seems highly unlikely in the face of other evidence. A few older sources and historians (including Thomas Jefferson) believed that potatoes had already migrated to North America by the time the Europeans arrived, and this theory can't be completely discounted. However the potato came to be here, whether by way of the European explorers or by way of pre-Colombian native migration, what is pretty certain is that it did not figure prominently in the Southern diet until the eighteenth century, and even then it was overshadowed by sweet potatoes.

Though potatoes are still probably not as popular in the South as they are in other parts of the country, the proliferation of fast-food fries and chips has tipped the balance of consumption over our traditionally favored sweet potatoes. But that isn't to say that we haven't long enjoyed potatoes in a number of ways. There are many potato dishes that are of course pretty much universal—those fries, for example—and mashed, scalloped, and baked potatoes. Good recipes for these favorites are commonplace and were included in my first book, *Classical Southern Cooking,* so I haven't repeated them here. Instead, I offer a few that you might not have expected to find on Southern tables.

Mary Randolph's
Potatoes and Onions ◀

This is mashed potatoes with an old Virginia twist. Mrs. Randolph left the proportion of potatoes to onions up to the cook's individual taste, but I've imposed mine here—a 2-to-1 ratio. You needn't feel bound by it. If you prefer a more subtle or even more robust onion flavor, adjust the proportions accordingly.

SERVES 6

2 pounds mature boiling potatoes of a uniform size
1 pound medium yellow onions
2 tablespoons unsalted butter
1/4 cup heavy cream (minimum 36 percent milkfat)
Salt
Black pepper in a peppermill (optional)
1 tablespoon chopped parsley or chives (optional)

1. If you store your potatoes and onions in the refrigerator, take them out at least half an hour before you cook them. Wash the potatoes under cold running water, scrubbing off any dirt without breaking the skin. Wash the onions briefly, trim off the roots, and cut a deep "X" in the root ends. Don't peel them. Put the vegetables in a kettle that will easily hold them and leave at least 2 inches of room at the top. Add enough water to cover them by about an inch, take the vegetables out of the kettle, cover it, and bring the water to the boiling point over medium-high heat.

2. When the water is almost boiling, add the potatoes and onions. Let it come to a full, rolling boil, then reduce the heat to medium low and cook at a bare simmer until the vegetables are tender. The exact time will vary, 15 to 30 minutes, depending on the size and age of the potatoes and onions. Also, one vegetable may take longer to cook than the other, so watch them. If either the potatoes or onions are done before the other, take them up and keep them in a warm spot until the other vegetable is done.

3. Drain off all the water and let the vegetables sit, uncovered, in a warm place for about 5 minutes. Peel the potatoes with your hands; the skins will slip right off. Trim off the stem and root ends of the onions and peel them. Force the potatoes through a coarse sieve or potato ricer into the kettle in which they were cooked. Either force the onions through the sieve or puree them in a blender (they won't go through a ricer). Add them to the potatoes along with the butter, cream, and a healthy pinch of salt.

4. Place the kettle over low heat. Stir and mash until the mixture is smooth and the liquid is incorporated. If the mixture appears to be too dry, add a spoonful or so more cream but don't overdo it. Taste and adjust the seasoning, and mound the potatoes in a warmed serving bowl. If you like, dust the top with a few grindings of pepper and one of the chopped herbs—or a little of both—and serve at once.

ILDA'S SCALLOPED POTATOES WITH HAM

It was my first night in Italy. Our class had spent the day sketching in the picturesque port towns of Portofino and San Fruttuoso. Soaked with Riviera sunshine and salty Ligurian air, we were very hungry, as only active young people can be. Already, I'd had my first espresso, focaccia, and *spaghetti alla carbonara*, and was game for anything our cook, Ilda, fed to us. She had long since gone home but had left a casserole for us to bake for our supper. She called it *casseruola al forno*, which only means "baked casserole"—not much of a clue. We popped it into the oven and made a salad. The aroma filled the house, rich and tantalizingly Italian; something very familiar about it kept teasing my imagination. At last we sat down to supper; the spoon pierced the crusty cheese and the creamy filling oozed out. I tasted it—and was enveloped by the memory of a dozen covered-dish suppers back home. Our exotic Italian casserole was only scalloped potatoes with ham, a dish I'd cut my teeth on.

That recipe came home with me, and now Ilda's version of this covered-dish standard, made with our own cousin of prosciutto—country ham—has become a tradition in my own family.

SERVES 4 TO 6

2 pounds boiling potatoes
3 tablespoons unsalted butter
2 tablespoons minced yellow onion
2 tablespoons unbleached all-purpose flour
2 cups milk
Salt and whole white peppercorns in a peppermill

Whole nutmeg in a grater
1 cup diced country ham (or prosciutto)
1 cup freshly grated Gruyère
¹/₄ cup freshly grated Parmesan (preferably Parmigiano-Reggiano)

1. Put enough water in a kettle to cover the potatoes and place it over high heat. Wash the potatoes under cold running water, and when the water comes to a rapid boil, add them to the kettle. Cover and let the water return to a boil. Reduce the heat to medium and cook until the potatoes are easily pierced with a fork. Drain and set them aside until they are cool enough to handle. Position a rack in the upper third of the oven and preheat the oven to 375 degrees F.

2. Put the butter and onion in a saucepan, and place it over medium heat. Sauté until the onion is softened and transparent, about 5 to 8 minutes. Sprinkle the flour over the onion and stir with a whisk until it is smoothly blended. Whisking constantly, slowly add the milk and continue whisking until it begins to thicken. Reduce the heat to low and simmer, stirring frequently, until thick, about 10 minutes. Season to taste with a pinch or so of salt, a grinding of white pepper, and a generous grating of nutmeg. Turn off the heat.

3. Peel the potatoes and slice them ¼ inch thick. Lightly butter a 9-inch square casserole dish and cover the bottom with a layer of potato slices. Scatter about a third of the ham over them. Spread a third of the sauce over this and top it with a third of the Gruyère. Add another layer of potatoes, ham, sauce, and Gruyère, and repeat with a third layer, finishing with the remaining sauce and Gruyère. Sprinkle the Parmesan over the top and bake in the upper third of the oven until the top is golden brown and the casserole is bubbly, about half an hour. Serve hot.

ℬAILEE'S LATKES

Until recently, many Southerners wouldn't have known a latke from a bagel. Yet potato pancakes have long been a standard in Southern cooking; it's just that they didn't generally come to the table accompanied by their Jewish name. That's never been the case in Savannah, where there has been a continuous and highly respected Jewish presence since the city's beginning. The first Jews arrived here barely five months after the colony's founding, and though their numbers have always been small, their influence on the cultural and social life of Savannah has been anything but insignificant.

Only one of Savannah's three congregations still keeps kosher, but there has lately been a renewed interest in Jewish culinary traditions even among Reform congregations, tempered though those traditions have been by a Southern accent. (When Congregation K. K. Mickve Israel holds its annual food festival, The Hard Lox Café, in Monterey Square, its telling slogan is "Shalom, y'all.")

For years artist and cooking teacher Bailee Kronowitz has brought the best of those traditions to the rest of us in Savannah with her intelligent and lively teaching. Her potato latkes are exemplary—traditional-tasting but a bit unorthodox in method. Usually latkes are made with hand-grated potatoes and onions, but Bailee prefers to chop them in the blender. Though the texture of the potato batter is finer than when hand-grated, there's still plenty of it—and needless to say the latkes are a snap to make.

MAKES ABOUT 30 LATKES,
OR 6 TO 8 SERVINGS

1½ pounds (2 to 3 medium) mature baking potatoes
½ pound (about 1 large to 2 medium) yellow onions
1 large egg, well beaten
1–2 tablespoons flour
Salt and black pepper in a peppermill
Vegetable oil for frying
1 cup applesauce (preferably homemade)
1 cup homemade Crème Fraîche (page 18) or sour cream

1.   Position a rack in the upper third of the oven and preheat the oven to 150 degrees F. Prepare a basin of cold water that will hold all the potatoes without overflowing. Wash and peel the potatoes, cut them into 1-inch chunks, and drop them into the basin of water. Peel and quarter the onions and set them aside.

2.   Lift one of the potato chunks out of the water bath, dry it, and put it in a blender. Put on the lid and process at medium speed until the potato is finely chopped. Drain, dry, and process the remaining chunks of potato, one at a time, until they are all chopped fine. Transfer the chopped potatoes to another bowl and process the onions in the same way. Add the potatoes back to the blender along with the beaten egg, put on the lid, and pulse until they are well mixed. Add 1 tablespoon of flour, and pulse until it is well mixed and slightly thickened. If necessary (some potatoes have more water than others), add another tablespoon of flour. Season with a healthy pinch of salt and a few grindings of black pepper.

3. Film the bottom of a frying pan (preferably cast iron) with oil (about ⅛ inch deep). Turn on the heat to medium high and heat until it is sizzling hot (375 degrees F.). Drop the potato batter in heaping tablespoonfuls into the hot oil until the pan is full but not crowded. Fry the latkes until they are nicely browned on the bottom, about 3 to 5 minutes. Turn and cook until the other side is evenly browned, about 3 minutes more. Drain the cooked latkes briefly on absorbent paper and then transfer them to a cookie sheet. Keep them in the warm oven while the remaining latkes cook. Repeat until all the batter is cooked, and serve the latkes at once, passing applesauce and sour cream separately.

Note: *The potatoes and onions should be finely chopped, but they shouldn't be a smooth puree, so don't overprocess them. The easiest way to keep this from happening is to pulse the blender rather than letting it run continuously.*

Bailee says that these latkes can also be made ahead and refrigerated. After they have completely cooled, cover them well and refrigerate until you are ready to serve them. Take them out of the refrigerator about half an hour ahead. Position a rack in the upper third of the oven and preheat the oven to 350 degrees F. Transfer the latkes to a cookie sheet and bake them until they are heated through, about 5 minutes.

*F*UNERAL SALAD

When somebody dies down South, the bereaved family is swamped with food. Will D. Campbell gives the best explanation for this phenomenon in his novel *Brother to a Dragonfly* (1977): "Somehow in rural Southern culture, food is always the first thought of neighbors when there is trouble. That is something they can do and not feel uncomfortable. . . . 'Here, I brought you some fresh eggs for your breakfast. And here's a cake. And some potato salad.' It means, 'I love you. And I am sorry for what you are going through, and I will share as much of your burden as I can.' And maybe potato salad is a better way of saying it."

Maybe it is.

I really don't know why it's always potato salad, so don't ask. Every cook I ever knew has his own particular potato salad for such an occasion—and usually the recipe isn't written down. You just make a big bowl of the stuff, throwing in things until it tastes right and looks as if it will feed a crowd. When my friend Adam Howard was growing up, his mother's version was called "Forest Home Salad" in polite company, but "Funeral Potato

Salad" at home, because the only time she made it was for somebody's funeral. This is my own Funeral Salad.

SERVES A LOT OF PEOPLE (AT LEAST 12)

4 pounds red-skinned potatoes
Salt
Dry white vermouth
1 cup chopped (1 small) sweet onion, preferably Vidalia
1/2 cup chopped (about 4) green onions
1 cup finely chopped celery
2 tablespoons finely chopped parsley
1/2 cup pitted Greek black olives, cut into thin strips
1/2 cup pitted green olives, cut into thin strips
2 tablespoons small whole (or coarsely chopped large) capers
4 hard-cooked eggs, peeled and chopped
1 cup Homemade Mayonnaise (page 53)
2 tablespoons Dijon mustard
1/4 cup wine vinegar
Black pepper in a peppermill

1.   Put enough water to cover the potatoes in a large kettle that will hold them comfortably and bring the water to a boil over high heat. Add a small handful of salt and the potatoes. Let the water come back to a boil, reduce the heat to medium, and cook until the potatoes are just tender, about 20 minutes. Exact times will depend on the size and age of the potatoes—some will take longer, some less—so keep an eye on the pot and don't overcook them. Drain the potatoes and let them cool just enough to handle. Peel them, cut them into large dice, and place them in a large bowl. Sprinkle them generously with vermouth and a pinch or so of salt. Let them cool.

2.   Add the two types of onions, celery, parsley, black and green olives, capers, and hard-cooked eggs. Add the mayonnaise, mustard, vinegar, and a few liberal grindings of pepper, and mix well until the vegetables are all coated with the dressing. Taste and correct the seasonings and let stand for half an hour before serving.

Note: Don't let a salad with homemade mayonnaise sit out at room temperature for more than an hour, and promptly refrigerate any leftovers, or you could have bacteria tapdancing on top of it.

Potatoes vary in density and absorptive capacity; the vermouth helps keep them from absorbing too much dressing, but even so, you may find that the salad is too thick if the potatoes are especially thirsty. If this happens, make a simple dressing of 2 parts vinegar to 1 part olive oil, mix it well, and add it by spoonfuls until the salad is the consistency that suits you. Taste and correct the seasonings. The added vinegar will naturally make the salad more tart and you may need to tone it down a bit.

BAKED POTATO SALAD

The dilemma is all too familiar; you had a barbecue last Saturday or there was a death in your family on Monday. It's now midweek, the visitors are gone, and you have 40 pounds of potato salad in the refrigerator. You can't face another ounce of the stuff on your plate. Hating the idea of throwing it out, I used to guiltily stow it in the back of the refrigerator until it had grown a nice junior-high science project on top and started to attack anyone who opened the door.

That was before my friend Jim King served me this solution to the problem, which involves neither mold, bribery, nor secret burials at midnight. Undisturbed by the surplus, Jim happily slapped it into a casserole, strewed a few buttered crumbs over the top, and popped it into the oven.

I know what you are thinking; but just wait until you taste it.

SERVES 6 TO 8

8 cups Funeral Salad (page 271) or any mayonnaise-based potato
    salad you happen to be swimming in
4 tablespoons unsalted butter
1 cup dry bread crumbs

1. Position a rack in the upper third of the oven and preheat the oven to 400 degrees F. Press the potato salad into a casserole that will hold it in a layer about an inch deep (a 9 × 13-inch dish).

2. Put the butter in a sauté pan and turn on the heat to medium. When the butter is just melted, turn off the heat and add the crumbs. Stir until the butter is evenly absorbed by the crumbs. Sprinkle the crumbs over the potato salad and place the casserole in the upper third of the oven. Bake until the potatoes are bubbly and hot and the crumbs are nicely browned, about 25 to 30 minutes. Serve hot.

WINTER SQUASH

There is probably no more confusing botanical history than that of edible gourds, which is of course what all squash are. They are part of a large botanical family that includes pumpkins, cucumbers, and all types of melons. These gourds have been cultivated and highly prized throughout the world since time immemorial. As to their origin, though, no one is really sure. There are theories placing their beginnings in both Asia and the Americas. Most botanists and historians agree that the varieties common in our country are either natives or hybrids developed from native stock. But weighty issues of origin matter only to historians and are of little consequence to most of us when we sit down at the table.

Though winter squash have been grown and eaten all along in the South, there was a time when they were thought of almost as a kind of Northern vegetable. For a Southerner, "squash" meant the yellow crookneck variety. Winter squash had come to be treated more as a sweetmeat than a vegetable, and when I was growing up, they were mostly made into pies or baked with brown sugar and spices, much like candied sweet potatoes. Both were popular dishes and I utterly loathed them. It was only after I was grown and had been introduced to savory dishes like the ones that follow that I began to like winter squash at all. Now they are one of my very favorite winter vegetables—and these recipes, some of my favorite dishes.

Baked Winter Squash with Sausage Filling ⪻

Cold weather in Savannah may not be as severe or as lasting as in more northerly regions, but when the weather here turns nasty, it's *really* nasty. The high humidity creates an icy dampness that seeps right through your clothes and sticks to your skin like a sheet of wet plastic. Nothing throws off that damp, icy mantle—except possibly a shot of bourbon—any better than this spicy dish. Like a well broken–in pair of flannel long johns, it envelops you with warmth and fills you up with a lingering sense of well-being.

SERVES 4

2 small winter squash (about 1 pound each), such as acorn, butternut,
    or kabocha
2 pounds bulk sausage or 1 pound ground veal or pork

2 tablespoons butter (if using veal or pork)
2 cups cooked Carolina-Style Rice (page 43)
1 medium onion, peeled and chopped
3 cloves garlic, lightly crushed, peeled, and minced
10–12 fresh sage leaves or 1 teaspoon crumbled dried sage (omit if
    using sausage with sage already in it)
Nutmeg in a grater
Salt, ground cayenne, and black pepper in a peppermill
1 lemon
1 large egg, beaten
2 tablespoons butter (4 tablespoons if using veal or pork)
¹/₂ cup dry bread crumbs

1. Position a rack in the center of the oven and preheat the oven to 375 degrees F. Meanwhile, wash the squash, split them lengthwise into halves, and scoop out and discard the seeds. Lightly grease a baking pan that will comfortably hold the squash halves in one layer and place them on it split side up. Sprinkle them lightly with a little salt and set aside.

2. Crumble the sausage into a frying pan and turn on the heat to medium. Brown the meat well and remove it from the pan. Drain it briefly on several layers of absorbent paper. Spoon off all but 2 tablespoons of the fat in the pan. Increase the heat to medium high. (If you are using ground veal or pork, brown it over medium-high heat in 2 tablespoons of butter.) Add the onion to the pan and sauté until it is translucent, about 5 minutes. Add the garlic and sauté until it is fragrant, about a minute longer. Turn off the heat.

3. Combine the sausage or ground meat, the onion, garlic, and rice in a mixing bowl. Add the sage (if the sausage doesn't already contain it), a liberal grating of nutmeg, and a pinch or so of salt. If you are using ground meat, add a pinch of cayenne and a few gridings of pepper. Grate into it the zest from the lemon, then cut the lemon in half and squeeze in the juice from one of the halves. Toss until uniformly mixed, then taste and correct the seasoning. Add the beaten egg and mix well.

4. Divide the mixture equally among the squash halves, mounding it up in the center if necessary. Melt the butter in a skillet over low heat. Add the bread crumbs and mix until the butter is evenly absorbed. Spread the crumbs over the squash and bake them in the center of the oven until tender and cooked through, about 1 hour.

BRAISED WINTER SQUASH

This is a cooking method that winter squash takes to like a duck to water. It brings out and enhances their savory-sweet flavor better than any other way of preparing them. Though traditionally served with a sturdy meat dish, such as roasted pork or grilled chops, the squash is meaty and satisfying enough to stand on its own as a main course.

SERVES 4

2 small (about ³/₄ pound each) or 1 large (about 2 pounds) winter
    squash, such as acorn, butternut, cashaw, or kabocha
3 tablespoons bacon drippings (preferable) or unsalted butter
1 large onion, peeled and chopped
1 clove garlic, crushed and peeled
8–10 fresh (or 5 to 6 dried) sage leaves
Salt and black pepper in a peppermill
¹/₂ cup Chicken Broth (page 23) or water
1 tablespoon chopped fresh sage or parsley

1. Split the squash lengthwise and scoop out and discard the seeds. Peel and cut the squash into chunks about an inch square.

2. Choose a lidded skillet (preferably cast iron) that will comfortably hold the squash in a single layer. Put in the drippings or butter and onion, and turn on the heat to medium high. Sauté until the onion is transparent, about 5 minutes, then add the squash and toss until they are glossy and hot, about a minute. Add the garlic, sage, a healthy pinch of salt, and a liberal grinding of pepper. Toss well and pour in the broth or water. Bring the liquid to a boil, cover the pan, and reduce the heat to a bare simmer. Cook until the squash is nearly tender, about half an hour.

3. Remove the lid and raise the heat to medium high. Reduce the liquid, shaking the pan and turning the squash frequently to prevent them from sticking, until the liquid is evaporated and thick, and the squash are just beginning to brown. Turn off the heat. Taste and correct the seasonings, transfer the squash to a warm bowl, sprinkle with the chopped herbs, and serve at once.

Winter Squash Country Captain

Country Captain is a spicy tomato-based curry that came into the South by way of England's East Indian trade. It isn't really an Indian dish, but an English adaptation of one. Since the early nineteenth century, Country Captain has been popular all along the Atlantic seaboard in every major Southern port from Baltimore to Savannah.

Usually, the main ingredient of Country Captain is chicken, but Charlestonians and Savannahians like to make it with shrimp. It's an excellent way to cook winter squash, too, since they take well to curry and develop a rich, meaty flavor.

SERVES 4

1 medium (about 2 pounds) winter squash, such as acorn, butternut, or kabocha

3 tablespoons unsalted butter or olive oil

1 large onion, peeled and chopped

1 large green bell pepper, seeded and chopped

2 large cloves garlic, crushed, peeled, and minced

2 tablespoons Curry Powder (page 31) or 1 tablespoon commercial curry powder

1 tart apple (such as Granny Smith), peeled, cored, and diced

2 pounds ripe tomatoes, scalded, peeled, seeded, and chopped as directed on page 117, or 2 cups seeded and chopped canned Italian tomatoes with their juices

1 teaspoon sugar

Salt

1 cup currants or raisins

1 tablespoon chopped parsley

4 cups cooked Carolina-Style Rice (page 43)

¹/₂ cup grated unsweetened coconut

¹/₂ cup toasted peanuts

1. Peel, seed, and cut the squash into 1-inch cubes. Set aside. Put the butter or oil, onion, and bell pepper in a lidded skillet that will comfortably hold all the ingredients and place it over medium heat. Sauté, tossing frequently, until the vegetables are softened but not browned, about 5 minutes. Add the garlic and curry powder, and continue sautéing until fragrant, about a minute more.

2.   Add the squash and apple, and toss until they are uniformly coated with the curry mixture. Add the tomatoes, sugar, a large pinch of salt, and the currants or raisins, and bring to a boil. Reduce the heat to a gentle simmer, cover, and stirring occasionally, cook until the squash are tender, about 1 hour. When the squash are tender, if there is too much liquid in the pan, raise the heat briefly and let it boil away. Turn off the heat and stir in the parsley. Serve hot over rice, with the coconut and peanuts passed separately.

Note: *Traditionally, this would be called a "two boy" curry because there are only two condiments. The condiment tray can have as many as ten "boys" and include chutney, Bombay duck, diced cucumber, mango, oranges, and bananas. Add any of these if you like, though in Savannah anything more than a five-boy curry is considered pretentious.*

TURNIPS

This common root vegetable is thought to be native to northern Europe, from whence it gradually migrated south and later was imported into North America, apparently with the earliest of the European settlers. It has been popular on both Northern and Southern tables at least since the early seventeenth century.

We Southerners do love our greens, and the leafy top of this vegetable is a particular favorite. There are some Southerners, in fact, who loosely refer to all greens as "turnip greens" even when they are really mustard, kale, and collards. The popularity of the greens is well known, but it isn't as widely known that we like the roots almost as much.

The simplest way to prepare turnips is to cut them into small dice and mix them with their greens in a single pot. In early autumn, when new turnips are at their crispest and most fragrant, we like them best prepared like mashed potatoes, with a little cream and butter for richness and a dusting of black pepper for added spice.

$\mathcal{T}$URNIPS STUFFED
WITH WINTER GREENS

This isn't an old recipe, but it has all of the old Southern sensibility about it. Its inspiration comes from Joan Cobitz, an artist and the bread baker for Brighter Day, our local natural-food store. A master cook as well as a baker, she occasionally cooks for private parties. When she was asked to do a Southern buffet, Joan—a Yankee from Chicago—immediately called me in to help. Once we decided to do something with turnips and greens that would be self-contained, the dish pretty much invented itself.

The best choice for the greens is kale; collards work, too, but only if they are very young and tender. Turnip greens, oddly enough, will not work.

SERVES 4

4 large turnips (about 2 pounds)
4 tablespoons unsalted butter (plus more for greasing)
1 pound kale or young collards
Grated zest of 1 lemon
$^1\!/_2$ cup dry bread crumbs
4 green onions, thinly sliced
Salt and black pepper in a peppermill

1. Position a rack in the upper third of the oven and preheat the oven to 400 degrees F. Trim off most of the tap roots and green tops of the turnips, but leave a little of both attached. Scrub the turnips well under cold running water and pat dry. Rub them with a little butter, wrap them in foil, and put them on a cookie sheet. Place the cookie sheet on the upper rack of the oven and bake until the turnips yield slightly when pressed with a finger, about 1 hour.

2. Meanwhile, stem and cut the greens into 1-inch–wide strips. Wash thoroughly and drain them, leaving some moisture clinging to the leaves. Put them in a large, lidded skillet, and turn on the heat to medium high. Cover and cook until the greens are wilted but still bright green, about 4 minutes. Turn off the heat and spread the greens on a platter to cool.

3. Put 2 tablespoons of the butter in a small pan. Turn on the heat to medium, and when the butter is melted, add the lemon zest and bread crumbs and thoroughly mix them with the butter. Turn off the heat. Transfer the mixture to a bowl and set aside.

4. When the turnips are tender, remove them from the oven, unwrap them, and let them cool enough to handle. Slice off the tops and with a melon baller or small spoon, scoop out the inner flesh, leaving a ½-inch–thick shell. Set aside the inner flesh for another use. Put the shells on a lightly greased baking sheet or dish and set aside. (Note: You can make it to this point up to a day ahead, but cover and refrigerate it if it's prepared more than 2 hours ahead.)

5. Put the onions and the remaining 2 tablespoons of butter in the skillet where the greens were cooked and turn on the heat to medium high. Sauté until the onions are softened, about 2 minutes. Add the greens, a liberal pinch of salt, and a few grindings of black pepper, and toss well. Turn off the heat. Fill the turnips with the greens, sprinkle them with the crumb mixture, and bake until the crumbs are golden and the turnips and greens are heated through, about 20 minutes.

$\mathscr{R}$OASTED TURNIPS

Even people who claim to hate turnips will put them away with enthusiasm when they are cooked this way. Roasting brings out the natural sweetness in any root vegetable. Turnips are no exception. Though they're especially good when cooked in the drippings of roasted lamb, pork, or turkey and served as an accompaniment to the meat, they are powerfully good all by themselves.

SERVES 4

2 pounds fresh young turnips
2 tablespoons lard, bacon or roast drippings, or unsalted butter
1 tablespoon chopped fresh sage or winter savory
Salt and black pepper in a peppermill

1. Position a rack in the center of the oven and preheat the oven to 400 degrees F. Scrub the turnips well under cold running water. Cut off the taproots and sprout tops. If the turnips are very young and tender, they shouldn't require peeling (in fact, the skin lends its own distinctive flavor), but if the turnips are older and the skin appears to be especially tough, go ahead and peel them. Cut the turnips into quarters and set them aside.

2. Put the fat in a cast-iron pan or ovenproof casserole that will hold the turnips in one layer comfortably. Put the pan in the oven until the fat is melted and hot. Add the turnips to the pan and sprinkle them with the chopped herbs and a liberal grinding of pepper.

Return the pan to the oven and roast the turnips, turning them frequently to prevent sticking, until they are uniformly golden brown, about 45 minutes to an hour. If they stick anyway, slip a metal spatula under them and gently work them loose. Drain briefly on absorbent paper, sprinkle with a healthy pinch of salt, and serve at once.

Note: *Though animal fats, especially drippings or lard, are best in this recipe because they help the turnips to brown and lend the best flavor and crust, strict vegetarians can substitute peanut or olive oil with reasonably good results.*

MARYLAND
BROWNED TURNIPS

This is a nice stovetop variation on roasted turnips when you don't want to crank up the oven. The turnips make a showy presentation if you go to the extra trouble of trimming them into olivelike ovals, as an old recipe suggests, but they do just fine cut into wedges. Just make sure their shape is rounded enough to roll around in the pan.

This recipe is from the Hammond-Harwood House cookbook, *Maryland's Way*, but was first published in the *Maryland Cook Book* (1892). It foreshadows the ominous tendency that later cooks had to add sugar to almost everything, but here the sugar has a distinct function beyond sweetening, as it helps the turnips to caramelize and become brown.

SERVES 4

2 pounds fresh young turnips
2 tablespoons unsalted butter
1 tablespoon sugar
Salt and black pepper in a peppermill
1 tablespoon chopped parsley

1. Over high heat, bring a quart of water to a boil in a kettle that will comfortably hold all the turnips. Wash the turnips, lightly peel them, and cut them into wedges. If you like, you can trim the wedges into ovals.

2. Drop the turnips into the boiling water, bring it back to a boil, and cook for 1 minute. Drain them well.

3. Put the butter in a large skillet (preferably cast iron) that will comfortably hold the turnips in one layer. Place it over medium-high heat. When the butter is melted and almost to the point of browning, add the turnips. Sprinkle them with the sugar and sauté, tossing them frequently, until the turnips begin to brown. Lower the heat to medium and continue cooking until the turnips are evenly browned and tender, about 10 minutes more. Season to taste with a pinch or so of salt and a few grindings of black pepper. Transfer to a warm serving bowl, sprinkle them with the parsley, and serve at once.

Note: *There's no real substitute for butter in this dish. Olive oil will work, but the turnips won't have that lovely dusky sweetness that is characteristic of lightly browned butter.*

FLORIDA CITRUS FRUITS

Just as the days become their shortest and darkest, Indian River oranges and grapefruits arrive in the market, bringing a bit of Florida sunshine to breakfast tables all over the country. It should be no surprise then, that Floridians, just as we Georgians sport that ubiquitous peach, emblazon everything with an orange. It's the symbol not only of the state's best-known industry, but of the sun, which is always supposed to be shining overhead. Actually, it rains a lot in the Sunshine State (which is why the citrus trees flourish), and the trees only bear fruit during the winter, but the carefree notion of endless oranges and sunshine endures.

In Florida's semitropical climate, citrus fruits have flourished since the Spanish introduced them in the sixteenth century. But it wasn't until the War Between the States that the fledgling industry began to develop in a big way. It actually got a boost from something that was designed to bring the South to its knees: Union blockades. With the South's supply of imported fruit effectively cut off, Floridians scrambled to fill the gap. The Florida citrus industry was on its way, but it was another century before it really took off. The development of frozen concentrated orange juice created a year-round market for what had previously been a seasonal product, and the citrus boom was on.

Today, the state, particularly the Indian River region, is known throughout the country for its citrus fruits, which are considered by many (and certainly by proud Southerners) to be the finest in the world. Though it is not the only major producer of citrus fruits in the country, whenever freezing temperatures dip south of the Georgia state line, threatening the ripening crop, the whole country holds its collective breath.

Dozens of varieties of citrus fruits are grown in the region, from juice oranges, which mainly supply the frozen concentrate industry, to exotics like honeybells, tangelos, and ugli fruit. While many of these citrus are marketed nationally, some are produced only for the local market, and others are not marketed at all. The fruits most commonly available to us and the rest of the country are Valencia, navel, blood, and honeybell oranges; tangelos and tangerines; pink, white, and red grapefruit; and lemons and limes. Unless a recipe states that a specific citrus fruit be used, you can use differing varieties of each type inter-changeably.

Of course, the best way to experience citrus fruits is firsthand. If you've never eaten a tree-ripened grapefruit, naturally chilled by a cool February night, then you have missed one of the world's great delights. But you don't have to be in Florida to enjoy this bit of Florida sunshine; just look for the Indian River label on the grapefruit in your market.

*A*MBROSIA

Appropriately named, this luscious fruit salad has been a traditional Christmas dish all over the South at least since the days of Sarah Rutledge's *The Carolina Housewife* (1847). The essential ingredients are oranges and freshly grated coconut, and it must have them both to be authentic, but depending on where you are in the South, other citrus fruits, and often pineapple, are added to the bowl.

Today, in the interest of novelty (at least, that's all I can figure), ambrosia has been subjected to all sorts of indignities, including sugar, which it does not need; packaged sweetened coconut, which it does not want; or worse, canned pineapple and lurid maraschino cherries; and—God help us—gelatin and nondairy topping. The fresh, clean flavor and spirited finesse that made real ambrosia's name so appropriate gets literally buried alive.

What follows is Annabella Hill's classic recipe, the critical ingredient of which is fresh coconut juice. When you are selecting a coconut for this recipe, hold it near your ear and shake it: it should slosh happily with plenty of juice.

SERVES 6 TO 8

1 small, fresh coconut with juice
1 fresh, ripe pineapple
6 large, sweet oranges, such as navels or honeybells

1.   Fit a fine-meshed wire strainer over a bowl. Using a skewer, ice pick, or Phillips-head screwdriver, punch out the stem scars that make the little monkey face on one side of the coconut. Invert the coconut over the strainer and drain all the juice into the bowl. The juice should smell of fresh coconut; if it smells musty, don't use either it or the coconut. Set the juice aside. Lay the nut sideways on an unbreakable surface (the patio, a bare concrete floor, the front walk—whatever). Tap it firmly with a hammer around the middle, rotating the nut, until it cracks and splits. Turn each half, pointed end up, and tap until the shell breaks apart. Pry the white flesh from the shell, peel off its brown hull with a paring knife or vegetable peeler, and shred the nutmeat with a grater. Set it aside.

2.   Holding the pineapple over a bowl to catch the juices, cut off the stem and sprout ends of the fruit and peel it. Cut out the core and slice the pineapple into $1/4$-inch pieces. The easiest way to do this is to cut the pineapple flesh from the core in vertical wedge-shaped sections. You can also use a special gadget that is designed for the purpose (it looks like a corkscrew on steroids), or if you're lucky, some grocers will actually peel and core pineapples for you. This allows you to slice the pineapple into rings. Put the sections in the bowl with the pineapple juice and set them aside.

3.   To peel the oranges: cut off the stem and blossom ends by cutting all the way through to the flesh of the orange. Holding the fruit over a bowl to catch the juices, peel them with a paring knife, just barely cutting through the outer membranes of each section. Cut the oranges crosswise into $1/4$-inch slices, remove the seeds, and put the slices into the bowl with their juice.

4.   Cover the bottom of a glass serving bowl with a layer of oranges, sprinkle it well with a handful of the coconut, and cover it with a layer of pineapple. Sprinkle the pineapple well with coconut. Repeat with more oranges, coconut, and pineapple until all the fruit is used up, finishing with a thick layer of coconut. Pour the reserved coconut juice slowly over the ambrosia and let it stand for an hour or so before serving.

5.   Combine the reserved pineapple and orange juice and drink it yourself—cook's treat.

GRAPEFRUIT AND AVOCADO SALAD ✦

A Florida classic, this salad makes a great first course for a fish dinner. You can also turn it into a fine luncheon main course by adding cooked and peeled shrimp. Allow about 1½ pounds of large shrimp.

If the grapefruit isn't very sweet, you can add a little sugar to the juice when you make the dressing, but go easy; the idea here is salad, not dessert.

SERVES 4

2 large pink grapefruit
2 medium avocados
2 tablespoons reserved grapefruit juice (see step 1)
2 tablespoons lemon juice
Salt
Sugar (optional, see step 2)
½ cup extra virgin olive oil
4–8 romaine or Boston lettuce leaves, washed and drained
2 tablespoons chopped fresh mint leaves

1. Over a bowl to catch all the juice, cut the tops and bottoms from the grapefruit and peel them with a paring knife, cutting all the way through the connective membranes to the inner flesh. Using a sharp knife, separate the sections from the membrane. Put them in the bowl with the juices and set aside. Peel, split lengthwise, and pit the avocados. Cut them lengthwise into thin wedges.
2. Combine 2 tablespoons of the reserved grapefruit juice, the lemon juice, a large pinch of salt, and sugar to taste (taste the grapefruit juice; if it's already sweet, it won't need much sugar). Slowly whisk in the olive oil, beating until it is emulsified.
3. Arrange the lettuce leaves on individual salad plates. Lift the grapefruit sections out of their juice, pat dry, and arrange them on the lettuce with the avocados, alternating in a fan pattern.
4. Pour the dressing over the salad, sprinkle the chopped mint over it, and serve at once.

Note: *The salad can be made an hour ahead up through step 2. Don't make it too far ahead or the avocado will begin to oxidize and discolor.*

JOHN EGERTON'S LEMON CURD

John Egerton is a journalist, historian, and dyed-in-the-wool Southern cooking advocate from Nashville, Tennessee. Through his columns for *Southern Living* magazine and his two excellent books—*Southern Food* and *Side Orders*—he has done much to preserve and advance the cause of traditional Southern cooking.

When I asked him for a recipe to include here, I told him that it didn't matter what it was, so long as it was Southern and a vegetable or fruit. With characteristic but unsurprising promptness, he sent three recipes. The surprise was that all three were for lemon curd, to which he is incurably addicted. When I reminded him that my book was about vegetables and fruit, *he* reminded *me* that lemons are fruit. When I said that perhaps I might want something a bit more, well, *green*, John shot back that I could make it with limes.

Clearly, lemon curd was what I was going to get.

And why not? There's nothing better or more Southern, for though it has English roots, it has appeared on Southern tables since the late eighteenth century. Lemon curd is the nicest and most traditional of fillings for lemon pies and tarts, and is singularly wonderful slathered over breakfast toast.

MAKES ABOUT 2 1/2 CUPS

1/4 pound (1 stick) unsalted butter
1/2 cup freshly squeezed lemon juice (4 to 5 lemons)
3–4 teaspoons (or more, to taste) grated lemon zest
1 cup sugar
3 whole large eggs and 3 large egg yolks

1. Prepare a double-boiler bottom with water and bring it to a boil over medium heat. Reduce the heat to a slow simmer and place the top boiler over, but not touching, the simmering water. Put in the butter and let it melt. When it has melted, add the lemon juice, grated zest, and sugar, stirring until the sugar is dissolved.

2. In a separate bowl, beat together the whole eggs and the yolks until they are smooth. Add them to the butter mixture, stirring constantly, and continue stirring until it is smooth. Cook the curd, stirring constantly, until it is very thick and the spoon leaves a distinct path in the curd, about 10 minutes. Turn off the heat and take the top boiler off the bottom.

3.   Continue stirring the curd until it has cooled somewhat and then pour it into another container and let it cool completely. Cover and refrigerate until the curd is thoroughly chilled before using it. It keeps well in the refrigerator for up to a month, though it is unlikely you will have it that long.

Note: *This amount of lemon curd will fill a 9-inch prebaked pie shell. Use the leftover whites to make a meringue for the top of the pie. It will also fill a dozen prebaked tartlet shells or provide three layers of filling for a 9-inch round layer cake.*

Working with eggs and butter in a custard can be a tricky business. Don't let the butter get too hot before the eggs are added or they could curdle, and keep the heat low. The custard continues to thicken as it cools, so don't try to cook it to the stiff consistency of a bottled lemon curd.

$\mathcal{O}$LD SOUR

The southernmost point in the South is, ironically, sometimes not considered to be a part of "The South" at all. But while the trail of islands off the tip of Florida that we know as the Keys are much influenced by their Caribbean neighbors, Key West nonetheless maintains a distinctly Southern sensibility. Perhaps that's due in part to the fact that it has long been a favorite winter hideaway for some of the South's great eccentrics, such as Tennessee Williams and everybody's strange uncle.

Key limes, the small, round, fluorescent yellow citrus fruit that can be found all over the Keys and South Florida, have long been a distinctive element of Floridian and Deep South cookery. They have a unique flavor that is miles away from that of common Persian limes and has no real equivalent.

Unfortunately, Key limes don't have a long season and they don't keep well. This recipe was devised as a means of preserving the juice for use when the fruit is out of season but, like its cousins the pickled lemons of the Mediterranean and the lemon catsups of northern Europe, it has become a distinctive and essential flavoring on its own.

This is Jeanne Voltz's recipe from *The Florida Cookbook*. She says it should never be refrigerated. Jeanne knows some Key West cooks whose Old Sour is from the starter they got more than 50 years ago as a wedding present; sitting on the dining-room sideboard in an old whiskey bottle, it has never, in those 50 years, seen the inside of a refrigerator.

Use Old Sour to add tartness to greens or as a condiment with any fish or shellfish. A few drops are all you will need—as one old cookbook put it, it ain't called "Old Sour" for nothing.

MAKES ABOUT 2 CUPS

16–18 Key limes, or about 8 regular limes and 8 lemons
1 tablespoon sea salt

1.   Roll the fruit well to release the juice, split them, and squeeze out the juice. Strain it into a measuring cup. You should have 2 cups, depending on the juiciness of the fruit. Put the juice into a pottery crock or glass jar.

2.   Add the salt and stir with a clean stainless spoon until the salt is completely dissolved. Cover the container with a double layer of cheesecloth or thin muslin, and secure the cloth with a tight rubber band. Set the container aside at room temperature and let it mature, undisturbed, for not less than 2 weeks. Jeanne recommends at least 6 to 8 weeks for proper fermentation.

3.   When the aging is complete, the sauce is ready for use. Pour it into a bottle, seal it tightly with a cork or screw cap, and store it in a cool, dark cupboard or the refrigerator.

Note: *Key limes have no equivalent. The closest you can come is to mix Persian lime and lemon juices together in equal parts, though even that is only a ghost of true Key lime flavor. While bottled Key lime juice is available at some groceries and supermarkets, it won't work for this sauce, since it's been pasteurized and won't ferment.*

CONFEDERATE BREAKFAST

This will give your morning orange juice a lift it's never had before. An oldtime Southern remedy for the morning after, it's also pretty good the morning before. It gives the hungover something to live for, and the still-sober something to hope for. Think of it as a mimosa with a kick like a mule.

SERVES 4

1 cup bourbon
3 cups orange juice, preferably fresh squeezed
4 sprigs fresh mint
Thin orange slices

1.   Combine the bourbon and orange juice in a pitcher, and stir well.

2.   Fill 4 old-fashioned glasses with ice. Pour the mixture over it. Garnish with the mint sprigs and orange slices, and serve cold.

Note: *My friend Dean Owens makes a version with frozen concentrated orange juice. Using the concentrate can as a measure, put equal parts undiluted concentrate, bourbon, water, and ice in a blender. For the really hungover, add a raw egg. Blend until smooth and serve in chilled cocktail or old-fashioned glasses.*

CRANBERRIES

Cranberries are a native American fruit, indigenous to the northeastern part of the United States. They aren't especially Southern, but they've been showing up on our holiday tables for centuries. Recipes for them were commonplace in old Southern cookbooks. Most of those recipes follow traditional English practice, substituting cranberries for gooseberries. Modern Southern cooks still use this fruit mostly as a condiment for the holiday turkey or as a relish for game, often pairing it with Florida oranges—a refreshing, and classic, combination.

PUREFOY CRANBERRY RELISH

The dining room of the old Purefoy Hotel in Talledega, Alabama, once had a national reputation for its fine table. Its Sunday dinners were practically a social institution. Though the hotel is long gone, Talledegans still talk of those dinners as if they had just been to one last Sunday. Much of the Purefoy's lovely cooking is alive and well in Talledega and frequently appears in the dining rooms of the city's many graceful antebellum houses, thanks to a cookbook written by Eva Purefoy, who for many years supervised the hotel dining room and the kitchen.

This is Miss Eva's recipe for the cranberry relish that used to appear on the holiday menu at the hotel. Its light, fresh taste has made it a holiday standard not only in Talledega, but all over the Southeast.

Lillie King, who gave me this recipe, chops the relish with an old-fashioned hand-cranked meat grinder, but you can use a food processor—just be careful not to over-process it.

MAKES ABOUT 8 CUPS

1½ pounds (two 12-ounce packages) fresh cranberries
3 whole oranges
3 small, tart apples, such as Winesaps or Arkansas Blacks, or 2 large,
    tart apples, such as Granny Smiths
2½ cups sugar

1.   Wash all the fruit and dry them well. Pick over the cranberries and discard any soft or blemished berries. Peel the oranges and set the peels aside. Slice the oranges crosswise into ¼-inch slices and remove the seeds. You can peel the apples if you like, but it isn't necessary. Cut them into quarters and remove the cores.
2.   Put the cranberries, oranges, orange peel, and apples through a meat grinder into a glass or stainless mixing bowl. Stir in the sugar, cover, and refrigerate for at least 24 hours. Stir again before serving, and serve it cold.

Food Processor Method: Cut the orange peel, oranges, and apples into chunks roughly the same size as the cranberries. Put them with the berries into a processor bowl fitted with a steel blade. Pulse the machine until the fruit is uniformly chopped fine. Transfer to a glass or stainless bowl, and stir in the sugar. Cover and refrigerate for at least 24 hours. Stir again and serve it cold.

Note: *This relish keeps for up to a month in the refrigerator. Don't leave the storage bowl sitting out; take out only as much relish as you need into a separate serving bowl, using a clean, stainless-steel spoon. Be sure that the storage bowl is kept well covered.*

DRIED FRUIT

Though Southerners have long stored apples in the root cellar or cold front bedroom to be enjoyed all winter, and today have access to Florida citrus fruit, which appear in the market around Thanksgiving and remain in season until the first strawberries begin to ripen, drying has long been a favorite way of keeping out-of-season fruit to enjoy all year round, and they remain popular on Southern tables to this day.

Stewed Figs in Wine

What dried fruit loses in succulence is more than compensated for by the rich concentration of its flavor. Here, that flavor is further enriched by stewing the figs in a sweet dessert wine. Once, stewed dried fruit was a standard winter dessert, but nowadays it is considered to be somewhat plebeian. Mind you, that misguided attitude does not prevent it from being deeply satisfying to eat.

SERVES 4

1 pound dried figs
1 lemon
1 cup Madeira, tawny port, or dry sherry
1 cup Bourbon Custard Sauce (page 59)

1.   Wash the figs under cold, running water and drain well. Pare a large piece of zest from the lemon, and set the fruit aside.

2.   Put the figs, lemon zest, and wine in a porcelain-lined or stainless saucepan. Add enough water to cover the figs completely, and place the pan over medium heat. Bring the liquid slowly to a boil, then reduce the heat, and loosely cover the pan. Stew gently until the figs are plump and tender, about 1 hour.

3.   Raise the heat beneath the pan to medium high, and let the cooking liquid boil down to a thick syrup. Turn off the heat. Remove the figs to a glass serving dish or divide them among individual serving plates. Cut the lemon in half and squeeze the juice from one of the halves through a strainer into the syrup. Stir it in and pour the syrup over the figs. Serve them warm or at room temperature with bourbon custard sauce passed separately.

MARTHA NESBIT'S FRIED PIES

For ten years, from the midseventies until 1986, the weekly food section of *The Savannah Morning News* was distinguished for its stylish writing and good regional cooking. Those were the years that my friend and fellow author Martha Giddens Nesbit was at the helm as food editor.

Martha left the paper to write her first cookbook, *A Savannah Collection*, containing recipes gathered during her years at the newspaper. Though privately published and only distributed locally, the book became a standard for local cooks, and visitors by the hundreds have carried it home to all corners of the country. Her second book, *Savannah Entertains*, has reached an even larger audience.

When I asked Martha for a taste that characterized her Valdosta childhood, without hesitation she answered, "Fried pies." Those homey pastries were a standard sympathy offering in her hometown. She explained: "Whenever there is sadness in a small Southern town, there are sure to be fried fruit pies. These crescent-shaped pastries are filled with stewed dried fruit and fried with love, often delivered on a cracked flowered serving platter with a gentle smile, to help the grieving keep up their strength." Martha says that they *almost* made you look forward to somebody dying.

MAKES 12 PIES

FOR THE FRUIT FILLING:
8 ounces dried fruit (peaches, apples, or a mixture of both)
1/3 cup sugar

FOR THE PASTRY:
3 cups (about 14 ounces) all-purpose flour
2 teaspoons baking powder, preferably single-acting
1 teaspoon salt
1 tablespoon sugar
2/3 cup shortening (see note)
1 large egg, lightly beaten
Peanut oil, for frying
Confectioners' sugar (optional)

1. Put the fruit in a heavy, stainless, or enamel-lined saucepan. Add the sugar and water to cover the fruit. Turn on the heat to low, and simmer until the fruit is very about 45 minutes to 1 hour. Drain off any cooking liquid that remains and mash t well with a potato masher or fork. Set aside.

2. Sift together the flour, baking powder, salt, and sugar into a mixing bowl th comfortably hold all the pastry ingredients. Add the shortening, and cut it into th with a pastry blender or fork until the mixture resembles coarse meal. Make a well center of the flour mixture and add ½ cup of cold water and the beaten egg. Stir to with a fork until it forms a soft dough.

3. Lightly flour your hands and divide the dough evenly into 12 balls. On a l floured surface, with a floured rolling pin, roll out each ball into a circle about ⅛ thick. Spoon a tablespoon of the fruit filling into the center of each round, then brus edges of the dough with a little water. Fold the dough over the filling to form a half-c gently pressing the moistened edges together with the tines of a fork to make sure the well sealed. If the edges are a little ragged, you can trim them with a knife.

4. Put enough peanut oil in a deep, heavy skillet or deep fryer to cover the bottom b inch. Turn on the heat to medium high. When the fat is hot but not smoking (around degrees F), put in enough pies to fill the pan without crowding. Fry until the bottoms nicely browned, about 4 minutes, then turn and continue frying until the pies are u formly browned, about 4 minutes more. Drain briefly on paper towels and, if you li dust them lightly with confectioners' sugar. Serve hot or at room temperature.

Note: *Martha and I have a running debate on shortening for the pastry. She uses o vegetable shortening, claiming that it is healthier than lard, but I use lard, claiming the rever Either one works fine. So will unsalted butter.*

It may take a batch or two for you to perfect making fried pies. Biscuit dough require certain knack that only experience can teach, as does perfect frying. I burned half of my fu batch, so don't get discouraged if your first pies aren't perfect.

If the prospect of frying the pies sends you into a fat panic, you can bake them instead, s my mother and grandmother often did. Position a rack in the upper third of the oven and pre- heat the oven to 350 degrees F. Place the pies on an ungreased cookie sheet, lightly brush them with melted butter, and bake until they are lightly browned, about 12 minutes.

As to serving them, Martha says that they should go on the table "between the layer cake with caramel icing and the fresh coconut cake." . . . Well, we should all be so lucky.

$\mathcal{B}$ IBLIOGRAPHY
AND READING LIST

➤

llowing is a list of books and manuscripts—Southern, Northern, English, French, and Italian—that
ve influenced this particular Southerner and have shaped modern Southern cooking in general.

Many of the antique books are still available; some have never gone out of print. Others are
vailable once again, either in transcriptions, facsimile reprints, or through continuous publications.
ve noted this wherever I am aware of them.

cton, Eliza. *Modern Cookery for Private Families.* London: Longman, Brown, Green, and Longmans, 1845 and
1855. (Reprint, Lewis, England: Southover Press, 1993.)

ndrews, Mrs. Lewis R., and Mrs. J. Reanney Kelly, eds. *Maryland's Way: The Hammond-Harwood House Cook
Book* (14th ed., 1995). Annapolis, MD: The Hammond-Harwood House Association, 1963.

unt Julia's Cook Book. Esso Corporation, n.d., c. 1936.

ailey, Lee. *Lee Bailey's New Orleans.* New York: Clarkson-Potter, 1993.

———. *Lee Bailey's Southern Food and Plantation Houses.* New York: Clarkson-Potter, 1990.

eard, James. *James Beard's American Cookery.* Boston: Little, Brown, and Company, 1972.

eeton, Isabella. *Beeton's Book of Household Management.* London: 1861.

elk, Sarah. *Around the Southern Table.* New York: Simon & Schuster, 1991.

ooth, Letha, ed. *The Colonial Williamsburg Cook Book.* Williamsburg: The Colonial Williamsburg Foundation,
1971.

remer, Mary Moore. *New Orleans Recipes.* New Orleans: General Printing Company, 1932. Referenced: 8th
(1942) printing.

ronz, Ruth Adams. *Miss Ruby's American Cooking.* New York: HarperCollins Publishers, 1989.

———. *Miss Ruby's Cornucopia.* New York: HarperCollins Publishers, 1991.

rown, Marion. *Marion Brown's Southern Cook Book.* Chapel Hill: University of North Carolina Press, 1968
(revision of the 1951 publication).

———. *The Southern Cook Book.* Chapel Hill: University of North Carolina Press, 1951.

Brown, Theresa Clement(ine). *Theresa C. Brown's Modern Domestic Cookery.* Charleston: Edward Perry,
Printer, 1871. Reprinted in a paperbound facsimile by The Pendleton District Historical and Recreational
Commission (printed by The Journal, Inc., Williamston, SC), 1985.

Bryan, Lettice. *The Kentucky Housewife.* Cincinnati: Shepard and Sterns, 1839. Paperback facsimile: Paducah,
KY: Troll Publishing Company for Collector Books, n.d. Hardcover facsimile with introduction by Bill Neal.
Columbia: University of South Carolina Press, 1991.

Bullock, Helen, ed. *The Williamsburg Art of Cookery*. Williamsburg: Colonial Williamsburg, 1938.

Burn, Billie S. *Stirrin' the Pots on Daufuskie*. Daufuskie Island, SC: Burn Books, 1985.

Child, Julia. *From Julia Child's Kitchen*. New York: Alfred A. Knopf, Inc., 1982.

Clark, Libby, ed., with Janet Cheatham Bell (food writer), and Jessica B. Harris (food consultant). *The Black Family Reunion Cook Book*. Tradey House, publishers, for The National Council of Negro Women, 1991.

Colquitt, Harriet Ross. *The Savannah Cook Book*. Charleston: Walker, Evans & Cogswell Co., 1933.

The Congressional Cook Book. Washington: The Congressional Club, 1927, rev. ed., 1933.

Cooper, Ben Green. *Savannah Cookin'*. Mableton, GA: Ben Green Cooper Press, 1967.

Cox, Eugenia Barrs, ed. *Low Country Cooking: A Collection of Recipes from Liberty County and the Georgia Low Country*. Hinesville, GA: Liberty County Historical Society, 1988.

The Creole Cook Book. New Orleans: The New Orleans Picayune, 1900. Reprint, 2nd ed., *The Picayune's Creole Cook Book*, with introduction and notes by Marcelle Bienvenu. New York: Random House, 1987.

Crump, Nancy Carter. "Foodways of the Albermarle Region." *Journal of Early Southern Decorative Arts*, Volume XIX, Number 1, May 1993.

Cusick, Heidi Haughy. *Soul & Spice: African Cookery in the Americas*. New York: Chronicle Books, 1995.

Darden, Norma Jean and Carole. *Spoonbread and Strawberry Wine*. New York: Fawcett Crest, 1978.

David, Elizabeth. *Elizabeth David Classics* (collection incorporating *Mediterranean Food, French Country Cooking*, and *Summer Cooking*). New York: Alfred A. Knopf, Inc., 1980.

———. *Spices, Salts and Aromatics in the English Kitchen: English Cooking Ancient and Modern, Volume 1*. New York: Penguin Books, 1970.

DeBolt, Margaret Wayt, Emma Rylander Law, and Carter Olive. *Georgia Entertains*. Nashville, TN: Rutledge Hill Press, 1988. (Originally published as *Georgia Sampler Cookbook*, 1983.)

DeBolt, Margaret Wayt, with Emma Rylander Law. *Savannah Sampler Cookbook*. West Chester, PA: Whitford Press, 1978.

Del Conte, Anna. *The Gastronomy of Italy* (American ed.). New York: Prentice-Hall Press, 1987.

DeMers, John. *Arnaud's Creole Cook Book*. New York: Simon & Schuster, 1988.

Donovan, Mary, with Amy Hatrak, Frances Mills, and Elizabeth Shull. *The Thirteen Colonies Cookbook*. New York: Praeger Publishers, 1975.

Dull, Henrietta Stanley. *Southern Cooking*. Atlanta: Ruralist Press, 1928. Facsimile by Cherokee Press, Atlanta, 1989.

Dupree, Nathalie. *Cooking of the South*. New York: Irena Chalmers Cookbooks, Inc., 1982.

———. *Nathalie Dupree's Southern Memories*. New York: Clarkson-Potter, 1993.

———. *New Southern Cooking*. New York: Alfred A. Knopf, Inc., 1986.

Edminston, Mrs. Jack R., and Mrs. James W. Heacock, Jr., eds. *When Dinnerbells Ring*. Talledega, AL: The Talledega Junior Welfare League, 1978.

Egerton, John. *Side Orders*. Atlanta: Peachtree Publishers, 1990.

———. *Southern Foods*. New York: Alfred A. Knopf, 1987.

Evelyn, John, Esq. *Acetaria: A Discourse on Sallets*. London: B. Tooke, 1699. Reprint, Brooklyn, NY.: The Women's Auxiliary of the Brooklyn Botanic Gardens, 1937.

The Ever Ready Cook Book. Savannah: The Rector's Aid Society of St. John's Episcopal Church, n.d., but before 1915.

Favorite Recipes from Savannah Homes, Many Before Unpublished: A Collection of Well Tested and Practical Recipes. Savannah: The Ladies of the Bishop Beckwith Society, 1904.

Fisher, Mrs. Abby. *What Mrs. Fisher Knows About Old Southern Cooking*. San Francisco: Women's Co-operative Printing Office, 1881. Reprint, Karen Hess, ed., Bedford, MA: Applewood Books, 1995.

Flexnor, Marion W. *Dixie Dishes*. Boston: Hale, Cushman & Flint, 1941.

Fox, Minnie C. *The Bluegrass Cook Book*. New York: Fox, Duffield & Company, 1904.

Garmey, Jane. *Great British Cooking: A Well Kept Secret*. New York: Random House, 1981.

Glenn, Camille. *The Heritage of Southern Cooking*. New York: Workman Publishing, 1986.

Gordon, Eleanor Kinzie (Mrs. William W.). Household notebook, c. 1858–1910. (Collection of the Juliette Gordon Low Birthplace, Girl Scouts of America.)

Grosvenor, Vertemae. *Vertemae Cooks in America's Family Kitchens*. San Francisco: KQED Books, 1996.

Gulf Fare, Favorite Seafood Recipes. Panacea, FL.: Iris Garden Club of Wakulla County, n.d.

Guste, Roy F., Jr. *Antoine's Restaurant Cookbook*. New York: W. W. Norton & Co., 1980.

Harper, Pat, ed., with Elaine Simmons. *Savannah Style*. Savannah: The Junior League of Savannah, Inc., 1980.

Harris, Jessica B. *The Welcome Table*. New York: Simon & Schuster, 1995.

Hazan, Marcella. *The Classic Italian Cookbook*. New York: Alfred A. Knopf, Inc., 1976. The title says it all.

———. *Marcella's Italian Kitchen*. New York: Alfred A. Knopf, Inc., 1986.

———. *More Classic Italian Cooking*. New York: Alfred A. Knopf, Inc., 1978.

Hedrick, U. P., ed. *Sturtevant's Edible Plants of the World*. New York: Dover Publications, Inc., 1972. Original publication: *Sturtevant's Notes on Edible Plants*, J. B. Lyon Company, Albany, NY: 1919.

Heritage Receipts from St. John's. Savannah: The Episcopal Church Women, St. John's Church, n.d., c. 1978.

Hess, John L., and Karen Hess. *The Taste of America* (3rd ed.). Columbia: University of South Carolina Press, 1989.

Hess, Karen. *The Carolina Rice Kitchen*. Columbia: University of South Carolina Press, 1992, including in facsimile the *Carolina Rice Cook Book* (see Stoney, Louisa Cheves Smythe, ed.).

———. *Martha Washington's Booke of Cookery and Booke of Sweetmeats*. Transcription with historical notes and "copious annotations." New York: Columbia University Press, 1981. (See also Randolph, Mary. *The Virginia House-wife*.)

Hill, Annabella P. *Mrs. Hill's New Cook Book*. New York: James O'Kane, Publishers, 1867. Reprint, Damon L. Fowler, ed. *Mrs. Hill's Southern Practical Cookery and Receipt Book*. Columbia: University of South Carolina Press, 1995.

Horry, Harriott Pinckney. Household notebook, 1770–1819. Published in 1984 as *A Colonial Plantation Cookbook: The Receipt Book of Harriott Pinckney Horry, 1770*. Transcribed with historical notes by Richard J. Hooker, University of South Carolina Press.

The Housekeeper's Friend. Fincastle, VA: The Ladies' Aid Society of the First Presbyterian Church of Fincastle, 1896.

Huguenin, Mary Vereen, and Anne Montague Stoney, eds. *Charleston Receipts* (The Junior League of Charleston). Charleston: Walker, Evans & Cogswell Co., 1950.

Kitchiner, William, M.D. *The Cook's Oracle*. London: Printed for Robert Cadell, Edinburgh, by Whitaker, Treacher, and Co., 1831. Also referenced: 1855(?) edition. (First edition, 1817.)

Krieger, Louis C. C. *The Mushroom Handbook*. New York: Dover Publications, Inc., 1967.

Leslie, Eliza. *Miss Leslie's New Cookery Book*. Philadelphia: T. B. Peterson and Brothers, 1857.

Lewis, Edna. *In Pursuit of Flavor*. New York: Alfred A. Knopf, Inc., 1988.

———. *The Taste of Country Cooking*. New York: Alfred A. Knopf, Inc., 1978.

Lustig, Lillie S., ed., with S. Claire Sondheim and Sarah Russel. *The Southern Cook Book Of Fine Old Recipes*. Asheville, SC: The Three Mountaineers, Inc., 1938.

Manning, Mrs. Stephen C. Manuscript receipt book, private collection. New Orleans, c. 1890–1910.

McColloch-Williams, Martha. *Dishes and Beverages of the Old South*. New York: McBride, Nast & Co., 1913. Facsimile, Nashville: University of Tennessee Press, introduction by John Egerton, 1988.

McCoin, Choice, ed. *300 Years of Carolina Cooking*. Greenville, SC: The Junior League of Greenville, 1970.

McRee, Patsy. *The Kitchen and the Cotton Patch*. Anniston, AL: Higginbotham, Inc., 1982. (Tenth printing; first edition, 1948).

Meldrim, Frances Casey (Mrs. Peter W.), and Sophie Meldrim Shonnard. Household notebook, private collection, Savannah, Georgia, 1890–1945. Most of this notebook was published in *Georgia Entertains* (see DeBolt, Margaret Wayte).

Mitchell, Patricia B. *Soul on Rice: African Influences on American cooking*. Macon: The Tubman African American Museum, 1993.

Montagne, Prosper. *The New Larousse Gastronomique* (American ed.). New York: Crown Publishers, Inc., 1977.

Neal, William F. *Bill Neal's Southern Cooking* (rev. ed.). Chapel Hill: University of North Carolina, 1989.

———. *Biscuits, Spoonbread, and Sweet Potato Pie*. New York: Alfred A. Knopf, Inc., 1990.

Nesbit, Martha Giddens. *A Savannah Collection*. Orlando, FL: Noran Printing Company (for the author), 1986.

———. *Savannah Entertains*. Charleston: Wyrick and Company, Publishers, 1996.

Ortiz, Elisabeth Lambert. *The Complete Book of Caribbean Cooking*. New York: M. Evans and Company, Inc., 1973.

Parloa, Maria. *Miss Parloa's New Cook Book*. Boston: Estes & Lauriat, 1885. (First edition: 1880.)

Peterson, Lee Allen. *A Field Guide to Edible Wild Plants: Eastern and Central North America*. Boston: Houghton-Mifflin Company, 1977.

Prudhomme, Paul. *Chef Paul Prudhomme's Louisiana Kitchen*. New York: William Morrow & Co., Inc., 1984.

The Quaker Cook Book. High Point, NC: The Women's Auxiliary of High Point Friends Meeting, 1954.

The Queen of the Kitchen: A Collection of Old Maryland Receipts For Cooking, From a Receipt Book Used for Many Years. Baltimore: Lucas Brothers, 1870.

Ragan, Bill. *The Georgia Cookbook* (3rd ed.). Milledgeville, GA.: Prestwood Graphics, 1993.

Randolph, Mary. *The Virginia House-wife*. Washington: Davis and Forth, 1824. (Revised and enlarged editions, 1825 and 1828.) Facsimile, Karen Hess, ed. Columbia: University of South Carolina Press, 1984.

Ravenel, Rose P., and Elizabeth Ravenel Harrigan, ed. *Charleston Recollections and Receipts: Rose P. Ravenel's Cookbook*. Columbia: University of South Carolina Press, 1983.

Rawlings, Marjorie Kinnan. *Cross Creek Cookery*. New York: Charles Scribners' Sons, 1942.

Reid, Catha W., and Joseph T. Bruce, Jr. *The Sandlapper Cookbook*. Lexington, SC: The Sandlapper Press, 1973.

Rhett, Blanche S., with Lettie Gay and Helen Woodward. *Two Hundred Years of Charleston Cooking*. Facsimile, Columbia: University of South Carolina Press, 1976. (First edition, 1930.)

Rudisill, Marie. *Sook's Cookbook*. Atlanta: Longstreet Press, 1989.

Rutledge, Sarah. *The Carolina Housewife, or House and Home*. Charleston: W. R. Babcock & Co., 1847. Also referenced: 2nd (1851) and 3rd (1855, John Russel, publisher) editions. Facsimile, with introduction by Anna Welles Rutledge, Columbia: University of South Carolina Press, 1979.

Saltonstall, Maxine, and Virginia Carroll. *First You Take a Leek*. Rutland, VT: Charles E. Tuttle Company, 1969.

The Savannah Cook Book. Savannah: The Ladies of Westminster Presbyterian Church, 1909. Not to be confused with the Colquitt book of 1933.

The Shadows-on-The-Teche Cookbook. Huntsville, AL: Southeastern Color Printing for The Shadows Service League, 1982.

Simmons, Amelia. *American Cookery*. Hartford, CT: Hudson and Goodwin, 1796. Facsimile, with foreword by Mary Tolford Wilson, by Oxford University Press, 1958; reprinted as *The First American Cookbook* by Dover Publications, Inc., 1984.

Smart-Grosvenor, Vertemae. *Vibration Cooking, Or Travel Notes of a Geechee Girl* (3rd ed.). New York: Ballantine Books, 1992.

Smith, E[liza ?]. *The Compleat Housewife: or, Accomplish'd Gentlewoman's Companion*. London: R. Ware, et al., 1727. Referenced: 15th (1753) edition.

Stoney, Louisa Cheves Smythe, ed. *Carolina Rice Cook Book*. Charleston: The Lucas-Richardson Co., 1901. Published in facsimile by the University of South Carolina Press as part of *The Carolina Rice Kitchen* (see Hess, Karen).

Taylor, John Martin. *Hoppin' John's Charleston, Beaufort and Savannah: Dining At Home in the Lowcountry*. New York: Clarkson-Potter, 1997.

——. *Hoppin' John's Lowcountry Cooking*. New York: Bantam, 1993.

——. *The New Southern Cook*. New York: Bantam, 1995.

Terry, Elizabeth. *Savannah Seasons*. New York: Doubleday & Co., 1996. Savannah's award-winning chef tells all—well, mostly all.

Texas Cook Book. Houston: The Ladies Association of First Presbyterian Church, 1883. Facsimile, with introduction by David Wade and Mary Faulk Kooch: *The First Texas Cook Book*. Austin: Eakin Publications, Inc., 1986.

Thompson, Lois and V. V. (Pete), eds. *Authentic Southern Recipes From The Colonial Inn*. Hillsborough, NC: The Colonial Inn, 1972.

Thornton, P[hineas]. *The Southern Gardener and Receipt Book* (2nd ed.). Newark, NJ: A. L. Dennis, 1845. (First edition, 1840.)

Toklas, Alice B. *The Alice B. Toklas Cook Book*. New York: Harper & Row, Publishers, 1954 (1984 edition referenced).

Tucker, Martha Goode. Household notebook, c. 1855–1868. Transcription, *Housekeeping Diary of an Antebellum Lady*. Milledgeville, GA: The Milledgeville Town Committee, National Society of the Colonial Dames of America, 1990.

Tyree, Marion Cabell (ed.). *Housekeeping in Old Virginia*. Louisville, KY: John P. Morton and Company, 1879.

Verstille, Mrs. Ellen J. *Verstille's Southern Cookery*. New York: Owens and Agar, 1866.

Voltz, Jeanne, and Caroline Stuart. *The Florida Cookbook*. New York: Alfred A. Knopf, Inc., 1995.

Waring, Mary Joseph. *The Centennial Receipt Book*. Anonymously published "by a Southern Lady" (Charleston ?), 1876.

Warren, Mildred Evans. *The Art of Southern Cooking*. Garden City, NY: Doubleday & Co., 1967.

Webster, Mrs. A. L. *The Improved Housewife* (20th ed.). Hartford, CT: Ira Webster, 1854.

Willinger, Faith. *Red, White & Greens: The Italian Way with Vegetables*. New York: HarperCollins, 1996.

Wilson, Mrs. Henry Lumnpkin, ed. *Tested Recipe Cook Book*. Atlanta: The Foote and Davies Company, 1895. Facsimile, with introduction by Darlene Roth, *The Atlanta Exposition Cookbook*. Athens, GA: Brown Thrasher Books, 1984.

Wilson, Justin. *The Justin Wilson Cook Book*. Gretna, LA: Pelican Publishing Company, 1976. (Originally published 1965.)

——. *Louisiana Home Grown*. New York: Macmillan Publishing Company, 1990.

Ye Old Time Salzburger Cook Book. Ebenezer, GA: The Georgia Salzburger Society, n.d.

$\mathcal{I}$ NDEX